MIND-FORGED MANACLES:

CULTS AND SPIRITUAL BONDAGE

MIND-FORGED MANACLES:

CULTS AND SPIRITUAL BONDAGE

Thomas W. Case

Fidelity Press
206 Marquette Ave.
South Bend, Indiana 46617

Copyright © 1993, Thomas W. Case

FIRST EDITION

All rights reserved. No part of this publication may be reproduced, stored in a retrieval system, or transmitted, in any form or by any means, electronic, mechanical, photocopying, recording, or otherwise, without the prior written permission of the publisher:

Fidelity Press

206 Marquette Ave.
South Bend, IN 46617

Printed at St. Martin de Porres Printshop, New Hope, Kentucky.

ISBN 0-929891-01-5

LC 93-070867

Cover by R. F. McGovern

CONTENTS

Note to Readers — 1

Foreword by Rev. Wm. Kent Burtner, O. P. — 3

Part I: Cultist to Catholic

1. Surviving the Sixties — 9
2. Inside Look at a Moonie Training Session — 27
3. Moonie Life: 1973 — 41
4. Moonie Life: 1974 & 1975 — 73
5. Rocky Mountain Dharma High — 113
6. Moonie Reprise: 1980 — 141
7. Coming Home — 169

Part II: Catholic Cultists

8. A Mighty Fortress Is Our Sect — 187
9. Dona Lucillia of the Flashes — 201
10. The Seer of San Vittorino — 221
11. The Legacy of Marcel Lefebvre — 237
12. The Keys of the Kingdom — 265

Acknowledgments

Parts of Chapters Two and Three first appeared under the titles "An Inside Look at a Moonie Training Session" and "A Summer with the Moonies" in the *New Oxford Review*, Jan-Feb 1988 and March 1988. Early versions of Chapters Eight, Nine, Ten and Eleven first appeared in *Fidelity*, under the following titles: "The Fatima Crusaders: Anatomy of a Schism" (Oct. 1998); "TFP: Catholic or Cult?" (May 1989); "The Rise and Fall of Padre Gino" (May 1992); "The Society of St. Pius X Gets Sick" (Oct. 1992).

Foreword

The Christian message, that God became flesh and lived among us, is no hiding place. It heals, gives meaning and comfort, and draws people to a new awareness of God, but it puts us face-to-face with our humanity, and with the challenge to embrace the broken quality of that humanity, body and soul, mind and heart.

Tom Case's journey is of a sort that none of us dare overlook. His account of his confrontation with the message of Christ begins with a journey through mental and emotional terrain foreign to most of us. Yet in an age when competing ideologies and controlling (and sometimes dangerous) groups vie for our attention, and that of our youth, his account sheds light essential for our minds and our hearts.

How could people in their right mind find their way into a cult, a group "that so dominates the personalities of its members that it crushes mental liberty and does violence to human souls?" How could they surrender their lives, choices, money, belongings, time, their very souls to a ruler at whom they would have laughed two weeks before? You have to have been there. Or had someone you care about dearly go there and leave you behind. Or you can listen closely to a fellow traveller on the road to faith. Then you understand.

Tom Case has given us, woven into the story of his struggle, an account of several groups, their history and behavior. The work at hand is not simply a book about curious groups, it is about ourselves. As Pogo said, "We have met the enemy, and he is us!" The search for ourselves, given the constantly changing fabric of our society, the erosion of moral values, and the subjectivism that marks our century, is perhaps more difficult than it has been in any age.

We all have a hunger for the things that only can be addressed by God. Recalling St. Augustine: " . . . and none can rest until they rest in Thee." The temptation to abandon the search and retreat into a comfortable place, free of challenges and pain, faces us all. To struggle with the ineffable yet ineluctable burdens of meaning, purpose, belonging, and relating is the most difficult of challenges, yet is the arena where the best of our humanity is most precisely revealed.

Yet this spiritual search is not the cause of people becoming cultists. The "devilish catch," as Tom Case would say, is that the cults are most clever at co-opting this universal need through their coordinated program of psychological and social influence control techniques. These tools exploit real spiritual issues, the universally experienced need for family, communion with others, and a sense of rootedness in the cosmos. They produce dependency on an absolute leader, alienation from family, friends, and belief, and fear.

In his personal wrestling with these elements, finding, losing, and finding again surrogate families, communities that show "glee when there was no happiness to sustain it, affection without the force of love, urgency when there was nothing to be urgent about," Tom Case was challenged not only to get out of a cult, but to get the cult out from himself. He finally came to the Catholic Church. But it was a hard coming.

As he struggled to find his way into the Church, Tom Case was confronted with what one could only label "disastrous pastoral ministry." Perhaps that he made it at all is a testimony to the power of the Holy Spirit working despite the duly appointed "agents" who presented themselves to him, priests and religious armed with vapid theology and politically correct catch-phrases.

The Church, for its faults, still shines through as an institution that has made allowances for the humanity of its members, the Body of Christ despite its broken bones. In spite of the confused state of so many in the Church, Tom found its core reality, and came to the Faith.

While the Church has accountability structures that minimize the chance of a cult operating fully within its midst, Tom Case's study reminds us that there are many ways by which the authentic search for the Truth is easily abandoned. He shows us how someone can lead Catholic minded people into a totalitarian group, take away their freedom, get them to pronounce ideas that are formally heretical and make them believe that they are saving their souls and leading the rest of us to God, all while they claim to be at the heart of the Church. Once we understand the nature of the cult experience, even this seemingly far-fetched scenario becomes understandable.

What you are about to read is more than the author's "twenty year marathon in pursuit of this or that false face of God." His book reflects our need to make friends again with the strengths of the Catholic tradition, refresh our own perspectives, and move forward confidently into a world that is full of confusion and superficiality, materialism and hopelessness. It is about a search for faith, for family, and for Truth that warns us of these pitfalls and reminds us that the Church, for all its difficulties, is a place of hope, strength and peace.

Rev. Wm. Kent Burtner, O.P.
San Francisco, California

Note to Readers

The word "cult" has several different meanings. It can mean the forms of worship (the rites and rituals) of any religion or religious sect. Thus we can speak of the cult of the Catholic Church, which includes the Mass, Benediction, the Stations of the Cross, and all the other official forms of worship in the Church. It can mean the rites and rituals and prayers connected with a particular devotion within a religion, along with the devotion itself. Thus we can speak of the Cult of the Virgin Mary, which includes the Rosary, other prayers and rituals connected with the devotion, and the emotions, thoughts and desires that go into the act of devotion.

It can mean a faddish adulation or involvement. Thus we can speak of the cult of French Dada art, or newspapers can report on a film which has a cult following.

It can mean a sect, a group of followers of a particular religious or political leader or philosophy or way of life. The connotation here is of groups that espouse alternatives to, or schisms from, established religions or majority view-points or the reigning political orthodoxy. Most numerous are those which have a religious orientation.

It can mean a subset of the definition above. That is, a cult is a sect that so dominates the personalities of its members that it crushes mental liberty and does violence to human souls.

The last definition is the one used in this book.

Part I:

Cultist to Catholic

Chapter One

Surviving the Sixties

In the early summer of 1973 I had been separated from my wife for several months. She was busy getting a divorce. I was living out of my pick-up truck, holed up on a parcel of land I owned in Mendocino County, California. My complacency—the complacency I felt in the married state (I had believed the marriage would be forever)—was shattered. For a couple of weeks I chopped down a jungle of wild rhododendron and manzanita, carving a park around the second-growth redwoods on my land. I walked in my little park and began to call upon God. One morning I had had enough of swinging my ax and mumbling prayers under my breath, and I ran up to the highest point on the property and shouted out over a deep valley and to the sky beyond. I found myself calling on Jesus and Mary and all the saints. I said: "God, I am through with women. Make me a saint."

Of course, I was not through with women, though I thought so in that time of distress. The prayer meant that to me, the only alternative to being married to a woman was to be married to God. This was especially so since I had been married and was no longer married. It's a lot different than never having been married at all. A vacuum is created in the pit of the soul that was never there before. But what does it mean to be a saint? I could only conjure up images of a monk's life, and I realized I'd have to become a Catholic first. I knew nothing about the Catholic Church, but it was strange that I had in a desperate moment prayed as a Catholic. Certainly no childhood training had ever countenanced calling on saints or the Virgin Mary.

I drove down to town and moved into a little hotel above the general store. I talked to a Catholic priest in town, a kind man, a sad man, who had been in a monastery himself—Trappist I think—for some twenty years. Now he was a parish priest in this diminutive backwater town, surrounded by loneliness and a thousand books. He lent me a few books about Christ and the Church. These I read in my little hotel room above the general store, and after a time I decided I could not become a Catholic. At that time I could not bring myself to believe the Church's doctrine of hell. I couldn't believe the merciful God would allow any part of His creation to be forever separated from him, free will or no free will. There were others things I questioned, but that was the big thing: the question of the cosmos at its end.

A kind of mental openness came over me and I said silently, "Well God, I tried and I can't do it. It's up to you."

I drove on down the coastal route to Berkeley and stayed overnight with an old college friend. She mentioned a group she had recently run into called the "New Education Foundation." She had gone to a dinner at their house and had been treated warmly. She had gotten "good vibes" from the place and the people. I decided to look the commune over—my radar was wide open to whatever God might send my way—so I drove down to the Dana Street House. (I call it the Dana Street House because that's how we in the Family named our domiciles. There was the Dana Street house, the Regent Street house a few blocks east, the Ashby Street house—famous for being the Reverend Moon's first residence in California—and later there was the Hearst Street house in north Berkeley.)

The door was opened to my knock by a young man in a business suit (but with unmatched socks) who told me to come back on the weekend and take part in a seminar.

This was my introduction to the Family. I was thirty years old.

I had a couple of days to kill before the weekend seminar, so I attended one of the lectures being given by Dr. Durst at various locations in Oakland and Berkeley. These lectures were open to the public.

The little hall was filled with perhaps fifty people. Tea and cookies were to be served afterwards. I was fairly interested in the lecture. Dr. Durst, a professor at Laney College, was weaving a synthesis of knowledge, sociological and scientific and philosophical, and even religious. Some ideas reminded me of Confucianism, with a dose of esoteric mysticism about the spirituality of numbers. I couldn't figure out why the first two rows of the audience cheered wildly at every third sentence, while the rest of us listened in interested silence. It seemed a bit odd, a little out of kilter with what was appropriate. (Later I was to find that intentional, acted enthusiasm is a hallmark of the Unification Church. The first two rows were filled by Moonies.)

Dr. Durst cut the lecture short, seemingly disturbed by the restrained attitude of the majority of his audience. We all headed out to the hallway for tea and conversation. A bubbly girl named Beth started talking to me about the Spirit World and Spirit Men and Sleep Spirits and other obviously Gnostic or magical fantasies, so I decided she was a typical "Berkeley crazy" but friendly and fun to be with. I offered her a ride home and she accepted. Home turned out to be the Dana Street House. I began to pump her for information about the "New Education Foundation" when I realized she had fallen fast asleep. So much for my great conversational charm, I thought. I woke her up when we reached the house, said good-bye and drove away bemused.

Saturday morning I arrived at the Dana Street house with sleeping bag in hand and $15 for the seminar fee. We were asked to refrain from smoking during the weekend, to open ourselves to the experience, and to participate as fully as possible in all the events. There was a lecture (given by Dr. Durst, now in his own element), comparing the world's religions, and then small group discussions, and then we all packed into cars and vans and rode to a park in downtown Oakland, where we ate lunch and played volleyball (back then it was benign volleyball instead of fierce dodge ball). The whole group of participants—thirty or so—had been divided into five or six smaller groups. Dr. Durst and Jeffy headed up the group I was assigned to. These groups stayed intact throughout the weekend. We went back to the house for more lectures and dinner and little musical skits each group presented; then there was singing and a couple of testimonials on the theme of "How God lead me to the Family." Sunday was a repeat of Saturday: more lectures, small group discussions about the lectures and about ourselves, volleyball, and meals.

I must admit I drifted through my first seminar (or, as we in the Family called them, training sessions) in a mild haze due to nicotine starvation. One very strong image I remember, on Sunday afternoon at the park. Our group was sitting on the ground in a circle (you always sit in circles at Moonie training sessions). I was hazily letting my mind drift away from whatever was being said in the group, and I kept noticing a very good looking, vibrant, charismatic woman in a group near ours. I was extremely attracted to her and involved myself in one of those romantic fantasies all lonely men are familiar with. What a thrill of pleasure I felt when she left her group and came over and said a few words to me! I was instantly won over by those smiling, compelling brown eyes. I definitely wanted more of her. This was Christina, who was to become my "spiritual parent," though my thoughts were far from the Spirit when I first laid eyes on her. I decided right then and there to stick around this group and see what would develop. It was good that I thought that way because I was flat broke and had no place to stay.

Anyway it seemed that being here was an answer to my prayer.

The next morning I was sitting on the couch in the living room of the Dana Street house. Christina bounced in and sat down next to me and fixed me with those warm brown eyes and said, "What are you going to do?"

"Well," I said, "I think I'll just hang around for awhile and relax and get a feel for the atmosphere, and, uh, I don't know ." I shrugged.

"It doesn't work that way." She smiled when she said this, but I was a little taken aback. I wanted a free ride for a while . Then I thought, these people really move, they really zing out and do it. Loafing is obviously not where it's at with these folks. I decided I liked the idea.

"Well, OK," I said. "Is there something I can do? Do you have a job for me or something? If you have a job for me to do, I'd be happy to do it."

"Let's think about it. We'll come up with something. You think about it for awhile and we'll talk later." She gave me a reassuring squeeze of the hand, popped up from the couch, and was gone. I really liked that woman. So active, so exuberant—and so interested in me. And about my own age, a little older than the average I had seen around here.

A little while later we sat down to our family breakfast. About thirty of us sat on the floor around a low table and ate oatmeal and toast and juice. Onni, a slightly plump, good-looking, very awake Korean woman presided at the head of the table. I thought of her as the dragon lady of this odd little commune. Names were called out for assignments to work groups. Some would be working with the Maintenance Company, some with the Gardening Company, and some with the Flower Teams. One of the leaders rose and said that there were a couple of temporary jobs available gardening at the Watergate complex down by the bay, and asked if anyone was interested. I remembered my little talk with Christina and decided this was a good opportunity for me. I raised my hand and said, "That sounds OK to me." Immediately there were cheers from around the table. And a winning smile from Christina. For Chrissake, these people sure over-react, I thought, but I liked it anyway.

So for two days I found myself digging weeds around the Watergate apartment complex, and then a couple more days pulling weeds from around trees on Shattuck Avenue in Berkeley (this was a temporary job with the Berkeley Public Works Department). I didn't mind it a bit, working in the hot sun, more or less left to myself (the Public Works people would drop us off in the morning and pick us up at night). I worked in a team with two other recent "New Education Foundation" recruits, and as it was all brand new to all of us, we all felt expectant and interested, and we traded talk of our past and our feelings about the spiritual life.

That very first day, cutting weeds around the apartments, I recall being happy and open to this bright new world. I had no doubt that God had arranged the whole thing. I had prayed for a way, and He had answered. "Sainthood" was a word that for me conjured up the image of a cowled figure, gaunt and desiccated, praying deep into the night in some wilderness retreat, learning (as Thomas Merton had said) "the Christ of the burnt men." That was quite a contrast from working in the sun in a modern California town, now and then wiping the sweat off my brow, stopping to talk with a pretty girl working with me. We had brought bag lunches and at noon we sat down near a sidewalk to eat. A slim, dark-suited, intellectual looking fellow came walking along and sat down with us. This was Noah, a computer programmer by day and Moonie lecturer by night. He was diffident, but friendly, and he asked us how we were doing, and held our hands and led us in prayer. I was embarrassed by these things (what if somebody should come along and see us praying?) We ate lunch together and I thought, hell, that's pretty nice of this bunch. They send someone out to reassure us, see how we are doing. I felt protected.

The first thing that happens to you as a Moonie is security. You are fed and housed, you have people around, you sing together and sit together and pray together, and someone is always coming around to ask how you are doing.

Why did that simple gesture—a guy coming around to eat lunch with us and lead us in prayer—why did that call up from me so warm a response? Well, I had never felt protected before. It was subtle, I didn't reflect on it at the time, but it went deep.

Czeslaw Milosz, the Polish poet who settled in the United States some years ago, said once that he felt terribly isolated here. He said that we in the United States have our political freedom, and that was good, but with that freedom came a cold neglect from the society. It is nearly impossible to understand what he means, this idea of a lack of care from the society, as if the government or the culture itself were a living being. It is something that goes beyond and beneath a particular political or economic system. It has something to do with the fact that our country is so new, created from a violent rupture just eight or ten generations ago. European countries go back four hundred, six hundred, a thousand years and more in their development of a certain spiritual climate, a particular cultural and national identity. The result of this long attachment to the land and the language is the feeling that to live within a country is to live within a home. We can't understand it, we who were born in the United States, but the expatriate poet's insight can make us take a look at why we feel so alienated in our vaunted freedom as we deny that alienation with the proudest and toughest talk we can manage.

We start out with a national insecurity because of our relative national youth, with a culture in which much is borrowed and not much is from ourselves. The organic cohesion we are missing could only come from a thousand years of living on this land. But there was a culture and a certain kind of propriety, maybe a little thin, that was in place here until around 1960.

I'll say it like this: I was happy twice in my life, in my eighteenth summer and in the first year of my marriage when I was twenty-eight. Connecting the two times is that in the first, I "went steady," and in the second, I was married. In my teenage years our family lived in a semi-rural suburb of Binghamton, New York. There were a few little gravel streets, a few blocks of houses, dairy farms down the road, and the Susquehanna River running through our back yard. The late 1950s was a world very different from the world we live in today. What you did as a teenager, besides the usual teenage rebellion from parental authority (meaning that we drank beer down by the riverside and raced cars in the hills), was to go steady. You were "somebody" in your peer group if you had a steady girl. Getting pinned, or going steady, was practice for marriage. Some guys married the girls they went steady with, other couples broke up. But that was teenage social life. Going steady was teenage happiness, breaking up was tragedy.

And once when I rounded up some wrong people to take to a football game in my parents' 1956 Ford station wagon, I heard it from my friends. Suzie Brown had a "bad rep." Today we would say that Suzie Brown slept around. Even when you went steady, you didn't usually "go all the way." That was for marriage, or a little bit before, when you were fully committed to each other and you knew you were getting married soon. Girls with bad reps were out; so were guys who got in too many fights, or who went from one girl to another too often. They weren't serious. They had a bad rep. Homosexuality, needless to say, was not something even in the consciousness. If by chance a "fairy" was around, he was mocked and avoided as something alien and diseased and evil. It is a measure of how far we've come that I can't turn on the TV in 1993 without hearing something about gay rights or gay pride or gay progress, or gay diseases described as anything but gay.

Another contrast of our world with that world which puts a cap on the difference. It is a statistic. In 1950, 3.9% of all babies born in America were illegitimate. In 1990 the figure had risen to 28%—after two decades of legalized abortion. One out of every five white babies were born out of wedlock, one out of three Hispanic babies, and two out of three black babies. If two thirds of all blacks are born illegitimate, what sort of teenage culture awaits them? We already know.

None of this 1950s teenage moral code had to do with what our parents taught us, at least explicitly, or what we got from religion, if we had any. It was there in the culture. It was what we walked into even as we got out from under our parents' oversight. It was basically monogamous, thoroughly intended to make boys into men and girls in women, and was all set up for marriage and making a family.

Going steady was teenage practice for married life. I was very happy going steady in that last year before I went away to college in the fall of 1960 and ran into something entirely different.

At first it wasn't that different in my mind, but the pressure on everyone in that liberal Ohio college was to enter the sexual drama, if we hadn't already done so. All of a sudden there were a lot of brilliant and voluble people around, from New York City, from California, from everywhere. I could talk my thoughts as I never had before. The girls were smart and they were nineteen instead of sixteen. So immediately there was all the complication of getting into real sexual activity, and folk dancing on Red Square in the evening, and sleeping bag parties in the pine woods in the moonlight. I took a potpourri of courses, moving in a year's time from science to history and literature, trying to figure out the human race. After a year of new excitements and profound pleasure and despair, the "best and the brightest" of us fed on intellectual resources like Kierkegaard and Camus and Sartre, Rimbaud and Ezra Pound, and *Who's Afraid of Virginia Woolf?* All these literary sources confirmed us in our brilliant wit and contemptuous manner and underlying misery.

I lost my virginity as a freshman to a girl who married another student a year later. Other loves came and went. The sexual scene became incestuous. A girl I was in love with might show up next month in bed with my best friend, and things began to fall apart. (The center could not hold.) Sartre's *Being and Nothingness* was more like nothingness than being. His *Nausea* became my nausea. I dropped out of college in 1963, in my junior year, more or less on a dare, and went to the golden city of San Francisco, where I lived with my girlfriend on Delmar Street in the Haight-Ashbury. We read Nietzsche and Dostoevsky and Thomas Mann, played Joan Baez and Blue Grass music on the record player, and nearly got drowned in the drug scene. Something held me back (thank God) from shooting up methedrine or heroin, but it was a close call. Some of my friends were not so lucky. Love fell apart in a mire of personal anxiety and existentialist Angst.

By 1967, things were weirdly religious. I would sit on the floor with assorted travelers in slum apartments, drinking wine and sharing chunks of French bread, and calling on the Holy Spirit. In another era, a week later, my companions and I would delve into hallucinogenic-fueled explorations of the magical and supernatural, or quite possibly the demonic. Once I prayed to a statue of Isis in a

Mission Street flat after a hit of LSD. From the phonograph came the strained, acid-enhanced sound of Bob Dylan singing, "I dreamed I saw St. Augustine, in utmost misery, searching for those very souls, whom already had been sold. I leaned my head against the glass, and bowed my head and cried." That's not it exactly, but it's close enough. I cried right along with the song. I cried for my soul and for the souls of everyone in the world, because I thought that on a particular day in September 1967 the whole world had passed under the shadow of Satan. In the next room a crazy woman prayed to a picture of Christ on the wall.

What I endured in the late 1960s, and what those friends I gravitated to endured, was a social alienation so extreme that we looked everywhere and anywhere for an experience that would make us feel we were connected, not to the society (we were divorced from the society), but to the magical and supernatural cosmos. Everywhere, that is, except in churches. When the Jefferson Airplane came to play in Golden Gate Park, and the Haight was swamped by teeny-boppers from all over the country, we all thought we were headed for a kind of joyful Armageddon. But that hot summer of 1967 was a swan song, or a siren song. Hard-faced drug dealers came in from New York City, and the Hells Angels came up from Santa Cruz. Cops who had joined in on the fun in the summer, smoking marijuana with bevies of flower children dancing in the street, in the fall clubbed those same dancers off the sidewalks. Within a year the Haight looked like a bombed out South Bronx, with clapboards nailed over the head shops and a few dirty posters drifting in the gutter.

Although I still carried with me the old teenage and post-teenage idea of love and marriage, it had all been swamped by the wrong sort of philosophy and literature, music that constantly incited the senses, too much careless love, and too many brutal departures in the cold dawn. People drifted in and out, off to Mexico City or India, back to Boston, up to Vancouver, searching for themselves. One lovely blond I loved for a week carried a paperback copy of *Steppenwolf* in her knapsack along with two changes of underwear and a stash of weed. "Going steady" was replaced by fierce, temporary psychological and sexual attachments to whatever person of the opposite sex came your way. It was "your old man" or "your old lady." It was not practice for monogamous sex and eternal relationships. It was practice for broken hearts and psychological ruin. My dream was still as always to get "my girl" into bed, fall in love, get married, and live happily ever after. It never worked out, and I never realized it was because the idea was sex today and love tomorrow instead of the other way around. Or more often, it was sex today and "finding yourself" tomorrow.

I'm not sure how to match what I experienced simply as a result of my going off to an extremely liberal college, and then later deliberately and desperately entering on an extremely disordered life, with the change that began to happen in the larger social ethic, to everyone, sometime around 1962. Can I plead innocence in view of the fact that my twenties pretty nearly matched the world's sixties?

I remember going home to visit one time at age twenty-five and finding my little sisters completely without that "going steady, practice for marriage" teenage culture I had enjoyed at their age. That culture had simply disappeared. What I was busy discovering in my twenties, they had discovered in junior high. We had broken the ground with LSD and peyote in the context of presumably religious experiences; the generation five or ten years behind us were tossing down peyote buttons with their Southern Comfort whiskey just for kicks. I was shocked, and I felt responsible. I was never a leading agent in the formless mess of the 1960s, but I got to the Haight-Ashbury three years before it was the Haight-Ashbury. I was right on the spot, creating it, loving or hating every minute of it. And if there was anything good in what we did—I'm thinking of serious (if unconventional) spiritual searches, poetry and poetic lyrics, the best rock music of the century, honest dreams for a harmonious and peaceful world, intense searches for perfect love—the larger contemporary society has tossed away, while it has embraced our drugs, our selfishness, and our sexual immorality. It has taken to its heart everything we did wrong and nothing we did right, perhaps because what we did right was mostly subtle and mostly a dream. It wasn't marketable.

Finally I moved back home, or in the neighborhood (now it was the Virginia suburbs of Washington, D.C.), got a job at the post office, and visited with my parents and sisters. I settled down a bit. And then I married a girl who ran with the bunch my younger sister ran with. She was nineteen, I was twenty-eight.

I don't think the nine years' difference in our ages was what made our marriage fail. I think it was the fact that my wife had run slam bang into the dope and sex culture at age sixteen or so, that I had helped create at age twenty-four. What I was in the process of rejecting, she was suffused with. She knew nothing else. Remember that it was not religion or my parents who drove in to me any notion of limits or propriety. (I was brought up Episcopal, but I stopped believing in anything Episcopal at age twelve.)

Whatever was in me from those sources I more or less rejected as a part of my ordinary teenage rebellion. But my ordinary teenage rebellion didn't take me very far away from the parental ethic, despite the beer blasts and hundred-mile-an-hour car chases. The parental ethic, the social ethic, and even the teenage ethic were still pretty much one and the same thing in the late 1950s. Teenagers could be "wild," but basically they were as socially conservative as their parents. But by 1970, the teenage ethic was the same as our self-indulgent, sex-adoring, marijuana-drenched San Francisco ethic. What I conceived was the end of my restless looking for something else, was for my wife just the beginning.

I had always thought marriage was for real, and forever, just like the Catholic Church says it is. At last I was married. I had a very happy year, feeling at last like a man. I loved my wife. Adventure wasn't dead in me, and my wife encouraged what was left of it. We went west on an extended honeymoon and then, with an idea of settling in, bought a ten-acre parcel of land up the coast from San Francisco. I tried to build a house and had in mind the notion of truck farming. That was a disaster titled "Poet in the Woods." But it was fun. It was the last expression of hippiedom, the back-to-the-land movement. We lived out of a tent for a while, drank wine with our next door neighbors on the other side of the ridge, then returned to Virginia when my wife got pregnant. I drove a taxi, then returned to work at the post office.

Our daughter was born in the Leesburg, Virginia, hospital while my wife was wide awake. We had gone through a program of natural childbirth planning; that time and the birth that followed were the closest, most exalted time in our married life. I was content and set for the long haul, planning to build a nest egg and eventually return to college. But then something happened. My wife became pregnant again, and immediately informed me that she was going to get an abortion. I couldn't talk her out of it, and as I stood there before that suddenly implacable woman, I felt our marriage crumble as my sense of fatherhood crumbled into the dust. All that wonderful, natural feeling of coming into my manhood as a husband, father, provider, and protector drained away in an instant.

My focus was not on the fact that a tiny new person would be destroyed—that came later in my education—but on the force of family, the continuity of life, and who should rule and hold it all together. The crushing blow was that according to the laws of the land, it was her decision and hers alone to make. Just as bad was that she could make that decision. She blasted my power of creating new life with her while the state blasted my rights as a husband and father. A few months later she left me.

I had to get away, far away, to save my soul, which is how I got to be standing on a hilltop on my land in California a couple of months later, desperately alone, praying a desperate prayer.

The spiritual search is of course real, since God is real, even if in the 1960s we got that all wrong, too. I was always searching for a spiritual way, and a home, even when all my living arrangements denied it. Something went wrong in the early 1960s, and I don't know why. If we search out the philosophical corruption stemming from Germany, with Kant and his progeny, or look to the long breakup of Christendom over four centuries, or look at ugly twentieth century changes in art and architecture and high-brow music, we will find a wealth of causes, as we see all of it percolate down from the academies and the coffee houses to the ordinary citizen. But why did teenagers stop going steady in rural towns all over America in the 1960s? Why did they stop preparing for marriage? Was it Nietzsche or LSD or the devil himself who finally broke through the firm tribal customs of small town America? Or was it Vietnam?

Artists and musicians and poets in colonies all over the world have always thrown off social conventions and tried to manufacture a garden of earthly delights. It comes with the territory. But how did our little sex and dope revolution in San Francisco come to flood the whole society? Even living in that uncommon artistic world, I held the instinctive creed that sexual intercourse is in itself an act of marriage. When that sexual union comes before accredited marriage, it may be wrong, but a legal marriage should always follow closely in any case. I got that knowledge less by teaching than by experience. Or rather I had it from the beginning, and it was confirmed by experience. But I lived for half a decade trying to deny it, playing along with the kings of clever. When I finally wrenched myself out of that milieu of sudden sex and careless love, I found it had washed over the whole country. Who took the lid off?

I don't know, but most of my adult life I have, like Czeslaw Milosz in America, felt isolated and unprotected—except for the year I went steady and the year I was happily married. The love of God or the search for God or the need for God has been the last and only thing that has kept me from falling into personal chaos. And one thing I brought out of the sixties was the knowledge, not only the faith, that God exists. There was a time in the fall of 1967 when I had to hold in my heart an ultimate reliance on the Absolute God behind all the occult forces, even unto death, because I was getting rocked around pretty severely by occult forces.

What occult forces? At the cost of sounding like a New Age freak, I'll have to say something about it. This was long before the new spiritual circus got rolling, marketing itself through conferences in Big Sur and Shirley MacLaine TV specials and feminist goddess courses in the Universities. I was a spiritual journeyman, an intellectual, and a poet investigating reality. When a poet sits down to write, he can receive lines and phrases from what seems like another dimension. The little hairs on the back of the neck rise up, and you feel a slight unearthly chill. The Irish poet William Butler Yeats talks about a river of eternal symbols in a dimension above the earthly plane. What happened to me, by my own volition, was to get tossed into a realm where I picked up influences from Egyptian religion, Germanic paganism, and the Arthurian legends. It was as if I were re-enacting the beliefs of my ancestors. Partially, it was an inward journey, since I believe we hold in our memories the memory of our ancestors, and even of the human race, as Carl Jung claims. But partially it was outside myself. I became convinced that there is a psychic realm "above" the earth which contains all that people have believed, true and false, and which exists independently as a home of spiritual forces, "gods" and "goddesses" and demons and angels, becoming more potent as they are worshipped more fervently. Some part of this realm is the creation of humanity, but some part of it is previous to mankind. In fact, humanity cannot create out of nothing. Humanity can move the pieces around, force things here and there to fit preconceived desires, and manufacture religions as ugly and sinful as we ourselves are ugly and sinful. Real prophets, on the other hand, are clean slates on which God writes. But what happens in that spiritual realm nearest the earth is a contention of the true and the false, of misbegotten entities and pure entities. It is an occult realm clogged with human and demonic junk, in which it is very difficult for the spiritual vagabond to find his way to the landscape of Christ.

I walked foolishly into that Chapel Perilous and was buffeted and even partially possessed by the spirits of my ancestors. A lot of very "coincidental" happenings made it all more than my own fantasy. I received messages from a higher or lower realm. I knew I was in a dangerous country. What brought me through without being killed and without going mad was my never-ending prayer to Jehovah, a name for the God who created and rules everything, the Absolute and ultimate victor over all those powerful and still existing excrescences of Canaanite, Egyptian, or European magic: or any magic anywhere. And then I received a "message" which said, "Stop this magic or we will kill you." And then I received a message that said, "Christ has conquered."

That was all, and it was everything. It put a stop to my unworthy and ill-prepared raid on heaven.

A little shift occurred, and I began to have a glimmer of the knowledge that acts of kindness and acts of truth are what straighten out that world which is a little above ours, make level the hills and valleys, and bankrupt the occult junkyard. And something more, that I know now but did not know then. The Church's system of sacraments—I'm thinking primarily of baptism, penance and the Eucharist—are from the wisdom of God. They bring protection to the unprotected human race towards which God is merciful. The Holy Grail is not off in some hidden forest of the mystic universe. It is the grail from which the blood of Christ is drunk at a Catholic Mass. The Eucharist slices through that whole inimical battleground of the occult worlds, and brings the Most High directly to us unworthy blobs of good and evil. We receive it best when we have no pride. The Church does not take kindly to amateur explorations of the spiritual cosmos, and for good reason. The amateur diviner not only can be swamped by evil forces, he will bring his own mixture of good and evil to further mar the soul of the world.

There is something else which may look unorthodox to Catholics, but I don't think it should. It comes from esoteric literature, and it says that the mystic working his way through the Chapel Perilous, when his mind is set on the highest realm, will sooner or later come under the protection of the Virgin Mary. I believe that, though it took another twelve years to come into my life. All of this means to me that when you hold out for the truth no matter what happens to you, you will eventually be visited by the truth.

The sixties turned to the seventies, I got married and divorced, and a hundred religious cults sprang up like poison ivy after a long summer rain to take the place of the vacuum of authority in our unprotected, disconnected, naked lives. Take a journey through the sixties like mine, give me the first solid happiness I had known for twelve years and then take it away in the most ego-crushing way possible, then give me God, Who I needed desperately, and a tribe, which I also needed desperately after all that proud and dangerous isolation of the spirit, and I was ripe for it. The Moonies gave me God and a tribe. They gave me a home. For someone else it could have been the Jesus Freaks braying on the corner, the Hare Krishnas chanting in the street, or a covenant community of Catholic charismatics babbling in the Spirit. It was not only us individuals deathly sick of our alienation from the social universe who succumbed to the siren song of the cults. It was and is whole families—ordinary, well-adjusted, religious families in small towns all over America, towns whose teenagers no longer drive cars fast and go steady, but who sit behind shades in dark rooms and smoke marijuana and "make love" to the sound of heavy metal rock music. The girls get pregnant, the guys move on, and the girls have abortions or illegitimate babies.

The cults started big time in the seventies because the sixties left so many of us high and dry and mortgaged to the core by free love. They continue in the nineties because now everyone is alienated from a culture which has no unity of ideas or care or moral substance or protection from things that go bump in the night.

Chapter Two

Inside Look at a Moonie Training Session

Touring the magical sixties as a precursor to my arrival at the doorstep of the Moonies is significant to my own story, but it can give the wrong impression. It can look as if the fodder for cults in the seventies and on into the present day is always the result of a disordered life, especially if that life was further skewered by an abortive marriage. I was indeed ripe for a cult, but what I consciously walked into was not to my mind a totalitarian society filling a vacuum of authority in my life. It was a small commune of interesting and friendly people. The Moonie hook to begin with was not discipline but affection. It was people who cared about me. And that kind of hook can hook anyone.

Was I brainwashed? Does the Unification Church brainwash its recruits? "Giving it up," as it pertains to religious or mystical experience, means giving up your separate, critical, worrying identity to a higher power. It is a voluntary act that often occurs somewhere within any genuine spiritual commitment. Being voluntary, it is not brainwashing. One may decide, however, that the Unification Church's method of recruitment is not a matter of you "giving it up," but of them taking it away from you. By the end of a weekend Moonie training session (called "seminars" for the benefit of the unenlightened), you are in a highly suggestible frame of mind. Why? What have they done to you?

You may realize that you have not been alone for more than five minutes out of the last forty-eight hours. An intense personal interest has been taken in you by someone, a sort of constant companion, usually of the opposite sex, usually the person who recruited you (that is, the person who *invited* you to a weekend *seminar*—the language changes once you are inside). This person has been at your side during the whole weekend, attending to your wants, pumping you for your comments and attitudes about the last lecture, asking about your family, your work, your desires and ideals in life, putting her arm around you in lectures, giving you little gifts, holding your hand as she looks searchingly into your eyes while you try to explain your life to her, and, likely as not, following you to the bathroom and tucking you into bed at night. She has been nice to you and has made you feel important; she has been a little severe with you if you have decided to act "laid back" or lazy or if you have rebelled against attending the next group session or the next lecture. If you say to her, "I just have to go off and think things out for a little while; I'll just go over and sit down by that tree over there"—she is apt to express her disapproval ever so mildly. She pouts a little and looks a trifle guilty, as if she has let you down somehow, as if she has failed you.

"No, no," you say, "it has nothing to do with you. I just have to have some time to *think*." She doesn't believe you. She pouts. Now you feel like you have let her down somehow. You contritely walk back to the group. After all, hasn't she done so much for you?—invested all her time in you? You, who have never had so much attention since you were a baby.

The day is drawing to a close. There is a large campfire. You are sitting with your group, hunched up together, shoulder to shoulder. Dinner is being served. Hot dogs smothered with melted cheese, baked potatoes, and a large, amorphous green salad. A plate is handed to you. You are about to begin eating when you notice that the other people in the group are passing their plates around the circle. You look up guiltily and pass your plate to the next person. You are getting the hang of it. Your "spiritual parent"—that sincere, pretty girl with nice legs who invited you to dinner yesterday—peels an orange and sections it, and hands it over to you. You thank her, smiling, a little confused. She smiles back, reassuring you. On a sudden, absurd impulse you pass half the orange to the dumb-looking, foggy hippie hunched up beside you (the guy you have been trying to avoid all day.) He turns a suddenly grateful face in your direction—and you think things are getting out of hand. When are we going to eat? What does this absurd little ritual of giving have to do with the real world?

Exactly. It is in contrast to the real world, of course. The contrast is *intentional*. This is not a ritual passage into adulthood á la American reality. This is a ritual passage into paradise. It has the quality of a dream.

All this personal attention, all these kindnesses and gestures of giving, all this praise and enthusiasm and friendly (but unsexual) touching, all this face-to-face nonsense (you always sit in circles at a Moonie training camp—no place to hide)—all this is a pollyanna fairy tale compared to the fare ordinarily served up by the world. Just when you think things have gotten a little bit too silly, a little too out of whack with expected human behavior, here comes another peeled orange at you—with a smile. Now, you'd be a pretty hard-hearted bastard not to join in with the spirit of things, wouldn't you?

This is all so silly. But it feels . . . so good. So what the hell. You have flash memories of how it was on jobs, in school, in college, the loneliness and sudden love, breaking into new realities, compromising, gaining and losing, but you kept your integrity . . . all *that* garbage of growing up becomes the bad dream, and this baby-ga-ga stuff feels wonderful. A security grows; love grows. You all of a sudden remember that you once read in an anthropology course about an African tribe of hunters with diminishing game to hunt, near starvation. Each member would, if he made a kill, call out to attract other members of the tribe; he would be incapable of eating if he had no one to share his food with. What a funny time to have such a memory! Then another thought comes unbidden into your mind: the tribal state of life is the natural and good state of life for mankind; where there is no such thing as an "individual" and the tribe is as if one person.

The campfire glows. The stars are coming out against a high, deep blue sky. Everyone now has a full plate in front of him, everyone eats. I am purring like a kitten, blown out with comfort. The group leader (Center Man in Moonie lingo) announces, "We have forty-five minutes to make up a skit to perform for the Family. Does anyone have any suggestions? A song we can write?"

My stomach contracts into a tight knot. Perform? In forty-five minutes? In a skit? On a stage? In front of a hundred people? Arrrrrgh! Somebody suggests a popular song, a melody to write new lyrics to. We go with it. Even I, desperate now to *give* something, come up with a rhymed couplet.

"That's not Principle," says the group leader. (What he meant was that my contribution was outside the bounds of what is appropriate for a spiritual community in conformity to the Divine Principle of the Reverend Sun Myung Moon—my rhymed couplet was a little risque. But he had made a slip of the tongue. "That's not Principle" is an *in house* slogan, an authoritarian bat used a hundred times a day in Moonie life to beat down any small demonstrations of independence or self-will.)

"Let's try to focus on this weekend," says the group leader. "Let's try to make a statement about our experience here." (You get the idea. First a lecture, then discussion of the lecture, an experience, then comment on the experience, recapitulation of the experience in dramatic presentation, concentration on and celebration of us, our thing, our sudden new life, in the exact here and now. Impressing it into each one of us.)

Some things are suggested. We move away from the song to a skit. It is five minutes to show time. Everyone is scrambling around for pencils and paper to write down the lyrics. It turns out we have a song *and* a skit. The group leader confidently merges the scattered melange into a whole, but I know this is all an impossibility. With two minutes to go, we begin to rehearse. It is time for our group to go up to the stage area. I have no idea of what is going on. We'll never be able to get across this complicated choreography. It will be a mess, a dismal failure, a humiliation.

One of us, the dumb hippie I have been trying to avoid, has been chosen to play God. He sits on a chair on a platform at the back of the stage. He expresses approval or disapproval at the events going on below. Below and at stage left a few of us are playing disgruntled, ultra-hip dope addicts. One of us who has a guitar plays our song: it expresses tough cynicism and despair. We sing along haphazardly. God expresses his disapproval. At stage right some joyful young girls are selling flowers. One of our gang glances up, moseys over to stage right, and buys a flower from one of the girls. She smiles. He smiles. God expresses his approval. (*He* knows who is selling those flowers. Heavenly children.) The audience cheers. We have been a success. We sing a Principle song ("Amazing Grace") all together now in the center of the stage. God climbs down off his throne and puts his arms around me and my spiritual parent. The audience goes wild with cheers. I sure feel good.

Other groups have presented their shows before us and have been cheered. Other groups have followed us and we have cheered them. The last skit is over. Everyone is exultant and exhausted. Even the cynics, while maintaining a superior mental stance, have gotten a kick out of it all. Oh yes, I am aware of these. I have watched them during the day, noticing when each one bends a little, taking cues from them for my own unbending. But now, like them, I am pretty unbent. All the groups come together now in a big circle around the campfire. We all grow quiet, and then begin singing a song that goes:

When true simplicity is gained

To bow and to bend we shan't be ashamed. . . .

and afterwards we move into a long, slow, full-throated "Jacob's Ladder," arms draped over each other's shoulders, being served marshmallows singed over the campfire. I am so relaxed, so fulfilled; I feel so warm, so good, so unified with my brothers and sisters. The stars twinkle overhead in a navy blue sky gone ecstatic in the presence of love.

And so, to bed. The men sleep in the Chicken Palace, so named because this is a farm in northern California with a large chicken house now used as a barracks. This is Boonville. If you have read any Moonie exposés, you know what Boonville is. Ladies and gentlemen, this is the place where your poor, innocent, naive sons and daughters are being cruelly brainwashed into an alien creed.

As I spread my sleeping bag out on the floor of the Chicken Palace, I trade a few words with another man, a man a couple of years older than me. He has left the Unification Church and come back, after spending some time in India at the feet of a guru. We commiserate over the fact that there are so few of us who are over thirty. (Most Moonies—in the early 1970s at least—were in their twenties.) We agree that most people our age have committed themselves to a life (such as it is) in some career or at least in some gainful employment (such as it is) and have become just a little too crusted-over, a little too much invested in their particular status quos, to be susceptible to something new and ideal and adventurous. More's the pity. Before I climbed into my sleeping bag, I made the sign of the cross on my chest. I apologized to my companion, saying, "I'm not a Catholic. It's just that, just that, I felt like doing this. Making some sign." He smiled. He knew what I meant.

I didn't know what I meant. I had prayed instinctively as a Catholic on a hilltop when I was in a tight spot after my divorce. Now here I was in a Moonie training camp once again making a

Catholic sign. It makes me think some part of me knew I would end up Catholic from the very start.

From the time we sat down to dinner to the time we went to bed, at most four hours had passed. In those four hours I had gone through all the extremes of emotion. I had felt bewilderment, absurdity, relaxation, silliness, serenity, love, sudden anxiety, terror, excitement, exaltation, deep calm, and unity.

I have a couple of questions. First of all, what genius (evil genius?) created Moonie training sessions? Secondly, and more to the point, is this brainwashing, or is it just that our separate, individual, defensive egos are an artificial construction from beginning to end? That what happens at a Moonie training camp is a sample, if you will, of the natural way mankind should be or can be? Is our susceptibility to this tribal mentality and giving up of ourselves indicative of a psychological weakness or is it a recognition of the lost paradise that is the rightful state of mankind?

Never have I felt so loved and loving—in a trans-personal or all-personal sense—as in a Moonie training session. These words, these descriptions, cannot get the flavor of it right, the sense not only of unity, but of being taken out of the mundane world of ordinary life, into a higher, deeper, more *real* world, that cannot help but elicit from us a gigantic "Yes!"—as if in our heart of hearts we knew that this new world is our birthright. A world that existed perhaps before the Fall of Man.

Isn't heaven supposed to be a place where everyone loves everyone else, where everyone delights in giving, and where there are no defensive barriers between people?

It is Sunday morning. Some idiot walks cheerfully into the Chicken Palace, creaking the wooden floorboards, playing a guitar, and singing, "When the red red robin comes hop hopping along, along . . . ." He passes down one alley and up another between the rows of sleeping bags. You bestir yourself and glance around, looking for something to throw at this singing idiot, this rude interrupter of your delicious slumber—but—wait a minute. You are suddenly awake, and, come to think of it, you feel refreshed, and—you catch yourself just in time from starting to sing along, to join in with this infantile ditty. Next, you think, he will sing, "You are my sunshine." He does.

You get out of your sleeping bag and stumble over to the door of the Chicken Palace, vaguely thinking about finding a place to urinate. You calculate that the creek is nearer than the outhouse, and formulate your plans accordingly. As you walk out into the bright and oddly happy sunlight—*who* is standing there to meet you with a joyfully insipid smile on her face but your spiritual parent! Ahhhhh . . . nuts. You mumble something about having to take a leak and try to wave her away but she takes you by the hand and walks you up the hill to the outhouse, and stands outside (standing outside *listening* to you, you think) and then when you come out she takes your hand again and leads you to the shower stalls, and you think, Oh Christ, it's happening again.

In spite of it's beginning to happen again, you feel a little devilish—you are not fully awake and self-censored, and you notice that your spiritual parent has nice legs and you would really like to take her down by the creek and play with her in the country way, but then you know she knows what you are thinking and she gets a mildly disapproving look on her face, and anyway the sunlight would no longer be happy with you and you remember God on the stage last night. You haven't had a cigarette in twenty-four hours; yesterday's events have made you relaxed, and you are getting aroused just by looking at this young woman—but you know it is not in the cards. So you walk hand in hand (chastely) with this girl you have fallen in love with down to the shower stalls and go inside and brush your teeth and take a shower (while she waits for you outside) and everything is, uh, nice . . . in a nicer , gentler way than you ever felt possible after your stumbling-around passage into adulthood.

Later I find, through turning the tables on this pretty girl and pumping *her* for information, that she has been strung out from Minneapolis to Timbuktu, addicted to heroin, raped by Arabs in the Sahara desert, meditated in the Himalayas, had once been a Nichiren Shoshu Buddhist (the Japanese sect of Buddhism where you chant for goodies to a sacred scroll on the wall), had been on LSD, peyote, hashish and methedrine; she had bounced and been bounced all over the world, and she has landed in a Moonie training camp being nice to me. I gain a sort of respect for her. Then I realize she could have been a kindred soul of that blond beauty I once loved, the *Steppenwolf* girl who felt the call of India and left me in despair in a flat in San Francisco in the bad old days. And I also had once been a

Nichiren Shoshu Buddhist, chanting to a sacred scroll on the wall, for a month or so in 1968. Now I was in a Moonie training camp, being mothered by the queen of the flower children. It seemed fated.

After breakfast (each with his group), we return to the Chicken Palace for a Sunday morning songfest. The sleeping bags have been removed. Twenty rows of chairs face a low wooden stage in front. You are sitting in the middle of a row; on either side of you is the rest of your "Trinity"—the small group you do everything with during the weekend. Each Trinity has its own row of chairs. On your right side is your spiritual parent. She massages your neck as the sun streams into the place and lights up the dust particles in the air. The guitar and tambourine players are warming up on the stage. Ragged songbooks are passed up and down the rows. You share one with your spiritual parent. On the stage someone grabs a microphone and we all break into a spirited rendition of "Higher Ground."

"Lord lift me up"—we all hold hands and pull each other to our feet—"and place me down"—a hundred buttocks hit the chairs (not quite in unison; this is a roughly humorous, amateur show of fun; people are laughing as they sing, looking around at each other; a bearded young giant in a motorcycle jacket has a silly grin on his face as his tiny waif-like spiritual mother drags him to his feet and drags him back down again)—"by faith on heaven's tableland"—people cross their arms and hold them out away from their chests, suggesting a—well, a tableland—"A higher plane, than I have found"—arms zoom around, dip and climb—"Lord place my feet"—stomp, stomp—"On higher ground"—we all climb up and stand on our chairs. The song ends amid a cacophony of cheers and applause and back-slapping.

After the songfest comes a lecture, then we break into our small groups for discussion and lunch, then a fierce dodge ball game (the sides assaulting each other not only with a dodge ball but with loud made-for-the-minute chants like "Holy Avengers bomb them for Father"), then a last lecture followed by a quiet dinner, all in a huge circle. Sunday is pretty much a repeat of Saturday, except on Sunday people are a lot looser.

All lectures are preceded and ended by songs, to establish a rapport between the lecturer and the audience, and to keep the level of attention and harmony high. In the Unification Church, group participation is fostered on every occasion. In what follows, I will present some themes of Moonie theology that one hears in the "Advanced" lecture series. (The "Primary" lectures, the ones you hear at your first training session, are largely an inoffensive introduction composed of vaguely Confucian philosophy and appeals to idealism.)

According to the Divine Principle (allegedly the product of the mind of Sun Myung Moon), God is dual. He is interior character and exterior form. Everything in the creation is likewise dual: interior character and exterior form. Everything is divided into two. The world is divided into Satanic nations and God nations. The Communist nations are Satanic; free nations are Godly. (Actually, all anti-Communist nations are called God nations, whether they are democratic or tyrannical.) The Bible is subjected to a peculiar symbolic interpretation. The Tree of Life in the Garden of Eden, for example, represents Adam. The Tree of the Knowledge of Good and Evil represents Eve.

At the center of religion is the great theme of man's departure from God, his exile, the road back, and the perils and difficulties of that return. This is the seemingly eternal story of human guilt and aspiration, whether the goal is called Heaven or Unity or Perfection or Happiness. The Unification Church seeks to conclude the story happily through a series of ritual, symbolic, faithful, and courageous actions on the world stage, wherein "Indemnity" plays a central part. Indemnity plays such a huge part that though the goal is heaven on earth (a Moonie heaven on earth), the methods are such as to exacerbate the guilt of the individual Moonie. But more of this later.

History is crucial, and for the Unification Church, history is mostly Biblical history. Cain and Abel, Abraham, Isaac, Jacob, Moses, and Jesus are all interpreted as figures in the working out of God's redemption of fallen man. God chooses his companions through accumulated tribal or racial merit (Israel's fidelity to the One God resulted in a high level of merit) and through individual merit, accumulated through obedience to God's will and acts of courage. After that it is up to the potential champion to follow explicitly God's often curious directions—such as, in Abraham's time, the exact rite of sacrifice—in order to establish a "Symbolic Foundation"; and also to demonstrate ultimate courage. A half-hearted commitment is bound to fail, allowing Satan to "invade "the operation. If this happens, the operation has to be repeated at some later date and under more critical conditions, after an indemnity has been paid.

Several major themes of Moonie theology can be gleaned from the above. Firstly, Satan has a pretty large control of things on earth. If God and man, working together, don't get it just right, Satan not only recoups his losses but actually increases his control of the earth. The theory of Indemnity is important here. Abraham's failure to execute the sacrifice of the animals correctly (he forgot to slice up the dove and the fledgling) allowed Satan (in the form of a raven diving down and stealing the birds) to mess up the proceedings. (See Genesis 15:9-11)

The message for Moonies is the crucial importance of following God's instructions exactly, even if some of those instructions may seem trivial or even evil. (Do you see where this can lead? Torture, murder, genocide—all can be justified if God demands it to defeat the wily Satan.)

From this comes the Moonie slogan of "Following Principle." God's champion must obey God exactly. The champion's followers stand in the same relation to God's champion. They must follow the champion explicitly in all their thoughts and actions. The same relation holds between the Trinity leaders or "Center Man" and Trinity members. So if a rank-and-file Moonie does not obey his "Center Man," he is guilty of a sin against God. He is not "Following Principle." The totalitarian structure goes in a straight line from top to bottom. If a Moonie fouls up, he is not only sinning; he is directly responsible for the failure of God's plan of redemption. He has allowed Satan to invade.

Abraham finally succeeded on the individual level (if not the symbolic level) by his great act of faith: his willingness at God's command to sacrifice his own son. And thus God could still use Abraham for his redemptive plan. But Abraham's earlier failure (the botched sacrifice of the animals) caused the 400 year exile of the Hebrews in Egypt.

Heavy indemnity for so slight a mistake! The Jewish diaspora and 2000 years of alienation and harassment after the time of Jesus is seen in the same light—an indemnity necessitated by their failure to "join with" Jesus. Is God such a harsh tyrant then? It would seem so. But Indemnity is not the same thing as punishment. Huge Indemnity when things go wrong is a consequence of Satan's huge power on earth. These niceties are however lost on a humane person contemplating the holocaust of the Nazi extermination camps, as if the Reverend Moon were somehow justifying the outrage. And somehow it seems that he is.

The niceties are lost in the Unification Church's theology too. Who, actually, is requiring these horrifying "indemnities"? God or Satan? It is not always clear. There is a legalistic smell to the proceedings. Satan gets off on a technicality, and is free to wreak further havoc. If it is not quite clear why the omnipotent God is so hamstrung by the powers of evil, the message is terrifically consequential for Moonies. Nearly everything is under the control of Satan. Every event becomes a matter of spiritual life or death. Satan is always just outside the door, waiting to invade. If a Moonie has an automobile accident, it was not caused by his inattention to his driving, but because Satan invaded. If a Moonie falls asleep at the wheel or in a lecture or Family Meeting, it is not because he has not had any sleep to speak of in the last four days, but because "Sleep Spirits" have invaded him. If a Moonie is all of a sudden possessed by a dislike for one of the group leaders, he is just that: possessed.

To return to the lecture, Satan is strong on the earth; God is weak. In fact, God is so weak that he cannot act without the cooperation of man. A much repeated statement: "God has 95% of the responsibility, and man has 5%. But man's 5% responsibility requires his 100% commitment." God will choose a champion, but then everything afterwards is left to the champion, and, just as important, the fidelity of the champion's followers. The whole equation is necessary. Jesus failed his mission because, though his obedience was perfect, the people failed to follow him. (Jesus was supposed to become a Messiah for the whole world in his own lifetime, and was supposed to have married and sired a perfect family as well.) The definition of Messiahship is *ex post facto:* Mr. Moon will have been the Messiah if the whole world follows him. Otherwise he will be just another failed champion, like Jesus. The hint is not lost on Moonies. Nor the terrible consequences of a failure of faith.

(But this coyness about the real nature of Mr. Moon is for public consumption, and for the second level of Moonie gnosis. At the first level, often lasting some weeks, Mr. Moon is not even mentioned by name. At the third level it is still only whispered knowledge, but certain knowledge, that Sun Myung Moon is indeed the Lord of the

Second Advent—with no ifs, ands, or buts about it. This is the last, greatest, binding secret for a Moonie: that the Lord walks on the earth today. Page 160 of the Moonie 120-Day Training Manual delivers up the secret for anyone to check out: "Then they can understand that Reverend Moon is Messiah, Lord of the Second Advent.")

History, which is essentially the spiritual history of God's redemption of man, is repetitive. If some scenario, some drama of redemption wasn't accomplished successfully the first time around, it will be repeated in its essentials after a symbolic number of years has passed. It will be repeated in order that a necessary *condition* is brought about so that a *foundation* can be laid. The condition may be ritual or symbolic or actual and political according to its type, and the foundation likewise. A Foundation must be laid for a Messiah to appear in the world. The 400 year exile of the Hebrews in Egypt laid the foundation for Moses to appear and lead the people to their Abrahamic homeland. The Babylonian captivity of the Jews foreshadowed the "Babylonian Captivity" of the medieval popes at Avignon. Both exiles are said to have gone on for 210 years before things got back in their proper order. Numbers are very important. Early on in history, Satan "invaded" the number "40," so 40 and its multiples (times ten) become significant in terms of redemption history—as does the number "21" and its multiples. If this kind of statement is patently absurd to a rationalist, it is not so to one familiar with traditional Gnostic or numerological doctrines, or to a certain kind of Bible Christian who reads significance into every date and jot and tittle of the Word.

Four thousand (forty times 100) years passed between the creation of Adam and the birth of Jesus. Forget that fossil traces of human beings have been discovered dating back perhaps 500,000 years. *Those* were "symbolic times," and in those times, time itself was foreshortened in relation to real time. *These* are the times of fulfillment, and the counting of years is now literal. A complicated conception, but in this manner differences between modern science and Biblical dating are sidestepped, or, if you accept it, understood and overcome.

It is more important to see that history is *spiritual* history in its fundamentals, and *these* are the end times. Now the world will be destroyed—not by God's fiat but by man's doing nothing to prevent it; or it will enter on the blessed era of the New Jerusalem. It is up to us.

At this point the lecture is over. Wild cheers erupt from the audience, hands are clapped, then held, one with another. Everyone stands and sings "God Bless America," swaying shoulder to shoulder, tears streaming down some faces. It is a riveting and exalting moment. It is the last lecture of the training session. Afterwards will be dinner, not now in separate groups but all together. Then there will be more songs, quiet now, everyone peaceful (if they are already committed) or undergoing a severe conflict of the mind and emotions (if they are not). And now come the gentle, heartfelt invitations to join the Family.

Chapter Three

Moonie Life 1973

That "inside look" was a look at how it was in Boonville, a year or so after I joined up. It is a portrait that can apply to anyone; anyone, that is, who finds himself on a weekend retreat in an isolated rural setting with a bunch of interesting, lively folks who seem to know the secret of communal happiness. In the summer of 1973, at least to my mind, things were milder, more relaxed, and unpressured. Maybe that was because we drove to a city park for games and picnics, and back to the Dana Street house for lectures and skits. The action was not as concentrated as it was later. As I say, I drifted through my first training session in a kind of fog, thinking not about what it was all about, but thinking how I could stick around for a while, have place to camp out, and maybe develop something with Christina. I was utterly unconscious of what was happening to me on a deeper level.

The manner of my initial contact with the Family became a cause for some awkwardness later on. Whenever you meet another Moonie the first thing you are asked is, "Who is your Spiritual Parent?" That is, who was the person who stopped you on the street and asked you to come to dinner or to a weekend seminar? This person forever after has a unique relationship with you in the mystical hierarchy that is the Unification Church. Because I had not been proselytized but had walked right in, I remained, you might say, an orphan. And if you don't think that should have bothered me, you have no idea of the tight and coded linkages that go into forming a group identity. I solved the problem later by claiming Christina (who had befriended me during my first training session) as my spiritual parent—affording me much status, since Christina stands right next to Onni and Dr. Durst himself as the most honored personages in the American branch of the Unification Church.

A word about origins. When I joined the Moonies there were about fifty or sixty members in the Oakland Family (the Dana Street house was in Oakland). At that time there was also a branch in Berkeley, on Euclid Street, and one in San Francisco, but neither of these were doing much in the way of growth. They lacked the scintillating energy of the Oakland Family. The seemingly supernatural power, energy and commitment of the Oakland Family was directly due to the dynamic mix of Onni (real name Yeon Soo Im, now Mrs. Moses Durst) and Christina Morrison (now Christina Sayer). At the beginning it was just these two.

The situation was this. The San Francisco and Berkeley centers were bogged down. Their members were grim and unhappy and lacked enthusiasm. Reverend Moon sent his lieutenant Onni to the San Francisco Bay Area to liven things up. Onni sat at a table on Sproul Plaza at the University of California and one day met Christina. There was an immediate, one might say ordained, spiritual attraction. For a while there were just the two of them, then Christina's brother and sisters joined, then some old friends from Ann Arbor, where Christina had gone to college at the University of Michigan. There were Jeremiah and Evey and a couple of others from what I called "the Ann Arbor contingent." Some of this contingent, I don't remember who, had been involved with the radical Students for a Democratic Society (SDS) at the University of Michigan during the halcyon days of the anti-Vietnam War movement. Then there were Jeffy and Noah and David, all from the University of Pennsylvania. There were nine or ten people in the core group of the Oakland Family, about a year before I joined.

At night we attended lectures upstairs in the Dana Street house. There was an "advanced" series which I was enthusiastic about since God was finally brought into the picture, and the Bible, and mention was made of the Second Coming of Christ. (In Moonie lingo the "Second Coming of Christ" was rendered as the "Lord of the Second Advent.") But this thing was only hinted at, providing a kind of excitement for us newcomers. Then, in my second week, there were History Parts I, II, and III. Much was made of the Biblical story of Jacob's deception of his elder brother Esau. Since Cain had slain Abel early on, apparently God must afterwards always use the second son as His champion. First sons had been "captured" by Satan. First sons of any family were of the lineage of Satan, second sons were of the lineage of God. Such was the dispensation of spiritual history.

More importantly in the story of Jacob was the very act of deception in connivance with his mother to gain the birthright. Translated into our present idiom, this means that the forces of God must necessarily use deception against the forces of evil, and not only for pragmatic reasons, but so as to undermine the symbolic dispensation of Satan. Pretty "advanced" stuff!—but pretty worrisome, too. It seemed to make out a case for playing Satan's game to defeat Satan. But do ends so radically justify the means, when ends and means are not as separate as they seem? It would seem rather that to play Satan's game is to play on Satan's side.

In the Moonie view of things, what seems good, for example a legitimate and morally functioning bureaucracy or government or communications network, may in fact be working according to the Satanic world dispensation; while a murderous general practicing genocide in some Latin American dictatorship may in fact be acting for the triumph of God's dispensation.

The problem is of course how you sort out the good guys from the bad guys. Perhaps Mr. Moon would tell us. (Mr. Moon was now beginning to be mentioned in advanced lectures as perhaps having some connection with the "Lord of the Second Advent." It was all very low key, by suggestion and innuendo: this was about three weeks after I joined the "New Education Foundation.")

It soon became apparent that you sorted out the good guys from the bad guys quite easily on the basis of whether they were Communists or not. Communist nations were promoting the Satanic dispensation, anti-Communist nations were promoting the dispensation of God. Two societies could be mirror images of each other in terms of such things as totalitarian government, enforced conformity, cult of the leader, and murderous goon squads—but the tag-line "Communist" or "anti-Communist" made the one an image of Hell and the other an image of Heaven. North and South Korea come to mind as perfect examples, and these examples were constantly brought up in lectures—not, of course, as I have described them (mirror images). My description was applied to North Korea, while South Korea was called "free" and "democratic" and a "God nation." The mind must be kept focused on symbolic dispensations, and off the realities of power and life and law in a nation. (The first editor of the Moonie-owned *Washington Times* resigned when his editorial critical of the South Korean government was spiked.)

But let us return to a small upstairs room in the Dana Street house in the first week of my residence. It is late evening, after a day's work and after a dinner where we had encouraged invited guests to sing songs and reveal their souls to us, and finally invited promising ones to come back on Saturday morning for a weekend seminar. Now the guests have gone. It is quiet in the house and I am attending a lecture on the Cause of Crimes with Patti and one or two other newcomers. Patti was often hysterical and would break into giggles at the oddest times. But not now. Jeremiah, who ran the Maintenance Company, gave the lecture. There was a poster on the wall picturing a tree. On the tree were branches with apples dangling from them, each apple labeled with a "crime": murder, war, theft, adultery, envy, lust, lying, insincerity . . . obviously this was the Tree of the Knowledge of Good and Evil. I sat next to Patti and traded glances with her as the pointer pointed and Jeremiah talked.

Apparently social factors had nothing to do with the cause of crimes—we must go behind society to the individual because society is made up of individuals. What is in each of us, then, to make for crime? It has a historical basis. We must go back to the Garden of Eden. In that Garden, the Archangel Lucifer seduced Eve, and Eve in turn seduced Adam, and thus began a lineage of human evil, transmitted to each generation through the sexual act. The sexual taint of the Fallen Angel infected the human race from the beginning, and thus we remain, fallen and criminal . . . the Augustinian theory of original sin presented right up front in sophisticated post-hippie Berkeley! I was bemused and at first contemptuous.

(In fact the theory is close to Catholic dogma, except for the Moonie designation of the exact sin of the angel, and the notion that the human sexual act itself, in any context, is tainted with diabolism. The differences are crucial, however. The Moonie view comes closer to Manichaeism, with the whole material and sensual world, as it were, given over to the Evil One.)

After the lecture Jeremiah said to me, "I was nervous when I saw Patti there. She loses control and laughs hysterically whenever Satan is mentioned. You being there seemed to calm her down." I made nothing of that comment except to think that Patti liked me and I liked her, and apparently I had some kind of steadying influence on her. She was red-haired and freckle-faced and had a nicely formed body, and she would grab me by the hand and drag me upstairs to lectures. Was I sexually attracted? Of course—but the very closeness of us all, jam-packed thirty or forty in one two-story house, and all the frenetic activity, day in and day out, had the effect of wiping out physical lust in favor of fleeting emotional contacts. The notion of "making love" was there subliminally, but unmanifested, while gestures and smiles traded here and there made all the difference. You might say the love game went down a notch, where a hand grabbed and held was more than sufficient. It was an ascent into childhood.

Ascent? Perhaps. An "ascent into childhood" means that the disordered emotions and mixed motives of sexual love are rejected—thankfully?—for a pre-pubescent state of life. Patti held my hand, and I held hers, and that seemed enough in that jammed together scenario, with everything kept at a high pitch of emotional and social activity, where you were never alone and could never rest except when you were asleep.

I say much of this in retrospect—there wasn't much time at that time for reflection. But I was bothered at how swiftly and easily we all seemed to slip into an *ersatz* childhood. Perhaps it is a natural human reaction to living twelve to a room—something in our natures that quells the sexual urge in such scenarios in order to keep out the jealousy and rage that can quickly turn into mass mayhem. In any case the Cause of Crimes (we heard that lecture and all lectures over and over again) was premature sex—Adam and Eve were supposed to have grown up before they made love, the consequence being that the human race is sexually mature before it is emotionally mature—in fact it never got a chance to be emotionally mature. Besides that, the origin of this premature sexuality is something alien and inimical to human beings.

Oh, it was not all childlike. I sat in lectures night after night and stared at the hair and bodies of women seated in front of me, and fell in love or lust, and stopped listening to the lecture. I would snap out of my fantasy at the end of the lecture when we all sang a rip-roaring spiritual song and thumped each other on the back and then tumbled off to bed, the men in one room, the women in another, lying in sleeping bags on the floor, the sleeping bags nestled up against each other—to be awakened in four or five hours for group calisthenics in the schoolyard next door and breakfast and work assignments.

That was a typical day: up at six, calisthenics, breakfast presided over by Onni, work all day (most people sold flowers), home at six in the evening hopefully with a guest, dinner and entertainment followed by a lecture for everyone given by Dr. Durst; then send the guests home and go to advanced lectures given by various trinity leaders, then usually a late night trinity meeting. Live a schedule like that for one week and you feel like you've been living it all your life.

Following Center

Following Center is the password to understanding how the Unification Church works. It all starts with God's chosen champion. He is the "Center Man." He is the subject; his followers are the object. All things in the universe are in a dual relationship—subject to some things and object to others. All things exist in a give-and-take relationship. The flower gives nectar to the bee and receives pollination. Similarly, the ideal society exists in a give-and-take relationship. Everyone is subject in some relationships, object in others. (To avoid confusion, it should be made clear that in the special idiom of the Divine Principle, "subject" is the higher of the two, "object" is the lower.) God is Subject; mankind is His object. In relation to nature, mankind is subject; nature is object. The husband is subject; the wife is object. The parents are subject; the children are object.

To make the relationship of subject and object clearer, you should conceive of the subject as focus, as center, as in the nucleus of an atom. The object, in a sense, revolves around the subject, as the electron revolves around the nucleus. The object surrounds, follows, sustains the subject. The object implicitly obeys the subject.

God's champion is the chief subject. He is the paramount Center Man. All his followers are objects in varying degrees. The subject-object relationship continues down to the base of the Family hierarchy. In a "Trinity," the smallest group entity in the Unification Church, the leader is your "Center Man." (The smallest groups were ideally to contain only three people, a subject and two objects—thus the name Trinity—but since there were always many more followers than leaders—and recruitment always outpaced leadership training—reality intruded to constitute groups of an average of seven to fifteen members.)

The arrangement is carried over into every activity. On a work assignment, for example, there might be four or five people from several different trinities. A Center Man (usually the senior Moonie) is chosen from among the people in the work group. He is the leader for that particular assignment. He is the *ad hoc* boss. To follow his direction is to "Follow Center." If you dispute anything with your Center Man you are "Not Following."

It is a week and a half since I have joined the Family. I have finished up my jobs at the Watergate Apartment complex and the Berkeley Public Works Department. Christina asks me if I want to sell flowers. I groan inwardly. Selling is the most distasteful thing I can imagine doing. I say "No."

She says, "How about the Maintenance Company?"

"What do they do?"

They have a rug cleaning operation, an apartment cleaning operation (readying apartments for new tenants), and a night-time restaurant cleaning operation. The business is expanding rapidly because "we always show up on time for our appointments, we do the job rapidly and thoroughly, and we charge less than our competitors."

The apartment cleaning operation sounds OK to me, so I find myself later that morning in a white van speeding over the San Francisco Bay Bridge, crouching among brooms and mops and pails, singing songs. Somewhere in the Sunset district of San Francisco we pile out of the van. There are four of us—the Center Man, another young man, a girl about twenty years old, and myself. We walk into the manager's office and sing "You Are My Sunshine" to him. He grins. I am embarrassed as hell. The manager gives us a list of three or four apartments to clean. We get our mops and brooms and cleanser and sponges out of the van and attack the first apartment. Attack—I mean our Center Man, a nervous young fellow, attacks it. He rushes in and has oven cleaner spread around the oven and Ajax on the bathroom floor and half the living room swept before I get up the gumption to ask him what the rest of us are supposed to be doing. He looks hurriedly around and mumbles something, and then goes back to whipping his broom around the floor. I see that the wall sockets are uncovered, then I spot the covers in a corner. I pick them up and decide to screw them back into their places over the sockets. We have no screwdriver. I look around and finally find a knife. I do the best I can with the knife, but I realize after awhile that some of the screws are missing. The job is left unfinished.

We are on our way to the next apartment. I suggest we split up into two teams of two people each, to make better use of our personnel. This suggestion is turned down—we should all stay together in a group to keep the spirit high—in any case, what would one team do without a Center Man? At the second apartment the girl, at least, has found something to do. She has swiftly grabbed the sponge, bucket, and Ajax before the Center Man can get his hands on them. I finally pick up a broom, thinking we should really have a vacuum cleaner. The broom doesn't have much effect on a pile carpet. After a few frustrating sweeps I am bummed out. I toss the broom in a corner and say, "I'll be outside. I'll wait until you finish." I stomp out and sit down on a curb. I pull out a cigarette, carefully secreted on my person for just such an occasion. (I have struggled mightily to quit smoking, but have not been successful.)

Smoking is forbidden in the Family. It is a vice, and any vice is a doorway through which Satan can enter. And that becomes a self-fulfilling prophecy. I periodically sneak cigarettes, feeling guilty, mad at myself for my inability to overcome the addiction and then angry at the Family. For the lifetime of the cigarette, I am separated. I feel crummy, I feel—bad. I feel rebellious. If I find another Moonie to do this bad thing with, we are immediately in a conspiracy. Some of the other new recruits also find it difficult to quit smoking, and every once in a while we meet late at night out behind the shed in the yard behind the Dana Street house and smoke. The criticisms of the Family or certain people in the Family (especially leaders) or methods or even the Divine Principle itself—the criticisms we have buried and strained against expressing—just naturally come out at such times. We are making a "Negative Base." This is an odious sin.

Little, insipid rebellions like this assume mighty proportions when your opportunities for evil are so limited. Even this early in the program we are getting the message pushed into us that every act is significant for the triumph of good or evil. Everything is magnified to take its place in the cosmic war of God and Devil. A critical thought when one is tired—and a kingdom is lost.

I am smoking the cigarette on the curb, mentally swearing at the incredibly stupid people I have joined up with. The absurdity and artificiality of the "Center Man" business. The idiot Center Man rushing into the job before handing out assignments or sharing any knowledge of techniques. These damn kids.

Just then the girl sticks her head out the door of the apartment and sees me. "You are acting like a child," she says. I blow up. How dare this girl talk to me this way? She is only twenty, and I am thirty years old. I have had a lot of experience in life and I know when something is ridiculous and when it isn't.

I yell at her, "You just go back and do your stuff with your idiotic Center Man. Obviously there is nothing for me to do. And if you or anyone else talks to me like that again, I'll just walk away from this organization." I am acting like a child. She is young and pretty and blond and I am attracted to her.

I realize that, of course, I will have to go back to Oakland with the others tonight. I have been cantankerous, perhaps nit-picking. My rebelliousness has put me out of favor with the Family. I am alone, and weak in my aloneness. I have pulled myself out of the subject-object relationship. I have rebelled against it, like Lucifer rebelled against God. God is the Father, and the Father means Authority. If God is anything in the Unification Church, He is Authority. If you rebel against authority you are cutting your own throat.

So it was already in me. There was already something working deep inside that provoked a severe conflict between self-identity and tribal identity. This is where we begin to realize what a cult does. It is not simply a conflict between my conscience and the dictates of a teaching authority. You can be taught, and the teaching goes into you, and becomes your teaching—but that is all a part of teaching, and you are still yourself. Here I am talking about something else. It starts in the first training session. It hits you on a deeper level, so that, without realizing it, your psyche begins changing, until your very sense of self depends on the favor of another something. Call it the genie of the cult. Or just call it the will of the leader.

I think we must penetrate deeper, to avoid a false impression. It is not a matter of a person getting shaky in the mind and feeling insecure and needing approval. Not necessarily. A person may think of himself as hard-headed, in control, strong in himself. But soon, all of his arguments are arranged around defending his cult or his organization. All his critical faculties are directed against those opposing his sect and none directed within his sect. His very identity, without his realizing it, is now tribal. His whole psychic life is bound to the cult. So if his leader says to drink cyanide, he drinks cyanide (I refer to the Jonestown calamity in The People's Temple some years ago). It is a reasonable thing to do, according to his tribal self. There are priests in the Society of St. Pius X who have been drummed out and vilified by superiors, but they cannot break away mentally. Their very psychological identity is bound up with the Society, even when the Society has treated them like dirt. (We will take a closer look at the Society of St. Pius X later in the book when we examine Catholic sects.)

It is the most self-assured, unreflective, psychologically stable people who are unable to recognize what is happening to them, and who make the best Moonies, or Khmer Rouge, or company men. When people ask me how on earth I could ever have been a Moonie, the implicit question is how could I have been such a psychological misfit as to succumb to a cult. On the contrary, I thank God I was self-reflective enough to break away, though it cost me to do so. It's easy to get into a cult. The people are nice; they welcome you; they are reasonable folks; the philosophy they live by seems all right. It's getting out that's tough.

That night I have a talk with Christina. She listens patiently to my criticisms. I say, "Look, I don't mind not running things. I don't mind somebody else running things unless they run them poorly. If I am running things, and I see that somebody else has more expertise—say, we're on a painting job and somebody else has worked before as a house painter—I would delegate the authority for the job to him. I would let him be the Center Man for that job. That way you avoid a lot of wasted motion and frustration. With this arbitrary Center Man structure, you have no flexibility."

She agrees with everything I say. She thinks it's great the way I can see through to the core of things. She is sad that so many of us in the Family are so stupid. I should try to realize that many people have no real idea of give-and-take. If I only knew how *impatient* she got with people sometimes.

She is on my side. By now I am comforting her, letting her know I realize how this is all an experiment, how tough it is sometimes to get things happening right, especially when you are trying to make something radically ideal work on the practical level. I sympathize with her. We are having an adult conversation.

She says, "How would you like to drive the truck for a flower selling team?" All of a sudden my negativity has disappeared. Drive the truck? Sure thing! Christina sure is a smart woman. She has copped to my need for status. I will be a Center Man!

For someone who has not been Following Center very well, I'm making out OK. Actually, I think Christina is handling me with kid gloves. I am older than most of the recruits, and understandably less malleable. I am also intelligent and filled with ideas; I could be of some greater than normal value to the Family. I think Christina likes me specially.

The next day I drove one of the white vans to San Francisco to pick up our flowers at the wholesaler's. I have five or six young people in my team. There is loud singing in the van, but I refuse to join in. I make it known that since I am driving the vehicle, I am responsible for everyone's life. I refuse to be distracted. I am Center Man.

After we pick up our flowers—carnations and roses—we drive to the Marina area of San Francisco. There I let out one "flower child" at a time, spaced out over a half mile. While they are gone, I prepare more bundles of flowers, then drive back along the route and meet my charges where I let them off, and each takes more bundles. We repeat this procedure several times during the day.

The high point of that day was when one of the flower selling girls said, "You sure get back to pick us up on time a lot better than Alex did when he drove." (I'm a good Center Man.)

I am conscious of an added dimension adhering to every event connected with the Unification Church. Everything that occurs seems to point beyond itself. Everything has a shimmering quality of super-importance.

Christina is giving a lecture upstairs in the Dana Street house. I am sitting with twenty, or so, others. As I gaze at Christina, a pleasant feeling develops in my forehead in the region of the fabled "third eye" or psychic opening. And I am thinking, "This woman is blessed."

I am washing dishes with a young woman in the kitchen. I feel strongly that I have been here before; that I have known this woman in some past life—or rather I am translated to a feeling of time out of time, a momentary waking-dream state, the effect being to make a mundane experience into something extraordinary, memorable; a knowledge of having been here before—will be here again—the forces of time all driving to this moment. Did I dream this woman? Did I dream standing next to this woman, washing dishes? Are the words we are saying now to each other repeated from an earlier conversation, dreamed or lived before?

(During *déjà vu* experiences, the mind habitually comes up with these two answers: "it happened before," or "I dreamed it," at the same time knowing, somehow, that neither of these answers is correct.)

You are conscious that you have lived more than this particular life or that *now* you live more than this particular life. You are aware of parallel events in other dimensions, of situations ordained, repeated (until you get it right?).

It may be that there are key moments in life when dimensions cross, heightening the here and now experience to a place out of time, charging the moment with supernal importance.

It is about three weeks since I have joined the Family. A bunch of us are driven from the Dana Street house over to the large San Francisco headquarters to help prepare for a special event. Fifty Japanese Family members are to arrive and spend some days here in special study and ceremony. I help out with painting and cleaning. (But things are uncoordinated. Some people rush about in a fever of energy while others stand around wondering what to do.) I am in a huge, empty auditorium, and on the far wall down in front is a huge red and white banner emblazoned with the words UNIFICATION CHURCH, and in the middle, dominating the whole arena, is a gigantic picture of Reverend Moon. For the first time it hits me that we are taking part in a serious, world-wide effort, possibly with the sanction of God Himself.

Later I am teamed up with a young, pretty girl to make up beds for the visiting students. She is from the San Jose Family (sixty miles south of San Francisco). We share notes on our Family experiences. We are in an upstairs hall with fifty bunk beds lined up in rows. After we make the beds, brand new sleeping bags will be placed on each one, gifts from the San Francisco Family to the Japanese students. I criticize the cost and the waste. Why are we making up the beds with sheets and blankets and pillows if the students will be sleeping in sleeping bags anyway? Why all these brand new sleeping bags? Couldn't the money be put to better use?

All of a sudden an interior voice says, "Give it up. Just give it up." Immediately I experience an absolute bliss, a certainty of heaven, a knowledge of eternity and eternal love, a knowing that all of us, all the people, all the universe, will be in bliss, in heaven, that we are *now* and always *have been* and always *will be* in a place of infinite open joy, pure serenity, absolute security, and comfort, always have been and always will be in the Holy Mountain, the New Jerusalem. In that momentary glimpse of eternity, the world of pain and suffering we live in simply did not exist.

I "came back" and ecstatically resumed tucking in the corner of a sheet on a bunk bed in a loft in San Francisco under the auspices and protection and direction of the Unification Church, U.S.A.

This is powerful subjective evidence for the truth of the Unification Church, is it not? And yet I had had a similar experience some six years earlier while sitting in a restaurant, discussing something or other with a friend, staring up at a mural on the wall portraying an immaculate landscape: it hit me then too. This former experience was during the "summer of love" in the Haight-Ashbury district of San Francisco in 1967. That time had been for me a riot of tasting and testing a multitude of odd spiritual experiences. Some of those experiences were wonderfully auspicious. Some were not.

For some reason I didn't continue as a driver for the flower team. I spent at most a couple of days at it. Maybe Alex complained about my taking over his job. In quick succession I sold flowers for a few days (I hated that, and did very poorly at it), worked with the Gardening Company mowing lawns and pruning trees for some weeks, then did some more apartment cleaning. It became known that I knew how to bake bread, so I volunteered to take on that job for the Family. I made thirty loaves a day, more on Fridays in preparation for the weekend training sessions. This was my favorite job with the Family. I remember standing over the stove in the upstairs kitchen at the Dana Street house, peering out the window and across to the Catholic convent next door. From time to time I would see some nuns moving silently around the courtyard during what was presumably their recreation period. I felt spiritually akin to the nuns, feeling that I, too, was living a life devoted to God. I liked the fact that I was providing bread for "my family. "I would steal a couple of eggs out of the refrigerator and throw them in the batch, and substitute honey for molasses in the recipe when no one was watching. I also changed the recipe to all whole wheat flower instead of half white and half wheat, and added powdered milk on occasion. All the Family members liked my bread. They would tell me about it, not in public ceremony, but in little private asides, and this was important to me since I knew it was genuine.

One day I was in the kitchen making up a batch of bread (I used a trick I had learned before—pouring oil on the counter to keep the dough from sticking rather than using dry flour—the oil would soak into the dough and enrich it). I was lost in a reverie, liking myself for adding these extras, knowing they added to the food budget, but also knowing how little things, like special , delicious bread to eat, made a big difference in morale. The kitchen abutted Onni's bedroom. She walked out and told me, "You are bad. You don't believe in the Principle."

I was nonplused. She was right, in a way. I had talked with Christina the day before, sharing with her my troubles with this complex system of theology. In one sense the Principle was at least mathematically beautiful. It seemed to be the product of a masterful mind, a mind trying to combine all knowledge into a complete package. It was just this that also bothered me. In its ordering of all things it necessarily simplified them, and maybe got it all wrong as well. I expressed it, I think, something like this:

"I am a poet. I build mythologies in my mind. I can agree totally with the Principle, or I can make up a system of my own, agreeing or disagreeing with the Principle on any point. The Principle can be seen as just another mental creation."

I saw no connection, for example, between Abraham's botched sacrifice of the animals and the 400 year exile of the Hebrews in Egypt. I thought it was arbitrary to say that the Tree of the Knowledge of Good and Evil represented Eve, with the implication that evil comes from women. Many other points in the Principle seemed an arbitrary imposition of symbolism on mysterious realities.

You can see that instead of becoming more and more of a true believer, I was becoming less convinced. I was tiring of the constant group participation, group lectures, group singing, group praying, and what began to seem like contrived communication. The pleasure I got from private and spontaneous praise (for my bread) began to show me the fallacy of intentional, always public praise . Something began to seem hollow about the whole thing.

Though it felt very nice initially, there was something unreal about wildly cheering a wretched off-key singing performance with the same intensity as one cheered a melodious, quality singing performance.

Constantly acted-out positive emotion and approbation begins to wear out one's sense of integrity, or let's say, one's sense of discrimination, or let's even say, one's sense of self. When the emotional reservoir begins to get used up and when the body is pushed and pushed so that you always feel worn out, the mind gets frazzled and the speech pro-forma, and you end up with the glassy-eyed one-dimensionality so apparent to Moonie-watchers.

This said, I will return to my private reverie in the kitchen, lovingly baking bread for my people. One day Noah, the lecturer who had joined us for lunch on my first day of work in the Unification Church, rushed into the kitchen, opened the cabinet near me, and pinched some salt out of a little bowl. He hurriedly tossed the salt onto the loose-leaf binder he was carrying, and sped away.

What the hell, I thought. This guy is really strange. Then I dismissed it out of mind. My attitude towards the perverse event was the same attitude I had displayed when confronted with Sleep Spirits by Beth after Dr. Durst's lecture the night after my first contact with the Moonies. A bit of private aberration. (It takes all kinds.)

As in the case of Sleep Spirits, I was to learn that Holy Salt was an integral part of Unification Church theology. The salt had been blessed by Father Moon. Noah had thrown a pinch of it on his lecture notes to help ensure a successful lecture.

Underneath the Divine Principle there is a good deal of Korean magic.

One more event in the kitchen before I leave. Onni said to me one day, "You should work in the daytime and bake bread at night."

"Right," I said. "When do I sleep, by the way?"

She gave me a hard look and walked away. What a fanatic, I thought. Onni and I began not to like each other. Which was trouble, since she was Center Man for the whole Oakland Family.

I think you understand by now (and perhaps I understand it for the first time now) that during my days in the kitchen, stealing eggs to enrich the bread I was making (putting one over on the powers-that-be)—looking at the nuns in the courtyard below, relishing our common "saintliness" and feeling good and fatherly, but a little removed from a centrality of commitment, that I was already preparing my departure from the Unification Church. If only it had been so simple and had not kept torturing me for eight years.

About that time I complained to Christina that I was not getting enough sleep. Twelve of us brothers slept in sleeping bags on the floor of a tiny room near the back of the house. For some reason people would come in at all hours of the night, stepping over the sleeping bodies, sometimes stumbling. Or an alarm clock would go off right next to me at three o'clock in the morning. I didn't question these comings and goings in the middle of the night. I was just getting mad that they were causing me to get only three or four undisturbed hours of sleep a night. I think I was working for the Gardening Company at this juncture and baking bread in the evening. I was pretty exhausted.

Much to my surprise Christina suggested I move into the house that Dr. Durst owned in Piedmont (a wealthy little city within the borders of the city of Oakland). There I would get a good six hours of sleep a night, and I would be with older Family members who would have a more mature influence on me. She had once again immediately pandered to my wishes. I imagined that she was a little impatient with me by now. I felt guilty. After all, I got more sleep than most of my brothers. I didn't feel right about getting special treatment. I was pretty selfish to demand so much comfort while my brethren were denying themselves to build a new world.

"Building a new world!"—a constantly heard slogan, a pervasive conversational phrase, calculated to engender enthusiasm in the worn out bodies falling asleep on their feet in Family meetings or tumbling into bed for a couple hours of precious rest after a twenty hour day.

Later I found out why there were these comings and goings in the middle of the night. Prayer meetings were often held for leaders at midnight. The brothers would wrestle with each other for a half hour or so, building energy (and dissipating sexual need, I think now in retrospect). They would pray, all together, but with individual prayers, deeply emotional gut-wrenching moaning and shouting prayers. Only the most strenuous emotional praying could break through the Satanic shield covering the earth and reach the ears of God. The brothers would cry out their faith and dedication, comforting the tears of God, abandoning themselves to His will. Then there would be a group prayer for every new Moonie. I once saw a long list. My name was on it. The trinity leaders would pray over each name, pray for our faith and fidelity.

At two or three a.m. the prayer session would be over, and the leaders would catch a few hours sleep. Thus the stumbling over bodies in my room at night.

As I write this, I flash on that state of abandonment, of heart-gripping prayer in the small hours of the night, of getting up at five in the morning to direct the day's events, that *using up of yourself*, that sleepwalk, that hypnotic state of everything given over to the karmic well of Father Moon.

Very early in my stay at Dana Street I saw a curious declaration written on the door of the sisters' sleeping room. "Get rid of all sleep! All for Higher Purpose!"—signed Beth, my crazy friend. No wonder she had fallen asleep in my truck that first night in Moonieland.

Heavenly Deception

An unfortunate phrase in the Moonie lexicon if you are a defender of the Unification Church, but its usage at least suggests that Moonies do know the difference between lying and telling the truth. I first heard the slogan in 1975 when I was trying to edge my way back into the Family. I was angry when I heard it and told the young man that if he thought what we were doing was a lie, he was in the wrong place. I didn't realize that the slogan was another of those linguistic curiosities that had been taken from somewhere in the Principle and had become common parlance.

The scriptural authority for "heavenly deception" comes from the story of Jacob and Esau. Although Jacob tricked Esau, he was the one chosen by God to advance the dispensation. Deception is therefore required on *our* side to fulfill some arcane symbolic necessity. In practical terms, it is a matter of the ends justifying the means.

I do recall, quite clearly, saying to Christina a few days after I joined up, "The end does not justify the means." I also remember her troubled disagreement. I don't recall in particular what was bothering me, but I must have noticed some fast and loose attitudes towards the truth very early in my stay. I was worried that a lot of little lies could very easily pyramid to the One Big Lie. Once you have the habit of lying it becomes difficult to lose it. But no, a "Higher Truth" justifies a lower lie. Thus "Higher Truth" was the tandem slogan to "Heavenly Deception." "Higher Truth" was a favorite expression of Onni's.

I didn't join the Unification Church. I joined something called the "New Education Foundation"—a mild enough name. It was weeks before I even realized we were more than a small local commune, idealistic and vaguely religious. It was weeks before I heard mention of the Unification Church or Father Moon. By then I was pretty well tracked into the life. We went through a series of name changes in the summer of 1973. What would be most appealing to idealistic young people? A name that stuck was "Creative Community Project." The Boonville camp, a hundred miles or so north of Oakland, was just being re-established at that time, and that name would be an effective lure to entice people to spend a weekend or a week at our model "Ideal City." Boonville was of course never to be a city, ideal or otherwise, but our brochures pictured a futuristic development with lots of open space, green grass and trees and gardens.

I must admit I got a kick out of the double language—innocuous names for the seduction of outsiders, but calling a spade a spade "in house." We knew they were training sessions, not seminars. The nice liberal academic world from which we gathered our troops had its appropriate language, but once inside, the language and the world both changed towards a tighter, combative, military focus. We were in a war, after all.

It was a few weeks after I joined the Unification Church that I first heard the name Sun Myung Moon. We were all called to a Family Meeting one night after the guests had been sent away, and there Christina gently told us the story of our "founder," a Korean gentleman who had prayed mightily to God for direction and who had suffered terribly at the hands of the Communists in North Korea. While incarcerated in a concentration camp, he had shared his meager rations with his fellow prisoners, rations which were hardly enough to keep one man alive. For some miraculous and providential reason, the Reverend Moon was kept alive....

Later on we received more of the story. At the age of sixteen, Reverend Moon stood on a hilltop in Korea and had a vision. Jesus appeared to him and said, "Finish my work." This vision was in 1936. In subsequent years the prophet prayed earnestly for an answer to the age-old philosophical question: where does evil come from? The answer he got, after many spiritual trials, was that Lucifer, previously the most perfect and beautiful of God's creatures, became an enemy to God because of the envy he felt when he saw God's love poured out no longer to him alone but to the new creation, Adam. So he flew down to the Garden of Eden and proceeded to mess up the proceedings.

(This is more or less the Catholic and Protestant Fundamentalist position, so the question arises as to why the young prophet didn't simply consult a local priest or minister.)

Reverend Moon, Lord of the Second Advent. I have a flash image of this ranting lunatic with his army of sleep-walkers. I see duplicity and stonewalling and out-and-out big lies; I see vast wealth at the top of the hierarchy and wretched poverty at the bottom; I see a ubiquitous "do as I say, not as I do." I see everything that can go wrong with a religion presented right up front in the Unification Church.

Sexual contact of any kind is forbidden in the Unification Church until forty days after marriage, and, as often as not, couples are split up in separate cities or countries for long periods of time just after they are married. And marriages are allowed only at the whim of Mr. Moon. Five years or so pass between "Blessings," mass marriages performed by Mr. Moon. Your mate may be someone you know, but more likely it will be a total stranger.

I saw Onni and Dr. Durst, now heads of the Unification Church in America, necking in the front seat of their Lincoln Continental before they were married.

Alcoholic beverages are forbidden in the Unification Church. In 1974 I took Christina out for a pizza dinner and we both had a glass of wine. (This was when I was out of the Family.) She told me that Onni made a delicious wine for private consumption.

Father Moon requires a brand new sheet to sleep on every night. He requires a brand new glass to drink from at every meal, and brand new plates to eat from. This is for purposes of ritual purity. Moonies sleep thirty in a room on a hard floor in sleeping bags. Their clothing is communal, catch as catch can. Flower selling teams that are on the road, moving from city to city, are apt to subsist on a diet of day-old bread scrounged from bakeries along with stale cupcakes and Danish twists. Every now and then, on special occasions, they may be treated to ice cream or a McDonald's hamburger, for which they are hugely grateful to their Center Man.

On Christina's suggestion I moved into Dr. Durst's house in Piedmont. Dr. Durst, Jeffy (one of the Trinity leaders), myself and a couple of others slept on the floor. We usually got to bed around midnight and slept undisturbed—thank God—for six hours. As I woke in the morning I would see Dr. Durst kneeling on top of his sleeping bag, head down, praying silently.

Our breakfasts were generous—fruit, hot cereal with honey and milk, and very often toasted bread with melted cheese on top. We would start breakfast with a Bible reading.

I was looking for a job in those days. I talked to several bank vice-presidents. I could go on these interviews with confidence because I was not doing them for myself, but for the Family. Because of this, I felt a sort of larger self than self, a freedom and lack of inhibition. I found it easy to sell myself when I was not selling myself for myself alone. I was part of a spiritual atmosphere, in a spiritual home.

One thing at Dr. Durst's house bothered me very much. Dr. Durst was divorced but had his two boys living with him, ages four and six. The four year old was a bit of a hellion. (They usually are.) Michelle, a Family member, would come over every morning and house-sit with him. When he would get out of hand, he would be punished by being locked in a closet for an hour or two. As I walked in, I would hear his cries and pathetic weeping coming from the closet. The experience would leave him in a state of terror.

I felt that this kind of punishment was extremely harmful to a child and said so. It also reflected badly on the Unification Church. Is this how parental love works in the Family? This was another indication of a sinister difference between Moonie theory and Moonie practice. Primarily, though, I was sympathetic towards the child, and angry with Michelle. Michelle told me that Onni had mandated that kind of punishment.

Poor Michelle! Poor Dr. Durst! Poor Hymie!

One day a new young Family member with a broken arm moved in with us. I asked him why. (Most of the Piedmont house residents were leaders or relative old-timers like me.) The youth said he had been told to stay here for the length of time it would take for his arm to heal and for the cast to be removed. It would not look good for the guests invited to dinner to see a Family member with a broken arm, so he was moved out of the Dana Street house for the duration.

I moved back to the Dana Street house. I'm not sure why; I think I felt the need to get back into the thick of things again. At Dana Street a dinner, songs, and lecture would be presented for potential recruits. Everyone sat on the floor, kneeling or cross-legged. During the dinner we Family members would sit with the recruits (surrounding and isolating them from each other) and sound them out. I resisted doing this. Only occasionally did I have enough enthusiasm for our cause to gain the spirit of clever intention, those techniques of the touch on the arm, the eye contact, the expression of profound interest in whatever this wonderful new person had to say. It was too swift a turnaround for me. I had been seduced by affection and kindness, now I was to seduce. You must understand, though, that I did not see it like that if I was spiritually committed. That commitment was not just a mental act, but a state of grace where you *knew*, and you knew that you were doing this person an extremely valuable service. Every once in a while I was able to give myself up to that exalted higher ground, but most of the time I felt we were just manipulating people. Certainty and skepticism traded places on a daily basis.

I had received enough hints of that exalted state of consciousness to first, give my truck to the Gardening Company (it was worth about $800) and then sign my land over to the Family. Actually, I signed it over to Onni. The equity in the land was about $3000. There was really no question in my mind that I would give the Family my truck or my land, or willingly endorse my paychecks from my various jobs over to the Family. It was the Family, and I more or less knew what was expected. I knew that this was a commitment that included anything monetary, and I accepted that implicitly. Even in the first training session I think I realized as much. It is difficult to explain to a materialistic society, but I was in a sense looking for a chance to get rid of money. My ideal was to labor and to be fed and sheltered without the artificial middleman of a means of exchange. A "vow of poverty" was not at all difficult for me; it was a pleasure. I had gained a society that fed me in more ways than one. Here I was among spiritual people living the life of the spirit: what need did I have for my own money?

Giving up my few assets was the easiest thing for me to do. There were other things I couldn't do. I couldn't sell flowers . The week or so I tried, I remember the rose thorns sticking into my hands, my anger and frustration at that, and the extreme embarrassment I felt when I tried to con somebody into buying a flower from me. I could never really get it out of my head that selling is conning. Perhaps I could have gotten over that inhibition if I had really believed that we had a pearl of great price to sell.

But we *lied* when we sold flowers. We were a Christian group engaged in a special project to help runaway children. Or we were a drug rehabilitation group. Or we were a city-sponsored group raising funds to help incorrigible teenagers. Or all of these things at once. I remember saying these things to a little old lady whose door I had rapped on in north Berkeley, and hating myself for it. We sold leftover roses that had been laying around the house for days and which were two hours from wilting. This was often late at night, after the dinner and lecture, and we went from bar to bar in the darker sections of town. I say "we"—but I didn't. I refused. I would go upstairs and make up a batch of bread, and concern myself anxiously about our small-time duplicity.

And I never brought a "guest" home for dinner. I had one hell of a time trying to proselytize anyone. I could add an argument if another Moonie was there, but I could never initiate a contact. The one or two times I tried I felt foolish as hell. I was jealous of these brazen kids who could. I felt it as a lack in myself. I wished I could get into that larger uninhibited space where ease and certainty followed.

I remember one day going along with some other Family members to our table on Sproul Plaza on the U.C. Berkeley campus, trying to join with them in some happy sunshine song or other. The table next to ours was manned by the Young Socialist Alliance. I felt *really* out of place. Not that I have any love for the Y.S.A.—I did believe our theory was better. When you leave God out of your theory of the cosmos, you open the door for Satan (or any old unnamed evil)—I believed that much. But my temperament was more like theirs—contemptuous, cynical, critical. A flood of memories washed over me. This same campus in 1968—the anti-Vietnam war marches I had been on, the clashes with police, the tear gas, the Oakland cops barring our way on Adeline Avenue and standing idly by while Hell's Angels charged our parade and beat up on bespectacled professors and women with babies in their arms. And now here I was trying to be ready to talk about a strange God who required Indemnity and trying to sing "God Bless America" to sniffy co-eds while the mute sun beat down on the comedy.

An effeminate young man sat down on the seat next to me. He asked me about the Unification Church (how did he know?—since our placard said only "Creative Community Project" and talked about an "Ideal City"). He talked to me about God and Jesus Christ and the spiritual life. After a half hour or so of this, be blessed me with a smile and told me how he had been saved at a Baptist camp meeting in North Carolina some months ago. He was so happy. Jesus was his Personal Lord and Savior. He was certain of Heaven.

At this point a fellow Moonie, a young woman, turned and whispered in my ear, "I thought he was up to something like that."

But I handled the situation nicely. I congratulated the young man on his salvation, and asked him, "But what are you going to do now? What are you doing for the salvation of the world? Don't you think Jesus wants us not to just sit on our duffs in a state of bliss, but act to bring about a heaven on earth for everyone?"

He was taken aback. "I never thought of that," he said.

"That's just what we are trying to do," I said, "we are trying to bring about an ideal world."

He walked away, defeated—at least temporarily. Well, I thought, we can beat the Jesus Freaks anyway.

Back at the house we prepared for the weekend training session. I was frightened. I was frightened of the Saturday night performance. The lectures were OK, the dodge ball was OK (it was dodge ball now instead of volley ball). The small group discussions were OK. The only thing that was *not* OK was the mini light opera to be created during an anxious dinner and performed in front of a hundred smiling but (I thought) critical souls. I had utter stage fright. Just thinking about it made my bowels hurt.

I decided I needed some practice. Before our ordinary weeknight dinner, when songs were requested from guests or Family members, I got up in front of the room (the room packed with fifty Family members and guests kneeling or sitting with hands clasped around knees) with two other Moonies and tried to sing. I got halfway through the song and lost the key and lost my voice. The others in my group were shy too, they had lost it, and we all dribbled down into a thin wail. Luckily another Family member sitting on the floor noticed the disaster and joined in strongly, giving us the strength to finish the song with less than total humiliation. I was eternally grateful. A moment or two later I was sitting on that same floor next to our benefactor, Jeremiah, while a guest guitarist, a traveling hippie who was full of himself but had no talent whatsoever, sang and played a song for us—horribly. After the song was over everyone cheered. I began to cry (I was still shaken by what had happened before). Jeremiah put his arm around my shoulder.

"What's the matter?"

I choked it out—"That guy was terrible . . . and . . . they cheered him anyway. You people are so damn . . . *nice* . . . all my life there was this damn *judgment* . . . you people are so damn *good*."

This was a couple of weeks *after* I had begun to see something sinister in hollow praise for indifferent performances. Everything changes when you are in the spotlight, needing forgiveness, needing help, needing . . . love. On the other hand, something violent was happening to my soul. It seemed that as my skepticism grew, so did my need to be accepted, and my need to be exactly and totally in the midst of the tribe. Without judgment—your critical judgment of others or others' critical judgment of you—there is bliss. But at what a cost? Lose yourself in the bosom of Abraham and be turned out like a rubber doll in the armies of the night?

Something is very right, and something is very wrong—both at the same time.

The first dream I had occurred about a week after I joined the Family. I was in the front seat of a coup with Onni, making love to her. There was just the coup, the darkness, the windshield split in two like on old-style Model A Fords, me on top of Onni. We were both excited. She was protesting my aggression, saying, "What about my boyfriend? My boyfriend?"

And I was saying, "Don't worry, don't worry about him."

The scene shifted. There was darkness all around. There were streets and hills and we were running up and down. Most of the Family members had become Nazi storm troopers, blond and husky, and they were chasing us. I was running as fast as I could next to a hedge, rounding a corner with Jeffy. Jeffy and I were the only male Family members who were on the other side. The Nazis were chasing us. They had declared war on sex. They were after the women. We ran down a hill. It was raining and dark, and the ground was slippery. Down in the next valley the Nazis had caught one of the sisters. They were accusing her of sex. They were closing in on her. She was backed up on top of a flat rock, cringing, trying to hide herself. The rock turned into an iron cage with her inside. The Nazis were running near. They were brandishing torches. They were going to burn her in a bonfire. I couldn't believe it! The girl was Rachel, who had complimented me on getting back to the pick-up point on time when I drove the van for the flower sellers.

It was too late. The Nazis were after Jeffy and me too. We ran up a defile in the cliff and got away. It was the end. All the women had been marked for destruction, and all the men had turned into brutal Nazis. They were killing all the women for the crime of sex. Only Jeffy and I made our escape.

Was this dream, surreal as it was, precognitive? Rachel, a couple of weeks later, was to give me a human moment on my first day as Center Man. Two years later I caught a glimpse of Moses Durst lying on top of Onni in their Lincoln Continental just inside the Boonville camp, before they were married. Jeffy had been one of the University of Pennsylvania contingent, a friend of David's and a friend of Noah's. When I lived at Dr. Durst's house a month or so after the dream, Jeffy lived there and made melted cheese on toast for us in the morning. He was working on a doctorate at the University of California between Pioneer missions when he would drive flower selling teams across the country and feed them on stale bread and once in a while a hamburger. Later he established and ran the Aladdin delicatessen on College Avenue in Berkeley. He was deprogrammed in 1976.

And I was to notice that a goodly number of male recruits, especially the most laid back long-haired hippies, turned into perfect little order-taking and order-giving fascists once they joined the Family. If there was one thing that bothered me more than anything else, it was the facility with which the most individualistic young men became divested of personality and imbued with the most rigid ultra-conformist false face once they fell in with the princess Onni and her leader, the Lord Mr. Moon.

(The women seemed to find their appropriate Moonie status without so great a change in themselves. *Pace* the feminists, I think females are more naturally suited to the nest than are males, and it is male aggression that must be quelled in a beehive scenario and changed into something else lest jealous rage and violence erupt and destroy the hive.)

The second dream was all in brown. I was responsible for bringing someone to a training session—and it was already half over! I was supposed to get him to come across the bay to the old, decrepit house in San Francisco where the training session was taking place. The house had a staircase. We had to get to the second floor. There was a buzzer to ring. Upstairs there was a button to push that would unlock the front door and let us in. It was a dilapidated old two story house divided into flats, like the flats I used to live in, in the Fillmore district of San Francisco. Now I was trying to get my recruit on the phone, but the connection was poor. I had been derelict in my duty. I had missed a day already, and now I was trying desperately to get him to come to at least part of the training session. If I could push the button (I was inside now), I could let him in. As I crept near the button I saw that the ivory was cracked. It was old and chipped away and had not been replaced. I pushed on it anyway. It didn't work. The downstairs door remained locked. It became impossible. Everything was too old and dilapidated to work. Dim singing was heard on the other side of the door, but it was too late for us to get in. I felt horrible. I had almost gotten this guy to attend the training session, but had failed, through my own laziness. I had forgotten to call him at a crucial time.

(And in the morning I told the dream to Christina in our Sunday morning small group. I was apologetic. This was the Sunday morning of a training session. We had pancakes on the stoop at the back of the Dana Street house. The Sunday morning small group breakfast was the occasion for the Center Man to ask if anyone had had a dream last night. This was the introduction to the spirit world. Did you have a dream? Do you think it had any spiritual significance?—and then: Does anyone think there could be a world of spirits? All very mild, very circumspect, very seductive, leading you into the doctrine slowly. In the advanced lectures you learn that everyone has a "spirit man." This is a sort of higher self, or perhaps a guardian angel, who lives in the unseen universe, and is your connection with God.)

Moonies are strong on psychic proof. There was a Christian mystic lady in town, giving a lecture down in San Leandro. I chauffeured Onni, Christina, and Susan down to the lecture. Onni had the address of the place and was asking to see if we knew how to get there. Susan would nervously declare that we should take a right here, a left there. She hadn't the slightest idea where she was leading us. I finally saw through the act and stopped at a gas station to ask for directions. I followed the attendant's directions, and we finally arrived at the lecture hall a half hour late. Onni was peeved. She humiliated Susan, shouting at her that she was "stupid!" Did Onni compliment me for finally getting us there? No. She only had time to embarrass the young lady.

I mention this incident because it is typical of Moonie behavior—a kind of cringing obeisance so frightened of the wrath of the overlord that practical reality is lost sight of. "Can you do this?—Get us there?"—"Oh yes"—then you try to muddle through. Nearly always it would have been better to admit ignorance in the first place and incur a lesser wrath than the wrath that comes after a mission is botched. This kind of thing occurs generally in overly authoritarian sects. Brother Gino Burresi's nuns (more on him in a later chapter) were never to interrupt their superiors if the superiors were talking to someone else. A young nun burst in, to report a fire raging on the property. But her superior was talking over some business matter with another nun. So the young woman waited and waited and waited. Finally the superior turned to her impatiently, was told about the fire raging outside, and angrily berated the messenger. It is not as if the young nun, if she had been clear-headed, would not have broken the rule in the face of an emergency. But her soul was so stricken by her re-education that no emergency could compete with the horror of breaking a rule. Her intimidation before a superior consumed everything. In the same way a Moonie, always in an "object" relation to a "subject," becomes so brow-beaten that he is utterly intimidated by the "subject's" will. I have heard Moonie men so denuded of personality that they parrot the high, Asiatic, chirping voice of Onni without realizing it.

We scrambled into the full lecture hall and caught the last part of the mystic's performance. Afterwards Onni invited the lady to come to a restaurant with us. The mystic was famous for her ability to see auras—those wispy radiations surrounding a person which give an indication of the spiritual character of that person. A pure white aura means a Christ-like figure. A gold aura was next best, then clear blue, and so on down to the muddy dark or violent red colors exhibited by the lower human types. The mystic could allegedly look at the photograph of a person and see the color of that person's aura. This is what Onni was intent on testing. Over dinner she pulled out a picture of Father Moon and thrust it towards the lady, commanding her to see what she could see.

The circumstances were not the best. The restaurant people wanted to close shop, and were grudgingly suffering our presence . We were munching on half-warm hamburgers. The lady did her best, stared and stared at the photograph, and finally declared she could see some gold flares emanating from the visage.

This is what I remember. The lady's wanting to please, Onni's disappointment, and an embarrassed drive back through the night, everyone silent, keeping to his own thoughts.

Another training session is coming up. I am frightened and unhappy. I am thinking I may just skip out on the skit after the Saturday night dinner. I am unsure about the Principle, I am unsure about my life, I still have not conquered my addiction to cigarettes. Cigarette smoking has become a symbol of my inability to fully commit myself to Father Moon and this whole adventure. As long as I continue to smoke cigarettes I am not fully a part of the blessed company. Quitting smoking would seem such an easy thing to do for the love of God. For that very reason all the negative thoughts I have, all the uncertainties, frustrations, and antagonisms collect around the act of smoking a cigarette. For the first time I begin to think seriously about leaving the Unification Church.

I have just heard that I have been hired to work at the post office in Moraga—a little bedroom community about ten miles east of Oakland. (Not all Moonies work as flower sellers or in Moonie-owned businesses. A small proportion have "outside" jobs. Noah, for example, is a computer programmer. David works for an engineering firm. Joanie is a nurse. Some Moonies have been pursuing studies at the graduate level, hoping to become lawyers or theologians.)

But an outside job for me means an avenue of escape. Within a week or two of work at the post office I will be able to put money down for an apartment in Moraga. And Jeffy has promised me the use of his car, a grey-blue Volkswagen on its last feet, to drive to and from work—that is, ostensibly from Dana Street to Moraga and back. Michelle and I are fighting over use of the car, but Jeffy has promised it to me. After all, I gave my truck to the Gardening Company. And just yesterday I learned that Nick had wrecked it. Moonies are always wrecking their cars. They are always falling asleep at the wheel.

I have the use of a car and in a couple of weeks I will have the money to get an apartment. I am angered at all the lies, about misrepresenting ourselves when we sell flowers, about our devious methods of recruitment, about the psychological manipulation. I am worn out with the lack of any privacy or any time for reflection or relaxation. I am deeply troubled by the slick anti-Communism that refuses to see any evil in the dictatorships on the Right. I realize that the theory of universal subject-object relationships translates into dictatorship at every level of being. Where is there room for independence or freedom or self-reliance or initiative in such a "heaven on earth"?

How have I reached such a point only two months after that mystical experience in Moonie headquarters in San Francisco? I guess I had seen too much go wrong. I had a growing antipathy towards Onni's autocracy, I was worn out working and getting too little sleep, but more importantly I was beginning to see a hollow pit developing beneath all the forced cheer and forced enthusiasm everyone was expected to exhibit all the time, which drowned out genuine feelings and took away the capacity for clear thought, and made the whole operation seem artificial and at times robotic.

It is Saturday morning. We all hop into vans and head out for Tilden Park, singing all the way. I skip the dodge ball game and sneak a cigarette over by the trees. I am in conflict. Commit myself in spite of all the things that are wrong with the Unification Church—or leave? I am afraid of whatever course I may take. The evening is approaching. We pile back into the vans and return to Dana Street. Dinner is being served. The skit is being discussed. I see that it is not going too well (I am contributing nothing) and I despair of our group's ability to get it ready on time. This is what always hits me. We just don't have enough time and here this idiot is suggesting something patently absurd and this other idiot is talking about his past life, blissfully unaware that we have a play to perform in fifteen minutes. And the trinity leader is not cutting off the talk and making us get on with it. But mainly, as usual I am afraid of getting out there in front of a hundred people and singing something. I decide I will cash out on this one.

We have decided on something, we are ready to go. We will move out to the stage area and sit with the other groups, watching and applauding the other performances as we wait our turn. I can see it all happening in the near future. As we get up from our dinner and move out, I slip away. I walk out the back door and around the block. I walk around the block three or four times. I pause beside a tree next to the sidewalk and smoke five or six cigarettes. I am dreadfully unhappy. I am betraying the best chance of my life. I wander back to the kitchen area at the back of the house and realize that the skits are still going on, and our group has not been called to perform yet. I see a pamphlet called "Master Speaks" laying on a side table, and I pick it up and take it to the bathroom to read. Suddenly I am excited. Here is the man himself, Father Moon. But what is he saying? It sounds like out-and-out raving.

I walked over to the living room where the skits are going on. By listening intently at the door, I know our group has finished its skit. I open the door and walk over to my group. The Center Man sees me and expresses concern. "Where were you? What's the matter?"

I sit down beside him and start to cry.

"What's the matter?", he says again. I say I have just read "Master Speaks" and "it sounds like the ravings of a paranoid madman." I am sad and crying for myself. I look up with longing, look for some comfort from my Center Man.

He looks back at me with understanding. He is compassionate. He sends love and concern and sympathy in my direction. He puts his arm around my shoulder. He starts out by saying, "I know what you mean. Look, the first time I read that stuff I felt the same way. I felt like you do. But I decided to stay with the Family longer. I asked questions. I kept with the lectures, and I finally understood. I understood that Father loves me."

I kept crying. I bought it all—and I didn't buy it for a minute. I had no doubt as to my Center Man's sincerity. I thought, sure, you buy it now. You stayed and went through it over and over and over again until you had no argument left. I have just read Father Moon saying, "I will think for you. Give me your minds." I love you Jeremiah and I love this place and I think if this place is taking me for a ride, any place can take me for a ride, maybe everything in life takes you for a ride, there is so much affection here, so much love, I love you all—but *give up my mind*?

I walked out and around the block again and knew I was going to leave and felt—not that I had been betrayed, but that I was betraying myself—or that both things were happening. Despite that fatuous dictator—but it is wrong to think that—that misguided maniac Mr. Moon—no, no, that's not right, these people love me so much, and I love them, I am destroying what God led me to, I am betraying my own prayer—but I did read that garbage, didn't I?—but didn't I read it just at the time when I was already preparing to leave? So what? It's right down there in black and white, isn't it? The guy wants me to be a zombie for him—no, something's wrong with that idea—didn't I, just a week ago on Saturday night, singing "Jacob's Ladder" with the whole Family, be come totaled-out in bliss and love for everyone? Isn't that so strong and so real?

Didn't picking up that "Master Speaks" give me just the ammunition I needed? Wasn't I already in a negative frame of mind? Didn't I read it in the wrong light? Wasn't it taken out of some context that would make it OK? It is black as hell tonight, and the sidewalk and trees are dark and ugly. This is real, horrible aloneness. I walk around and around. I cannot stand this. I will go back. But I know I have made up my mind to leave. I am going to throw away my own salvation. I am hell's minion. If only I could destroy my goddamn judgmental, critical brain! Too late. It's all set. It's bigger than me. I'm walking out on the only thing in my life that has ever meant full reality and purpose. I fell into my sleeping bag that night just about the saddest I have ever been.

I don't remember Sunday. A few mornings later I remember we had to get a number of cars ready for a trip to San Francisco. We always had a hassle with the cars, because the keys were always mixed up. Somebody would have to run up and down the street with a bunch of keys in his hand testing out each key on each car.

Breakfast was over and I stood looking on while Jim (who had joined the Family the same day I had) argued with Noah.

"That car isn't running," said Jim.

"Well, use the blue one."

"I can't find the keys to the blue one."

Noah is flustered. He has to get a certain number of cars running. "Then start up the old Chevy."

"Which Chevy?"

"The old green one."

"I tried to get that one running yesterday. I couldn't fix it."

"Just do it."

"But I can't."

"YOU ARE NOT FOLLOWING."

The phone calls came exactly on time. For one minute out of twenty-four hours I was standing next to the phone just off the kitchen. The phone rang. It was for me. Yes, the post office would hire me. A day or so later I was standing next to the phone again. Just at that moment I had walked in. The phone rang. It was for me. Confirming my employment.

That phone took calls for maybe fifty people. Given the hundreds of calls that came over that phone, given the fact that in the constantly changing melange that was Family life, phone messages rarely got to people, given the fact that by coincidence I was right next to the phone on both days at the exact time and no other, what or Who do you think caused me to get that job? What or Who was easing my departure from the Moonies?

The job started at 4:30 a.m. every day. It was a half-hour's drive to Moraga, and a half-hour's getting ready to go. I set the alarm for 3:30 the first night. I sleep-walked down to the kitchen, thinking to grab a cup of coffee before I went. And who was in the kitchen waiting for me, but Christina with a bowl of hot cereal and cup of coffee with honey in it?

This is what I mean about the Family I left, but that would not leave me alone. Gestures like that are worth all the gold and striving in the world.

Cults are a lot easier to join than they are to leave.

Chapter Four

Moonie Life 1974 & 1975

I left the Unification Church two and a half months after I entered it, fighting with myself, relieved and unhappy at the same time. The ostensible program had been to live at Dana Street, and commute to Moraga every morning; instead, I scrounged around for my few belongings one afternoon and transported them to Moraga in the old Volkswagen I had borrowed from Jeffy. I got an apartment and moved myself in. I didn't return the car to the Family for five months.

What had that summer been like? A phantasmagoria, a dream-life, punctuated by flashes of anger and sharp love and unity. Every day was a new life, every week a millennium in the mind. After I left it seemed that time raced on ahead in compensation for the dream life. Every day went by in a minute, every month in an hour.

It may seem from these scribblings that when I was a Moonie I cried too much and too easily. After all, I was an adult man, more or less sane, thirty years old, and had been through a marriage and a divorce. Perhaps I should have been made of stronger stuff, not so emotional, not so easily moved. But if there is one thing I want to get across in this story of a cult experience, it is the emotional wringing out, the pushing of the whole character to extremes of conflict, the sounding of the depths of who I was and what the human race was. The package deal of Unification Church theology was conducive to certainty and mental peace, but just because it was such a package deal it was prone to be jettisoned with the least disappointment in the character of the higher-ups, or with the least anger at something going wrong. I said before that I was most bothered by ebullient and colorful young men turned overnight into cloying team-players, but I think there was something worse. It was how we *all* forgot overnight that what had got us into the Family was someone paying loving attention to us, seemingly for ourselves alone, and how in a week's time we turned it around, paying loving attention to someone else, not for themselves alone, but in order to get them into the Family. It was too damn easy for us to get intentional and clever and come up with techniques to make another person feel he was the most important person in the universe. We weren't taught these techniques in so many words; they came naturally.

But it was not all techniques. It was being allowed to release and manifest the need to love other human beings. That is why it came so naturally. If I am not out for myself, but promoting a tribal otherness to which I have given myself, I can without taking thought on the matter easily seduce you, a person pathetically alone, into the higher vision. It is deceitful but at the same time it is genuine. It is genuine because the wish to love you is genuine, but it is false because the only *effective* opportunity I have to love you, to really stand you on your hairs, is when I am not loving you for yourself or for myself but for the cause.

Still I have not gotten to the bottom of it. Psychologists and sociologists have not gotten to the bottom of it. Being in a cult and then being out of a cult is not just a matter of being programmed and then being deprogrammed. That is, it is not just a matter of trading in one set of pushed-in mental certainties for another set of pushed-in mental certainties. It does have something to do with the human sense of identity. The cult experience is *sui generis*, it is unlike any other, but I think everyone in this life, whether or not he claims to be self-reliant, is grounded by an identification with his work, or his company, or his country, or his Church. People who grow up and leave their families and become "autonomous," in reality send out tendrils of themselves so that they become entwined in a larger "family," be it company or cult. This is not just a matter of conscious or unconscious loyalty but a matter of identity, so that an attack on my company or my country is an attack on myself.

But these outwardly spiraling facets of identity are multi-layered, like my present identity in the Catholic Church. There is a distance as well as an identity between me and the various structures of the Church. In a cult experience you lose that distance, and lose something of yourself, until you are no longer you, but a mouthpiece for the genie of the cult. I would say that a group is a cult insofar as its members are possessed by the genie of the cult.

What is this genie? It is a demon manufactured by fierce convictions, strained emotions, buried psychological needs, unacknowledged spiritual tendencies, and unconscious perversities all condensing into a mental climate. That climate becomes a spiritual entity, sometimes called an *"egregore."* It is almost the anti-type of what the cult thinks it is. It becomes the special character of the cult. It dominates everyone in its venue.

In larger mass movements, such as Communism or radical feminism, *egregores* can possess whole societies. In tightly bonded tribal communities, they are small and sharp and more distinctive. They become more "realized." They mark a person as a glassy-eyed Moonie or a blank-eyed Scientologist or a barking Pentecostal flopping on the church floor, possessed by the spirit of his unacknowledged lusts.

But throughout this process, and immersed in it, is the need to love and the need to be loved. Psychologists wax eloquent about the need to be loved. But they have precious little knowledge of the need to love, and the conditions under which that need can be manifested. It seems that in the Moonie experience, the need to love *can* be manifested (and what joy there is in that!), but only if we, thou and I, are both pawns within a higher game. It helps that in the Moonie experience you live your life under orders—that way you don't have to call upon your personal character with all its self-doubts to manufacture some love. But is it really love if it does not come freely, from myself alone?

The intentional seduction of Moonie to Moonie, and Moonie to outsider, is released to operate because you are a Moonie and dedicated to a higher cause, a higher love. But face to face, it is deceitful, and that is perhaps why so many Moonies become more and more deceitful and faceless as time goes on.

I worked at the Moraga post office, my mental life a matter of dwelling on my ex-wife's betrayal of me and the Unification Church's betrayal of me—or my betrayal of the Unification Church. I shut out of my mind that chance for universal love, that subtle higher ground where the beast in the heart begins to recognize its own death and so strikes back with ferocity. Or where the center of the heart behind the beast tells you that what you have experienced is a bad joke.

But how could I rid myself of the songs? "Lord place my feet on higher ground"—that line, from one of our songs. All the songs appropriated from all the religions, that we had sung and sung.

"Amazing Grace." "How Great Thou Art." "God of all the Nations." "Jacob's Ladder." And the most inspirational and lovely of the contemporary songs: "You Light Up My Life." Even now, when I chance to hear one of "our songs" on the radio, I sigh, I am entranced, for a moment I want to go back. It is like the song playing on the radio the first time you ever kissed a girl, or playing on the jukebox when you are busy falling in love in college.

And not just the songs. Life as a Moonie had been a *dedicated* life, and communal. Now both dedication and community were missing. No matter how hard I worked, how much I read, how much I tried to reach towards God in the lone exercise of prayer and imagination, I could not get the Family out of my mind. I began to call Christina and meet with her and talk over coffee or dinner, and sometimes I would visit the Family at the newly purchased house on Hearst Street in north Berkeley. From time to time I would attend a Moonie function just to keep my hand in.

On one such occasion, in January 1974, Father Moon's right hand man, Colonel Bo Hi Pak, visited us at the Hearst Street house. He was there to warm us up for a visit from Father, who was touring the country that year. A hundred or more of us sat cross-legged on the floor while Colonel Pak held forth on the low stage in front. He exhorted us and berated us and lambasted us for not "giving enough." I was used to this kind of talk, having heard it from Onni often enough. But what was worse was his obvious contempt for us. It seemed like there was something racial in it. But no—he was equally contemptuous towards Onni. He was a perfect enactment of the Divine Principle's Subject/Object theory, slavishly devoted to his "general," cruel and merciless towards his subordinates.

A few days later Father Moon himself came to town to deliver a series of lectures at the Zellerbach Auditorium on the University of California campus. There would be three lectures, on Friday, Saturday, and Sunday. In the weeks preceding Father Moon's arrival, faithful Moonies decamped in droves to paper the city with advertisements, engender as much publicity as possible, and finally force free tickets on unwilling street people. With all the hoopla, more antagonism was fomented than amity, and the event drew not only Moonies and a disappointing number of the curious, but several small groups of ill-wishers.

On Friday night I escorted some Moonies to the place, and on the front steps I witnessed a pitiful scene. A local Jesus group had come to picket and admonish those who were walking into the auditorium that they were entering the pit of the devil. It was only three months or so after I had left the Family, and, my head still ringing with sounds of "You are Satan! The World is Satan!" (Onni's constant refrain), I was emotionally raw and sensitive to the criticism. Perhaps the little band of Jesus Freaks was right. They were gathered off to the side praying to their Lord just as I was about to go through the front door.

During events of this nature Moonie leaders are always running about with last-minute instructions and duties. Since Moonie society is one in which orders are given and obeyed, orders multiply according to the rising tension of the leaders. Noah came running out the main door with a typically anxious expression on his face, intent on fulfilling some suddenly imposed and most likely arbitrary directive.

The sun had gone down, and the entrance was illuminated by a flickering fluorescent light. A young girl from the band of Jesus people—she couldn't have been more than sixteen—ran forward perhaps to intercept Noah, perhaps only to yell imprecations. But just as she entered the area lit by the flickering white light—a few steps from Noah and a few steps from me—she fell to the pavement and went into convulsions. It was all so abrupt—the girl twisting there on the pavement and Noah rushing by, noticing nothing. It was as if the outraged spirit of Father Moon or of God had struck the girl down in her tracks. It seemed to me in that split second that I was witness to a supernatural tableau. But immediately afterwards I realized what had happened. The intense flickering light had set off an epileptic seizure in the girl. One of her group darted over and picked her up and drew her out of the light and over to the side area, where she kept thrashing around while her companions put their hands on her head and prayed for Jesus to heal her. I watched for a moment or two and then made a move in their direction, on the verge of shouting at them to force open her mouth and grab hold of her tongue—something I remembered from how to deal with epileptics. But she stopped convulsing before I had a chance to say anything. And then a couple of her friends looked up and glared at me with intense hatred, as if I—as if we—were veritable incarnations of evil.

Nothing more happened, but it was a frightening little scene, and I at least knew that the Jesus Freaks held us responsible for the girl's seizure, that we had practiced black magic on her, that we were the Anti-Christ. The Moonies rushing about were so boxed into their own idea of supernatural reality that they had noticed nothing, and that was as eerie to me as the event itself. It was as if they had blinders on, unable of focus on anything outside their immediate psychic cosmos, as if they were utterly entranced by the god who drove them around the race-track.

I attended the lecture for only a few moments. Perhaps the poor little band of Jesus people had scared me off. In any case I knew the lecture would be ill-attended, the audience unfriendly (except in those areas packed with Moonies), and the center of attraction, a seeming wild man kicking up his heels and gesticulating around the stage, while Colonel Pak stood at his side trying to translate at least some of the Lord's Korean jabber into more or less presentable English. I caught a glimpse of all that—the stocky Mr. Moon stomping here and there, shouting, waving his arms, while the audience sat in stony silence—before I slipped out.

On Monday I drove Onni and Christina and Jeffy and a few others out to the San Francisco Airport to join a column of well-wishers seeing Father Moon off. We arrived late, Onni screaming criticisms at us all the way—as if it had not been her negligence that had caused our delay. We found the departure gate, and moved towards the front of a long file of singing Moonies from all parts of the Bay Area. (The Oakland Family, headed by the strong-willed Onni, always horned in, took over, went to the head of the line.) Father Moon had some trouble with his passport, the delay sending chills of concern and anger up and down the spines of the faithful. He finally appeared after a half-hour, waved at us a couple of times, and disappeared into the tunnel leading to the plane. He was only ten or fifteen feet from us when he waved, and he looked tired and embarrassed at the noisily cheering honor guard. At that moment he seemed genuine, even humble, somehow like a real person with a real heart. The exaggerated dramatics and worked-up emotions of *everything* that went down in the Oakland Family seemed to drop away in the presence of this man. But perhaps I was indulging in wish-fulfillment. It was Father Moon's extravagant showmanship, after all, that set the style for the whole Unification Church—glee when there was no happiness to sustain it, affection without the force of love, urgency when there was nothing to be urgent about.

No wonder he looked weary. And maybe he was frightened of making a scene in the face of customs officials at the plush San Francisco airport, with all that meant in terms of the power of the official secular American Way of Life. For whatever reason, when I caught his eye I knew he would have much preferred to slip away without all the fuss. At that moment I even felt a little sorry for him.

That was my first and last close-up look at the Reverend Sun Myung Moon.

I had left the Unification Church but I still needed God. One Sunday morning I attended a Catholic Mass at St. Mary's College just down the road from where I lived. The chapel was jam-packed with people, and there was a mix of wealthy Anglos and poor Mexicans that I liked. There was indeed a mildly mystical feel to the proceedings, with the gray stone walls and a movie screen to the side of the pulpit where the words of the hymns were projected, and the black shawls on the Mexican ladies. But the experience was so terrifically anonymous compared to what I had known as a Moonie that it seemed not just a different religion, but a different universe. I never went back. I was still a Moonie by habit and memory.

Of course, I could not get the Unification Church out of my mind. To leave the Moonies whole-heartedly it is probably a good idea to undergo a violent disruption, such as a deprogramming—but I had merely snuck away.

One Saturday morning in the Spring of 1974 I decided to drive up to Boonville. The Oakland Family finally had a place where they could be separate from the city and its distractions and combine all aspects of the training session in a rural setting. I found the place a mile outside of town and drove down a dusty road past some dying fruit trees. This was shortly after the Boonville "Ideal City" had been established—or re-established; apparently it had been used briefly for training sessions in 1972. In 1974 there was no notoriety, no gate, no guards. I parked my car next to some others and walked down to a little bridge over a creek and towards the songfest. Evey was sitting on one of the back rows and turned towards me with a rush of recognition. "Tom! You've come back!"

I'm here, but have I come back? She loved to see me, I loved to see her. She supported me—I supported her. I had never touched

Evey, never been close, hardly ever talked with her. But she was one I'd marked out as spiritually sensitive, one of the intelligent ones, one with a great heart. There had been a lot of nit-wits, I thought, a lot of superficial idiots who just married themselves to discipline and a kind of glib discipleship; Evey was one who I perceived as having the gift of grace and an intelligent sense of spiritual realities. As Dr. Durst had represented maturity, so that I did not have to feel out of place among these "kids," and Christina had been that moving force that made you feel loved by her and important and powerful—you wanted to be a Galahad to her Joan of Arc—so Evey had been one who made you think you were involved in a truly God-loved effort. She was the sensitive.

Evey left the Unification Church in 1976. We traded letters once. In her letter to me she said she was saddened that her former friends in the Family thought she was in the snares of Satan, while the truth was that she still felt devoted to finding a path to God. She had been deprogrammed. In 1976 and 1977, a lot of Moonies left the Family; a year or two earlier had been the first public "taking notice" of Mr. Moon, the start of the deprogrammings and notoriety and news reports, the first real confrontation with this "alien danger" on our American shores. A lot of sincere Family members, caught in the publicity war of charges and counter-charges, betook themselves to a safer ground—or were taken. Jeffy and Michelle were deprogrammed in 1976, and David was preparing to leave on his own. These are some of that original group who had started the Oakland Family and had done so much to make it fly.

That "alien danger." It was alien all right, and dangerous to American ideas of democracy. But as I walked towards Evey, and smiled that wonderful smile of "Yes!" to her and squeezed in next to her on the bench, I felt again that *bon chance*, that giving of oneself to something alien perhaps, but perhaps so much better than the dreary getting and going of the world as it is. The skits were over and we all joined hands in a great circle and sang our love for God while the stars sprinkled in the beautiful blue night.

I ran into Christina a little later. I was so glad that they wanted me! In my life I have usually either isolated myself or had to push for love. I have "gotten off," in a sad sort of way, on the jibes of fellow workers while I sorted mail or packed cooking-ware in an import house, or traded insecurities among the "mystical company of poets" in Boulder, Colorado, but never have I been granted the sense of

"I want you" except in a Moonie training camp. Is this a pathetic confession to you tough and well-adjusted folks getting and spending your way through a grim universe? I think any one of you, inside that armor, would love some other adult to come to you cleanly and with no holding-back say, "I love you and I want you to be with me."

Christina wanted me. To work for an Ideal World. (Conditional love is better than no love at all.) I slept that night in the Chicken Palace, woke to a Sunday, and involved myself with the second day of the training session. When the company of Heavenly Children clapped wildly in the Chicken Palace, I clapped right along. I clapped louder. I decided to throw off that critical inhibition that had kept me in a state of wariness towards most of my fellow human beings. I joined in. After the lecture about the "Cause of Crimes" wherein it was stated that Lucifer had tainted all sexual love by his original seduction of Eve, I told Christina, "I'm worried. I'm beginning to believe this."

What happened, I think, in all that noise, those musical instruments braying out enthusiasm, the stamping feet and sweating bodies, the thin walls of the Chicken Palace trembling and filling the room with a communal power, and a young woman with small hands sitting next to me, putting her small hand in mine—what happened was that a kind of tiredness about my own "yes buts" and "this but not thats" descended over me, something clicked in, and I thought, I want to be with these people—and I consented to the theory of a jealous angel screwing things up at the beginning of time. It seemed a small concession.

(The trouble is that in all that happy crushing noisy scenario and the look of love from a person next to me, it was not the argument for the theory that got to me, but the scenario itself. Just about any theory of the origin of evil would have sufficed. Of course, the question "what went wrong" has never been answered sufficiently by rational argument, so maybe it's best to get it by drill or song or any milieu that produces a "willing suspension of disbelief." Despite Fr. Matthew Fox, O.P., and other feel-good Catholic heretics, the human race does know, whenever it gets honest, that something did go wrong in the beginning of time. The Moonie answer to the question is actually not all that different from the Catholic answer.)

What was so good was the release in my stomach, the contrast with the frustrated life all around me in the post office—those lives moving slowly towards retirement, a daily activity of work not so bad in itself, but requiring so much less than what everybody working there could have contributed to life if life would let them. I was at that Moonie training session after eight months of work in the post office, working with people who were using about ten percent of their human capabilities in the gaining of their livelihood. And I knew that this was the condition of most people and their work. Couldn't something on this earth offer something better?

It seemed to me right then in Boonville that it could.

But I went back to Moraga and to work. Months passed. I think it was about now that I began to write poetry again. (I had written poetry on and off since 1964 and had been published once or twice in small magazines.) In my new poems I considered the parameters of good and evil more often than I considered lost love, my old constant theme. At least I began to combine the issues and drove towards some mystical resolutions. I would often walk alone out to a rural area near Moraga and try to see God in His creation. I spent hours by a brook, or in a grove of trees, and sometimes I succeeded in becoming open to the infinity portrayed in small things. Especially, I loved trees and sky and tiny animals and the delicate symmetry of leaves. In my lonesomeness God allowed me to see the clothes He wears.

But I also knew that the most beautiful and provocative article of clothes God wears is a woman's face, and I was lonely because there was no face I could touch.

Another time when I took it into my head to drive up to the Boonville camp I found a locked gate across the dirt road and a couple of Moonie guards a short distance away. I pulled up in my little red Subaru and stopped, feeling that this gate was something I wanted to crush. I wanted to drive my car right through it. Instead I climbed out of the car and felt immediately suspected. The gate reflected on me. I was under observation. The tone of things had tightened up. I realized there had been trouble. The recent publicity flashed through my mind. A TV show on deprogramming. An interview with Dr. Durst on local TV, where he was asked about a couple of organizations he was involved with called "Creative Community Project" and "Ethical Management Project"; and he insisted that these organizations had nothing to do with the Unification Church. I knew better and the TV interviewer knew better. This was stonewalling, and it was tied up with the kidnappings and deprogrammings and the first public contentions, a story just beginning that caught hold of something basic in the infantile heart of America. The question was put immediately into the framework of parents and children, their mutual fight for ownership and autonomy. The question of adult liberty versus psychological control of adults was hardly touched on. (It was too touchy a subject.) The question of spiritual validity was not mentioned. Dr. Durst obviously felt that "you people would just not understand." So he stonewalled. He was bound to a Higher Truth.

The gate across the road meant that there was suddenly a chill to the proceedings. It wasn't just private deliberations any more, it was "which side are you on?" There was a scary excitement inappropriate to the subtle longing towards the place where God lives—a place blocked off by anger or fear. (I wish some Catholics I know would take that message to heart.)

The gate was opened after I convinced the guard that I was here to see Christina, my good friend, and that I was a member of the "extended Family." I drove on down the dusty road for several hundred feet and stopped at a conglomeration of brown wood buildings, unkempt vestiges of barns and coops and pens that had once been part of the thriving farm. It was August and very dry, and as I walked, little pools of dust rose up from the ground and disappeared into the general haze. It was hot. Five or six dirty children were playing or crying or whining around the area. I walked into the barn, and saw a couple of harried young women, and more children wandering around in the dust. The children—there were babies and toddlers up to the age of five or so—seemed uncared for, and a number of them were whining for attention. The two women whose charge they were talked to me, explaining that these were the children of Family members who lived at the Boonville camp or who were on missions. This is where they were housed. The two women were in their twenties, very tired looking, but they attempted to express a kind of gladness through baggy eyes. The idealism was intact, but the smiles twitched a little when a nearby two-year-old began to cry. One of the women went over and picked up the baby and cooed to it. It didn't help. She put the child down and walked over to the phone which was blaring loudly from a post in the center of the barn. She didn't ask for relief, but that was certainly what she wanted and needed.

Too much was being put on these women, I thought. And there was something out of synch. The women were good Moonies, but bad mothers. Moonie life had strained out any maternal instincts they possessed. To be a good mother you have to have your own warmth and your own power. The powerlessness and the strain communicated itself to the children, and they cried and were lonely and perhaps frightened. The women tried to be warm and kind, but somehow it didn't come off.

I walked out of the barn and looked at the children hanging around the fencepost or playing in the dust. Flies buzzed around my head. I was irritated and slapped away at my forehead, and I realized the children and the women were undergoing the same midsummer agony.

This was not right. Is this how the Family cared for its children? Shunted aside. An embarrassment. The Family was moving too fast—great things were to be accomplished—there was just no time to bring the children up, to spend the time to attend to their developing personalities, to give them individual attention and affection and guidance—for Chrissake, just to have enough adults around to pick them up and wipe their tears away.

In the Family's economy there was just not enough allowance made for the next generation. This generation would make or break the world, and the kids were not a part of the picture. Two harried, worn-out young women to be surrogate mothers for fifteen or twenty kids, while the kids' real parents worked the farm or attended lectures or sold flowers in distant cities. Not right. Something hypocritical here. Something thin about the whole effort when you didn't take the time to love the children. As if you didn't take the whole thing seriously in the first place. As if all the importance was in the picture show going on down the road in the dodge ball games and skits and seduction into "our" idea of God and the Ideal World, while the children who were the real continuity of life were shunted aside, burdens to "our" getting on with it. It was here that the spiritual validity broke down, because the key to spiritual validity is continued life and care, especially care for the children. I was unhappy for the kids. They were not being loved, while down the road in the training session everyone talked about love.

The sun was hot. I walked over to the trailer where Patti lived. She was glad to see me. I squeezed into a bench across from a little table from her, a little white table with flies dive-bombing us while Patti screwed the lids on some jars of fruit she was putting up.

Patti was the sometimes hysterical redhead who had befriended me a year and some months ago when I first joined the Family. She told me the news. First, she brought out a little card that said she was a member of the Unification Church. There was a quote on the card saying that she would follow the Reverend Moon through "Blood, Sweat, and Tears" to the making of a new world.

"Great," I said. "We've gone official."

She laughed. (We always understood each other.) Then she told me about "ECLIPSE," a group of ex-Moonies and superficial fellow-travellers which was fighting the Moon Church. They had a chapter in Boonville, and sometimes she would sneak out of camp and spend an evening with them smoking marijuana and reading their anti-Moon tracks. A few other Moonies in the camp also snuck out and spent evenings with ECLIPSE, letting their hair down, you might say, getting some relief. But they always had to get drunk or high to partake in these adventures. They must have felt terrific guilt. The people in ECLIPSE who had not been Moonies could not possibly understand. The Moonies who were playing a double game, trying to leave, but bound—they knew they were sucking up to the devil.

Patti told me the story of Mark, the tall thin man my own age, who had befriended me at a training session a couple of months earlier. He was the man who slept next to me when I had made the sign of the cross on a Saturday night after the group performances, the man who had commiserated with me over the fact that there were so few older people in the Family. He had been on and off with the Moonies for five years. He had gone off to India to sit at the feet of a guru for awhile, and then had come back to the Family. He remained restless and undecided, but bound. To keep him in the Family, so Patti told me, the higher-ups had married him to a rather plump, timid woman I had met. After the forty days were up—the days owned by Satan—they prepared to consummate the marriage. But the woman whined and prevaricated and finally refused. The marriage remained sexless. Mark was now spending weekdays at the camp and sneaking off some nights to spend a few hours with ECLIPSE. He was one of Patti's compatriots in uncertain complicity.

Patti offered me a taste of the hot peppers she had canned. They were hot as hell, and the water I gulped only aggravated the sensation. The flies buzzed around our heads. I complained about the stains on the table and floor of the trailer. Things spilled had not been cleaned up, probably for weeks. Patti made me remember how we had vacuumed the Dana Street house every morning, washed all the dishes until they sparkled, and how one day I had lifted the lid on the inoperative dishwasher in the kitchen. The inside was caked with mold and crud. It had been overlooked for months, though it stood in the middle of the kitchen, and was used as a table. All the surfaces of things were cleaned and cleaned, while the inside rotted. We would rush out and make a new world by love, while we forgot our children.

During the summer and fall of 1974, and on into 1975, I went on eight or nine training sessions at Boonville. I started a tradition. I would pick up Christina and a few others on a Friday evening or Saturday morning and drive them up to Boonville, and we would stop in town for supplies before driving down to the camp. One Friday night I decided to do something nice for the hard-working young people in the camp, so I bought fifteen half gallons of ice cream for them. After that, Friday night ice cream and cake became a Boonville tradition.

On the way back to Oakland on Sunday evening we would stop off at a roadside snack-stand in Cloverdale and have ice cream or milk shakes. One evening I pulled into the place and jumped out of my car and ran over and hugged Ginny. She had run towards me, too, and hugged me. It was a mutual enthusiasm. I hadn't seen her for a year. Though I had talked to her but little, it seemed we liked each other a whole lot (though I couldn't remember the incidents last year when we had begun to like each other—that was all a blur). My mind immediately began spinning towards the future, and marriage. There was joy in those days, but this was early on, before the locked gates and paranoia.

I lived and worked in Moraga, but kept up my contact with the Family primarily through luncheon dates with Christina. Several times I drove into Berkeley and picked up Patti and a friend of hers and escorted them around town.

In my conversations with Christina I talked about my idea of an extended Family—people like myself who wanted to contribute to the movement in some way but couldn't see themselves as twenty-four-hour-a-day members of the Family. I wanted to create a kind of "friend of the Family" association, something I vaguely envisioned as a liaison with the outside world. I suppose this was my attempt to break down that locked gate across the road that symbolized the ever-tightening "them versus us" mentality. I saw the gate as shutting off those inside, as well as those outside, from the love of God.

(Who am I kidding? What I really wanted was to recall and relive those exquisite moments of communitarian love when we sang "Jacob's Ladder" all together on a Saturday night—while escaping the false face, the obedience, the lack of sleep, the irritation of daily Moonie life.)

In any case events had gone beyond my fantasies of conciliation. The gate and the guards were there because there had been raids on the camp, kidnapping raids by deprogrammers, and bad feeling had been stirred up among Boonville residents by the "cult" publicity. Spies from ECLIPSE and other anti-Moon organizations had infiltrated the training sessions. That is why if you just drove up to the camp and honked your horn at the gate, you had to establish your credentials. You were under suspicion. It had not been paranoia on my part. The nice, happy road to God was gone.

Inside the camp we began to talk more and more of martyrdom. Every new religious revelation had been persecuted. Look at history. Look at the early Christians, the Quakers, the Mormons. Opposition from the world was proof that we were for real. At the same time it served to validate the "World as Satan" principle.

And yet had not the Family's very secretiveness and duplicity brought on the suspicion and opposition in the first place? Furthermore, as I kept pointing out to Christina, the "Us blessed, them Satanic" doctrine served to crush any self-critique, since everything we did, even if it looked bad, was ordained by God; and everything opposed to us, even if it looked good, was Satanic. The objectivity of things could get very shifty in such a self-serving cosmology. If we lied about something, it was necessary for a greater good. If "they" said something about us that was accurate, but showed us in a bad light, "they" were *ipso facto* motivated by Satan.

This is exactly what the Fatima Crusaders, the TFP (Tradition, Family, Property), and the Society of Saint Pius X do. Each of these "Catholic" sects will have their day in court further on in this book. I recently published an exposé in *Fidelity* (October 1992) of some of the rotten beliefs and practices of the Society of St. Pius X and was branded "a black agent of the Father of Lies" by Society Fr. Ramon Anglés. Girls in the Society's compound at St. Mary's, Kansas, were ordered to pray a Novena for my conversion. During the novena they were not to think about boys—this for its penitential effect on heaven. The penance was to be performed on pain of mortal sin. Children's souls are hostage to the perverted minds of their elders. Spirit of St. Mary's, shake hands with the spirit of Moonieville.

In such an atmosphere there is no such thing as reasoned criticism. In Moonieland *everything* is part of the crucial war between the forces of good and the forces of evil. Negativity is Satanic. On the practical level this has resulted in a stultification of some Moonie operations. People become afraid to suggest changes for improvement. Improvement implies that things aren't perfect as they are, and are thus subject to criticism. But criticism is the voice of Satan.

An example: some years ago one of the Korean Church leaders implemented a concept called "Home Church" in the New York City area. Moonies who did not live in centers, but in their own homes, were given a geographical area to cover. A certain number of houses in that area was the individual responsibility of each Moonie. Each day he would visit a different house in the neighborhood and attempt to make converts. There was no deviation from this activity, since no new directives came down from the leaders. The same people went to the same houses over and over again for years. Good Moonies, they persisted. The conversion rate was about zero. (You don't gain converts to the Unification Church by politely talking about how Jesus Christ failed his mission.) The drop-out rate among "Home Church" Moonies is not publicized.

I have traced a practical absurdity like this back to the pervasive sense of guilt about questioning which becomes an overweening characteristic of every Moonie's mind, and this from the large part Satan has to play in Unification Church theology. Satan is present not only in criticism, but in moments of unhappiness, self-doubt, or doubt about an order. Satan causes Moonie car wrecks, and is in the minds of TV newsmen or psychologists or police who dare raise a question about Moonie practices. Satan lurks everywhere where there is less than the highest pitch of fervor and prayer and love for the True Parents—Father Moon and his (third) wife.

Despite all my reasoned criticisms, the memory of the best moments called me back. So in the Spring of 1975, after more talks with Christina, I decided to try again to "willingly suspend my disbelief" and rejoin the Family. She suggested I move into the Ashby Street house. It was just now being refurbished, and a Trinity of about twelve members was about to move in. These were all generally older than average Moonies and had outside jobs. Since we all had our own jobs, we were a little removed from the centrality of the Moonie experience—an experience of uncertainty about tomorrow's job—it might be two days or two years on a flower selling mission, or a week with the Gardening Company, or a couple of days manning the tables on the University of California campus—a fluid situation, always with other Moonies, subject to change radically at any moment. Our Ashby Street Trinity, on the other hand, had definite schedules to keep on the outside, and we worked alongside non-Moonies. It was a lot different.

I remember distinctly the day in April of 1975 when I pulled into the driveway of Ashby Street house with a car full of my belongings. A couple of Moonie friends, among them Patti, helped me move my stuff in. We stashed it in a little room in back of the kitchen that I had picked out for myself. That little room was a Godsend, I thought, since, though I wanted to be in the Family, I definitely did *not* want to sleep jammed up in a room with ten other people. God was making things easy for me again. Patti and the others went off to other duties, and I was left alone. I spotted a hand lawn mower in the garage and decided to cut the grass on the front lawn. The sun was warm, and as I labored in my shirt-sleeves, I suddenly felt fine. The contentions of the mind ceased and I moved a little way into that blessed space of knowing I was doing the right thing, far from the doubts and the realm of charges and counter-charges that had befogged the whole issue.

I mowed the lawn happily. This was the front lawn of the house Reverend Moon had stayed in on his first trip to America. I had the place to myself for several days. (The rest of the Trinity was to move in later.) There was a big picture of Father Moon in the hallway off the kitchen, and another one in the little prayer room between the living room and the kitchen. I lived in the little room behind the kitchen, on the other side of the hall. I felt like I was at the center of things.

I spent the next few evenings (after I got back from work at the post office) cleaning up the yard, then painting the interior woodwork, then polishing the brass fixtures. I even polished the inside of the brass wall-socket plates before screwing them over the sockets. As I look back on this activity I confess it seems a trifle neurotic—the impulse to be thorough, then super-thorough. Then there was the knowledge that only God and I would know that the plates were polished on the inside as well. Probably I was trying to make amends for ever leaving the Family in the first place. There was something else to it, I think. I think I conceived of myself as a caretaker and corrector of the Family's faults—I remembered that dishwasher in the Dana Street house that had gone uncleaned for months. It was a symbolic act. I wanted things to sparkle on the inside as well.

The feeling of care for the house and renewed reverence for Father Moon didn't last too long. It was only a week or two before I was sneaking in six-packs of beer and putting them (inside paper bags) in the refrigerator. The refrigerator was right beside the doorway leading from the kitchen to the little hall and across to my room. This hall lead to the back entrance of the house, so in effect I had my own little apartment and private entrance. When the Trinity moved in I didn't bother joining their night-time activities. I stayed in my room, watched my TV, and drank beer.

During this time I wrote a long explication of parts of the Divine Principle—a painstaking work that talked a lot about the reality of symbols and of numbers as building blocks of the material and spiritual universe. This was all an attempt to make sense out of such statements in the Principle as "Satan invaded the number forty." I tried to interest Christina in the work, but there was never enough time in the ever busy, ever moving life of the Family for consideration of complicated mental ventures. Possibly, I thought, God had made the space and privacy for me to produce such a work. But I dropped it when I realized everyone was in just too much of a hurry to take a look at it. It would have been entirely up to me to push it forward and make the Unification Church leaders see it as something important in the long run—to have a commentary on the Principle that could afford a bridge between the science of the rational world and the science of the Divine Principle. In the haste and flush of things, I wasn't sure of its importance anyway.

The Trinity members didn't know what to make of me. Here was this man living alone in the back room—a Family member who didn't come to Trinity meetings or prayer sessions! There was some resentment about that. I did mix with other people now and then. One young man who had just joined the Family had quit his job and was looking for another. We spent several afternoons talking.

He was worried about whether or not to pay off his debts before making his final commitment to the Family. The Family needed the money, didn't it? I advised him to pay his debts first. I said something to the effect that God wants you to come to Him clean. In a karmic or indemnity sense, it was better to take care of old business before entering the new life. At least this is how I saw it. He agreed. He said a few days later that he saw me as a kind of father figure to him. He admired my wisdom.

I welcomed the compliment, though I was sure that if he had asked one of the Trinity leaders about it, he would have been told to give the money to the Family: nothing takes precedence over "building the Material Foundation." The Spiritual Foundation would die aborning without the Material Foundation to cradle it. The importance of money was constantly reinforced in everyone's mind.

Just before I moved into the Ashby Street house, I had been driving somewhere with Christina. She told me that she had recently had a long talk with Onni, and Onni had emphasized the crucial importance of money. Now Christina fully understood about the "Foundation of Substance." Suddenly she burst out with, "I would do anything for money!" I looked askance as a devilish impulse took hold of me. I nearly said, "Will you go to bed with me for $50?" I was a little disgusted with what I assumed was her dramatic exaggeration.

What I should have asked her is if she would be willing to sell roses every day and night for three years running, in all seasons, even in the dead of winter, in blizzards, in the northern provinces of Canada. Some Moonies did.

Christina had drawn me into her confidence. We had a number of dinners out together, and she had told me some secrets not for common knowledge, such as Onni's wine-making hobby. Christina was making me privy to the higher echelons. A "Blessing," a mass marriage performed by Father Moon, was due soon. Christina and I had gotten to the point of hinting around at marriage to each other. In fact, in the Moonies or out, the image of Christina and me together was always central to my desires about life in the Family. If not for Christina, I probably wouldn't have joined the Unification Church in 1973, or gone back in 1975 and 1980. For me, she was the archetype for the Family, and as I judged her, I judged the Family. As I felt love for and loved by her, I felt love for and loved by the Family. Sitting alone in my Moraga apartment before and after my second Moonie live-in experience, I would fantasize that a condition of my return would be marriage to Christina. I would imagine us together in places of high power and responsibility, and devoted to each other.

I was to find out later that perhaps a hundred Moonie men had similar fantasies, and the wind went out of a lot of sails when she finally married in (I think) 1981. She had been much more valuable to the Family as a knowing or unknowing tease.

More about money. On the first night I spent at the Ashby Street house alone, I remember being in an upstairs room, in a sudden turmoil. I prayed for a sign about the Family. What, exactly, was my commitment? Was this thing all false or all true? I saw a Bible lying nearby on a table. I decided to descend to that old trick of opening the Bible at random and blindly placing your finger on a verse. The verse said something about "giving gifts, and beneficence would result." That was a surprise answer, but yes, it meant that the Material Foundation was necessary and good. I had recently received a small inheritance on the death of my grandmother, and had put it in a Savings and Loan. A day or two later I withdrew the whole amount and turned it over to the Unification Church.

You must understand that I thought I owed my post office job to the Family. If I hadn't been in a confident frame of mind, I wouldn't have gotten the job. I actually received two job offers from the seven inquiries I made. But it was the interviews that were important. For myself, I might have been too nervous and probably would have blown the opportunity. But with the feeling of "not for myself, but for God," I was easily confident. And then there had been the phone calls from the postmaster, right on time, tracked to a mystical meaning. God had arranged it all, and He had arranged it through the Unification Church.

Of course the opposite meaning might also be true—that God had eased my way out of a pernicious false faith. For my gift to the Family, I received from Onni and Dr. Durst a mother-of-pearl tie pin, delivered by Christina to my little room in back of the kitchen. The fact that I didn't own a tie, much less a suit, demonstrates a kind of winsomeness about the whole transaction.

I turned over my paychecks from the post office while I lived in the Ashby Street house. It was only right. Then I wrote out a check for $1975.12 to "Mr. and Mrs. Moses Durst." (This was a wedding present.) The land I had turned over to the Family in 1973 was sold for "$1.00 and considerations" to Miss Im, not to the Unification Church—that is why I know Onni's real name. The total amount of money (including land equity and my truck) I gave to the Family I figured out once. It came to almost $10,000. But I knew that if I had sold flowers for the Family over the two-year period from 1973 to 1975, I would have generated much more money than that. It was my unique, outsider status and the sudden comparatively large donations that made it extraordinary.

One night soon after these gifts, at a Family Meeting (I was hustled out of sleep in my little room and driven over to the recently purchased Hearst Street house for the affair), Onni presented me in front of the assembly—perhaps 200 Family members—as one very special in the eyes of God, one who had given so much money without even enjoying the blessedness of Family life.

It felt good to be applauded, but Family life was just what I had been trying to avoid. For the wedding present I received another tie pin and a photograph of the marriage ceremony of Onni and Dr. Durst. "What a blessing," I was informed, "a picture of the True Parents [Father Moon and his wife] presiding over the marriage of our True Parents! [Onni and Dr. Durst]." I didn't care for it much. Now I had a glossy photograph and two imitation pearl tie pins I couldn't possibly have occasion to use. It was enough to drag myself into a pair of Levis and drive off to work every morning at 4:00 a.m.

But let us go back and set the scene of:

A Family Meeting

These were called without warning, usually at 10:00 or 11:00 at night. On this particular night I arrived in a car with several other Moonies garnered from Ashby Street house and Regent Street house. The meeting was held at the Hearst Street house, a large four-story building on the north side of the University of California campus in

Berkeley. It had once been a fraternity house and had been purchased recently by the Family with flower-selling money. It was still in the process of being re-painted (white) by the Family, new carpets were being laid, and little groups of people would be stumbled over on the staircases as they worked late into the night scraping off old paint and slapping on new. The downstairs, though, was more or less finished. New carpets and polished hardwood surfaces gave the place a well-appointed, solid, wealthy look. You walked up a stone pathway and up stone steps to the entrance. It was dark and the night was gentle and you felt peaceful as you opened the front door and took off your shoes.

There was a large hall, filled with jammed-together Moonies. A set of huge doorways was wide open leading from this hall to one transverse to it at the end, forming a "T." The transverse hall contained a long low table, so that there was a crowd of people kneeling down here below and a table surrounded by kneeling or cross-legged people, mostly Center Men, up above. Onni was seated at the middle of the table, facing us. She called for everyone to change places, to come forward and set themselves in order of their seniority in the Family, "oldest" Moonies in front. Trinity leaders hurriedly shifted people around. I crouched at the back, but Christina caught sight of me and took me by the hand up to the table in front. There I stood with Onni at my side while she told everyone of my great faithfulness. I went red in the face, but I stood there while we all sang a song about fidelity to God. Then we all sat down, and Onni gave a sermon. Many people brought out notebooks scrawled with the title: ONNI SPEAKS. It was a kind of little MASTER SPEAKS. Onni, obviously peeved at a recent expression of negativity, said, "Criticism is the voice of Satan!" Silence. Bowed heads.

"I will say it again. Criticism is the voice of Satan!" She glared at us. People squirmed. She said loudly, "Criticism is the voice of Satan!" Dead silence in the room, around the table, up and down the large hall.

Of course I had to pop up with the thought: isn't she criticizing us now? Patti began to laugh. She was sitting across the table from me. Ever since I had known her, Patti had had the unfortunate affliction of laughing uncontrollably whenever Satan was mentioned (which was often). Onni repeated her loud condemnations, and Patti's hysteria followed like an echo.

"Criticism is the voice of Satan!"

"Heh heh heh."

"Criticism is the voice of Satan!"

"Heh heh heh heh."

"Criticism"—louder now—"is the voice of Satan!"

"Ha Ha Ha Ha Ha Ha Ha—"

"PATTI, LEAVE THE ROOM!" (Onni Speaks.)

Patti hops up with her hand over her mouth, bubbling mischievously, hating herself, runs out of the room, stumbling over people in her haste to leave the arena of her shame and skips upstairs to her own private hell.

Onni glares balefully around the room. There is a lone Negress sitting at the table. All the rest of us are white or Oriental. Onni stares at her. "Prejudice is wrong! Prejudice is wrong! If you hate another race you are Satan! If you cut the skin [here she gestures with an imaginary knife] the blood is the same! It is RED! The Negro has the same blood as the white! We all have the same blood!"

If it is possible for a black-skinned woman to go red in the face, I'm sure that one did. Thanks, Onni, for telling us where it's at. Would we be sitting here taking orders from a yellow-skinned woman if we hadn't copped to that number long ago? Is this woman totally insensitive?

But pens are scrawling in notebooks. Onni speaks.

Onni launches into a tirade about laziness. "Laziness is Satan!" She may be right, but it is past 1:00 o'clock in the morning and some Trinity leaders are dozing off. What with Family meetings and 3:00 a.m. prayer sessions and getting up at 5:00 in the morning to organize the day's activities, they don't get much sleep.

"Jeffy! Wake up! Satan is in you!"

"I'm sorry." He looks woebegone and very, very tired.

"The Jews!"—she shouts, "The Jews! The Jews were burned in ovens because they *did not* follow Jesus! The Jews were massacred because they *did not* follow Jesus! The Jews paid the Indemnity because they *did not follow Jesus*!"

(Onni says everything three times. Three times makes it true. Jeffy is a Jew.)

"Wake up! How can you sleep?!" (Onni always speaks in exclamation points.)

David, sitting a couple of places down the table from me, nods off. His neighbor raps her knuckles on his forehead, then rubs his back, squirms her knuckles up and down his spine. Luckily, Onni has not noticed. David wakes up, whispers his thanks to his neighbor, and nods off again. David is a Jew. Half the Family in America is Jewish. Dr. Durst is Jewish. The Unification Church in America, you might say, is a conspiracy of Jews and Koreans, with some lapsed Catholics, Calvinists, and Seventh Day Adventists thrown in for flavor. Moonies are very good at telling each other how to be perfect. If there is one thing that goes down at a Moonie training camp more than any other (that is, after the weekend guests have departed and the old troopers are left to themselves), it is people trying to be perfect telling other people how to be perfect.

Conversation in the Kitchen of a Moonie Training Camp

"Use all the lettuce. You are wasting the lettuce."

"I'm only tearing out the brown parts. I refuse to make these people eat garbage." (I'm always trying to be a kindly uncle to my fellow Moonies. Uncle Tom, the man who bakes good bread for my Heavenly Children.)

"The brown parts aren't rotten. Think of the poor people starving in India." That old number. That's how your mother got you to eat those awful string beans when you were a kid.

She finds a new tack. "The water isn't hot enough."

"It's plenty hot. I'll burn my hands if it's any hotter."

"You should use rubber gloves."

"Fine. Go find me some rubber gloves. Make yourself useful."

"Oh, you're just not Following Principle."

"Who the hell is washing these dishes anyway?"

"You shouldn't use that kind of language."

"All right, *you* wash the damn dishes."

"I wasn't assigned to wash dishes. I'm supposed to slice vegetables."

"Then go do it."

"But the water is getting greasy. See, you're not really getting the dishes clean."

"OK. OK. I'll change the water."

"Make sure it's hot enough."

"Will you get off my . . . back?"

"You're not Following Principle. You shouldn't talk that way."

I storm off. If I had a cigarette, I'd sure smoke it now. I do my best, and there's always some critic nosing around. (This is how you act when there's no sex. And I sort of *liked* that girl. Nice legs. We could have gotten *married*, for Chrissake.)

Aside from Family Meetings I spent very little time with the Family. Evenings I sat in my room writing my explication of the Principle—with many associated ideas of my own concerning image and metaphor and symbolic mathematics. Often, our Trinity would be engaged in a prayer session when I tip-toed far enough into the kitchen to grab a beer from the refrigerator. Once when I went into the kitchen, a young woman was there who invited me to the prayer session.

Don't these people know I've been drinking beer? Do they see just what they want to see, or don't they care?—or are they intimidated by me? Does the fact that Christina visits me in the back room on occasion give me so much status in their eyes that they assume a hands-off policy towards me?

Association with Christina conferred status. When asked once by a recently recruited Moonie girl why I did not join in the Trinity meetings or prayer sessions, I said, "Ah, I'm only living here because I have my own job. Actually, I'm in Christina's Trinity." No more questions were asked. The girl gave a little gasp, and reverence wrote itself on her face.

"What a Blessing!" To be in Christina's Trinity meant you had a lot of ancestral merit. It must have been ancestral merit rather than merit gained in this life, because Christina was usually stuck with the difficult individualists or those, a little older than the average, who had built up careers of their own before running into the Family, and who, though less malleable than the youngsters, might be of some extra value to the Material Foundation. Christina once complained to me how difficult it was to get a lawyer into the Family. The Oakland Family had wined and dined and spent years trying to recruit a lawyer. By the Spring of 1975, they still had not been successful.

I stood there in the kitchen half-drunk, and allowed myself to be cajoled into joining the prayer session. I edged into the tiny prayer room with four other Family members. We knelt down in a circle and held each other's hands. Each of us prayed aloud in turn while a large picture of Father Moon looked benignly down on us from a little altar. When it was my turn I prayed slowly, trying to form my thoughts as I spoke. The gist of my prayer was the hope that God would attend to us and correct our mistakes and keep us attuned to the path He wanted us to follow. It was a hesitant prayer, with a number of pauses, unlike the forced emotion and parroting of Principle slogans that constituted the prayer of most Moonies. I suppose I felt again like a father to these children, and I wanted them to get the message that faults could exists inside the Family as well outside. From another viewpoint, I was just insisting on my own officious separation from the beehive.

I also kept thinking that in these close quarters, the others must have smelled the beer on my breath. Does it bode well or ill of the Family that no report of my beer-in-the-refrigerator game got back to the higher echelon? In any case, I was uplifted by the prayer experience. As I walked out of the little prayer room with the others, I glanced back with more than normal curiosity at the picture of Father Moon.

A Pledge Ceremony

I was just about to settle down to sleep one night when there was a swift rap on the door and one of the Trinity leaders came in. "Hurry up. We have a Pledge Ceremony."

"A what?"

"Pledge Ceremony. You have to wear a tie."

"I don't have a tie."

"I'll find one for you. Do you have a white shirt?"

"Yeah, somewhere."

"Suit jacket?"

"Yes, an old corduroy, I think its here . . ."

"That's fine, let's get going."

Five minutes later I was in the back seat of a car, tucking a crumpled white shirt into my jeans and trying to knot a tie in the dark without jamming my elbow into the young man sitting next to me. We drove for a few blocks and turned into a driveway nearly invisible between two mansions somewhere in the Berkeley hills. The doors of a gray wood gate were open to let us in and drive up a curving concrete path to a large split-level Japanese style structure, with sliding gateways and paths through crushed stone, and shrubbery lit by night lights.

Since his marriage to Onni, Dr. Durst had come up in the world. This million dollar split-level was a far cry from Dr. Durst sleeping on the floor in a sleeping bag alongside six other Moonies in his house in Oakland two years ago. This was silk sheets and the kind of privacy only the rich can afford.

We walked into a half-outside ante-room and piled our shoes with the others, then opened a broad sliding glass door into the house proper. I glimpsed large kitchens, dining rooms and bedrooms as we walked into the central living room, perhaps fifty feet by thirty feet, filled from wall to wall with kneeling Moonies, and at the front a long low table covered with gold brocades, and Onni and Dr. Durst, our own True Parents, dressed in finery, she in a white and gold gown and he in a white tuxedo. Both of them wore snap-on white gloves. I was bemused and didn't follow along too well as we chanted our dedication to Father Moon and performed a series of bows, heads scraping the floor, then back up to a kneeling position, then more bowing to the floor. We were facing Onni and Dr. Durst, and I really did not like bowing towards them.

I had been given no advance warning anyway, just this sudden plopping down in the midst of a hundred Moonies mouthing oaths which I did not want to utter. I was silent; I stumbled half-heartedly in the bowing and scraping—this non-compliance was easy since we were all so jammed together, and bowing all the way to the floor was nearly impossible. Mainly your head hit the back of the Moonie in front of you. I felt that this was too sudden an upping of the ante; I couldn't reconcile my more-or-less friendly talks with Dr. Durst, the talks that had meant a sort of fellow-feeling with him, with this Hollywood mock-up of an Asiatic court, complete with two splendid, doll-like figures smiling insensate smiles over a mass of groveling slaves. The glass wall on the side revealed a sparkling panorama of San Francisco at night. Where was I? What was this? Who were they? "They" had made a big mistake if they thought they could rope me in with such garbage. I was really irritated. Yes, respectfully follow a leader on a crusade to make a Heaven on earth; yes, take a gamble for the most radical good; yes, I had (I thought) sensed the presence of God on many occasions connected with this group. But this display of absolute monarchy, this blatant revelation of the huge chasm between king and peasants, these scrapings and bowings and choreographed humblings—the gorge rose, and I trembled with anger and lusted for our old-fashioned American war of liberation from arbitrary and self-serving tyranny. I was suddenly the lone, free, Marlboro-smoking man of the West against this chimera of an Egyptian court, these gilded pharaohs.

I remember it thus in retrospect, but that *was* the feeling half-sensed among this desperately idealistic crowd of young Americans, young people who were of the elite in intellectual sensitivity, hungering to make the world a paradise. Many of them—I knew some of them fairly well despite the necessity of snatching a few personal words from the hurry-up impersonality of work-pray-participate—many of them had joined the Family out of a penetrating sense of duplicity and hypocrisy in the world. I was mad and sad. Wasn't there duplicity and hypocrisy in this Pledge Ceremony? Wasn't I duplicitous and hypocritical even to be here? I stopped even trying to mouth the words.

And then each of us walked up to shake Dr. Durst's hand, and then Onni's hand. Only their hands were covered with tight little white gloves. Preserving them from our germs. I was very irritated. I passed right on by when it came my turn. I felt it was an incredible insult to make me shake hands with a person wearing gloves. If I had had the guts I would have spit in their faces.

But in the context of the crowd and the context of the signs I thought I had received from God and the context of my painful decision to re-join the Family, I had just about wiped myself out of any active rebellion. I walked stiff-legged past the two decorated dolls, our True Parents, and out to the stone path and put my shoes on and waited for my comrades.

"What's wrong?" Jeffy sat down beside me.

"Nothing. I just don't like it."

"What do you mean? What don't you like?"

"It's just not my style. That's all." That's all I could manage to say.

Right about then I began a policy of shutting myself off from other Family members. I was toughening up. No tears, no crying over disillusionment. Just a war that built and buried itself within me and a new level of cynicism in my soul.

That night I began to plot a second quiet escape from the Family. It would be easier this time. There were plenty of available garden apartments in Moraga. I would put my next paycheck in the bank instead of turning it over to Christina. I threw out my notes on the Principle and threw myself into bed feeling tough and unhappy.

A week later I was invited to Onni's house—the mansion hidden in the Berkeley hills—for dinner, as a token of appreciation for my money gifts. I was led into the living room and sat down in a deeply padded white swivel chair in front of a large-screen color TV. (Rank and file Moonies never saw a TV.) We watched the news. Onni was there, and four or five male Trinity leaders.

They were dressed in suits, and looked askance at my ragged blue jeans. I didn't care. I relished my unique position. This is what money can buy, you jerks (I thought). I don't have to play the game. I can walk into this palace in my Levis. Hah.

The fact is that these cruel thoughts were going on alongside proud thoughts that I had helped pay for this mansion. I was a Family member and I owned the place as much as anyone. We all owned it. There was no separate ownership in the Family. When you walked up that crushed stone path to the castle where Onni and Dr. Durst slept under silk sheets you gave no thought to their luxury. We were all in the Family, and this house was ours, not his or hers alone; we were all of one body, so who owned what on paper made no difference.

I sat down in that padded chair like I owned it. I graciously accepted a cup of tea and a sugary condiment from Onni. She asked me a few formal, gracious questions as if the stale-bread-eating flower teams did not exist. I answered easily and insincerely as if the sleeping bags on the hard floor were light-years away from my mind. Later we went into the kitchen where we had an intimate little dinner, just me and Onni and her house maid.

The house maid was a Moonie. She made the beds and did the laundry. Another Moonie house maid cooked ghastly Korean meals for Onni. I know. I tried to eat one of those meals at that little table in the kitchen. I tried a little raw fish and kimchee. If you have ever tried to eat kimchee you will understand my agony. It is a sort of rotted cabbage pickled in a sauce that makes you wish you had eaten the cabbage straight.

I decided to hell with it. I don't have to eat this stuff. I poked at it a little, and tried to engage Onni in conversation.

"Onni, the trouble with this symbolic division, I mean, well, the Communists are human beings just like we are, only they have the wrong idea...."

"You do not understand. Communists are not people. They are animals!"

Right. End of conversation. An English member of the Family, whom I have never seen before—tall, strident, unfeminine—sticks her head into the room.

"Don't you know"—a clipped aristocratic accent—"they are sitting over there in Russia throwing their psychic power at us? They are literally trying to kill us."

"Psychic power?"

"There are groups of people, mystics and psychics, sitting around tables in Moscow right this moment, shooting death vibrations at us.

You have no idea of the psychic warfare going on. Unification Church sensitives are focusing their energy to diffuse the Communist death rays. You should know how serious this is. We are fighting on *all* levels. They are trying to wipe us out!"

"Wipe us out?"

"Wipe us out. Wipe the Family out. Wipe out the United States. We are the only defense. The politicians don't even understand."

A couple of days later Christina tells me, "I can't wait until we get into politics!"

We ended the dinner with mutual insincerities, and I was driven back to the Ashby Street house, where I wandered around feeling half like a Moonie and half like a spy for the other side—whatever that other side was. I wondered why they had catered to me on such a crass level—the plush scenario, the color TV, a dinner in the inner sanctum. Didn't they realize that the only hook they had was the poverty-seeking, all-for-God instinct that had made me give all my money to them in the first place? Didn't they know that in accepting such special treatment, I was accepting a cynical frame of mind towards the whole Unification Church? Didn't they suspect that I would compare unfavorably the $1000 TV set with the myriad of drained souls who had paid for it and for so much more luxurious indulgence on the part of our leaders? Paid for it with a half-voluntary slavery to the Lord of the Second Advent? Oh, "we" owned it, all right. And then think about the burn-out cases, the young men and women on the road for four years, selling flowers and candles for the Lord, without love, without sustenance, with constant songs of hope and victory screaming in their heads.

Until they went blank and paralyzed in the mind.

World Day

The Family celebrates four holidays during the year: God's Day, True Parents' Day, Children's Day, and World Day. These are the only days off from work in the whole year, but they are filled with exhausting ceremony from dawn till late into the night. There's no rest ever for a Moonie.

Again I was driven to the "Onni Mansion." (It was owned by both of them, of course, but everybody knew who the real leader was. Dr. Durst is useful, a professor who can sound reasonable to the outside world, who always gives the Primary Lecture series, where he talks the liberal intellectual stuff that gets you mildly interested before you are socked with the twisted fundamentalism of the higher truth.)

I was to take part in a World Day celebration. The same large living room, the same glass wall looking out across the bay to the San Francisco skyline. High on a hidden hill where the Berkeley rich dwell and do whatever they do to worship the world's way in comfort and anxiety and hollowness in the center of the mind. But *our* rich house was in the hot cauldron of things. We were the center of the cross, the new beginning.

Some new beginning. A hundred or so Moonies from all parts of the country drifted back and forth from one wall to another, stoically mouthing "Happy World Day" to one another. Nothing else. Just "Happy World Day, happy World Day," in a mass of moiling, tired, drained people. Even worse than that. A short, unshaven refugee from an insane asylum (why was he here?) makes a move to clutch my hand and wish me a "Happy World Day." He misses. I push my hand through the somnambulant mist and grab his.

"Happy, happy World Day," I shout at him. He registers dismay. For I had destroyed the ritual phantasmagoria, repeating the word "happy"; I had cruelly varied the slogan and added a contemptuous, winning smile. If there was ever a zombie Moonie, he was it. He was probably fresh from a two-year Pioneer Mission, selling roses sixteen hours a day to make a new world.

There was nothing to the celebration but a nervous song from Noah (on orders from Onni) and a drifting, slow-moving crowd, mouthing "Happy World Day" as they wandered about in the best clothes they could manage to scavenge, a shimmering mess of ill-fitting linen on the women, and blue or black greasy suits on the men. It was a celebration of sleep-walkers. I couldn't help being cruel. "Happy World Day"—my hand was grabbed and moved up—stop—and moved down—stop—with a kind of grin gone beyond trying, into some nether world of paralysis.

"What's happy about it," I said. Just a twitch of mental register. "Ha, ha," tried to crawl out of the set-piece mouth facing mine—but didn't quite make it. I kept smiling winningly. My attitude was not proper, of course. But I felt myself awash in a sea of . . . washed brains. And I saw the two gilded Egyptian monarchs hold court up near the table. I moved slowly through the sleep-walkers over to them. I shook a gloved hand.

"Happy World Day," said Dr. Durst.

"Happy, happy World Day," I said.

"Grimace," he seemed to say to me. It was worse because there was a personal interlude. I suddenly came face to face with Ginny of the light brown hair, the woman I had hugged and lusted for a year ago at the Cloverdale snack-stand on the way back from a Boonville training session. She had been sent to New York, to Barrytown, to the big time, where Father himself ran the scene, doing God knows what, a 120-day training session, nine months on the road. This I gleaned from her tightened mouth and bleary eyes. Women back from a year at Barrytown or on the road often had gained weight, had pasty skin, sores around the mouth, and a deep vertical line in their foreheads. They were somehow immobile, and couldn't laugh. It was as if they'd learned a terrible secret.

"Tom! Oh! It's so good to see you!" she called out through the mist. I wanted to put my arms around her.

I wanted to say, What's happened to you? Why have you gotten fat in the backside and why is your linen dress all out of whack? Why has your body gone flaccid and your eyes gone bug-eyed?

But I said, "Hi. How are you? It's really good to see you. Where have you been?"

"Oh yes. It's good to see you." She squeezed my arm. "Happy World Day," she whispered to me and nearly cried.

"Come on," I said. "How are you really?" Meaning, what have they done to you?

"I'm so glad to see you here," she said. "So glad . . . Happy World Day . . . ."

She disappeared off into the crowd, trailing her newly large bottom with her. I trailed off into the crowd, stoically trailing my newly vacant self with me. The atmosphere was hypnotic. Many Family members who had come in through the Oakland Family and had gone on the better things were here. It was a kind of reunion. "Happy World Day," I cried to these long lost souls. A deep melancholy took hold of me and wouldn't let go. The vibrant woman I had liked—really *liked*—a year ago, had turned into a blobby, formalistic ghost of herself, with a muted heart inside still begging to glimpse someone real who could make her real.

I didn't bother shaking the gloved hands of the pharaoh and his wife again. I moved through the sea of "Happy ... World ... Day's ..." to the door, seeking my girlfriend. She was nowhere to be found. I thought of searching the whole place for her, but thought, No. It's too late.

Nowhere is the price of souls so great as on the mountain of a great hope. Satan must have scraped the skins to the bottom on this one.

I pushed my way through the zombies and managed to get home somehow. Was I a zombie too? Probably. I took my zombie self back to bed in the Ashby Street house where my own boxed reality consumed me, and I escaped a few weeks later to a fit place for the pity pot, a bachelor apartment in Moraga with California wine to comfort me and violent dreams to worry me.

Probably I was able to see the World Day Zombie Parade for what it was, because I was a Moonie with an outside job. The blur I remembered from the Summer of 1973, when I was a full-time Moonie, without much sleep, jerked around from one job to another, always wrapped up in Family life without a moment of my own—all that was what these people had endured for years. And worse. Moonies on Mobile Fund-raising Teams never slept in the same place two nights running; they ran—literally ran—day and night to sell and sell and sell; they ate poorly; they had nothing but their Center Man and five or six other Moonies to be with, constantly singing, constantly chanting, praying without letup. They are the ones who were psychologically brutalized. I was let off easy. And especially in my second go-round with the Moonies, I was awake, alert, and mentally functional. So I was able to see what I saw.

A Moonie with his own job must really believe in the Principle and the cause and Mr. Moon, in the sense of holding these beliefs rationally, so he can rationally defend them to a non-Moonie. You don't need that kind of faith when you are in the swim of Moonie life in a total sense. There, you believe in same way you believe a song that you can't get out of your head. It's always there as a litany, but not something to think about, because you are not really capable of rational thought. Your thinking process has been reduced to songs and slogans and a few ritual phrases. Anything more would mean you would have to have a separate mind, an ego of your own. In the middle of Moonie-land, in the World Day ceremony, you have lost all that.

That second departure was not the end of my association with the Unification Church. The "bad joke" epitomized by the zombie parade on World Day faded in the memory in favor of remembered kindnesses from Christina and others, and the beautiful feelings of unity I had experienced when we sang a song of love late at night at the end of a training session. I kept in touch with Christina and Patti and one or two others. Sometimes I would drive into town and pick Patti up on a street corner and we would play hooky together, she filling my head with wild stories about her mistreatment at the hands of Onni. Once (she said) she had been cleaning a small table in the mansion and had dropped something on it, chipping a tiny piece of veneer off the edge. Onni had screamed at her that she was "destructive" and "unfaithful" and "Satanic."

I knew somehow that Patti's continual screwing-up and her bouts of hysterical laughter at the mention of Satan were parts of a deep insight. She knew that the beast is in every heart, and that Moonies—pre-eminently Onni—ignorantly or hypocritically threw that beast onto whatever lay outside them. Patti took the heat because she couldn't do otherwise. She was too intelligent and too sensitive, and so was the perfect "fall guy." She was the court jester who couldn't help mocking the princes and the courtiers.

A month or so after World Day I went out to dinner with Christina and the Moonie house maid (the house maid who had sat silently while I tried to engage Onni in conversation over a dinner of raw fish and kimchee and death vibes zapping us from Moscow).

We had pizza in a Berkeley restaurant. When Christina went to the ladies' room, I asked the woman why she had joined the Moonies.

"After my husband left me I sat in a room drinking wine for a year," she said. "Then I ran into the Family."

From such fodder does the Family gain its warriors. And out of such loneliness the world has shown itself bankrupt. The society is a ship of wealth for those who stay on board, but for those who slip off, there is nothing but the green sea and a bottle of wine. This woman was no child. She was in her thirties. She had no parents to snatch her out of any mind-stealing cult and return her to the bosom of the nuclear family. There was no nuclear family. She had no brothers or sisters or aunts or uncles to give her a lifeboat. She was too grown up, socially conceived as an independent agent, to climb on board anyway. Divorced people with shattered hearts often look for a "support group." She found the Family. Or the Family found her.

"House maid to an Asiatic princess?"

"I was drinking myself to death. There is hope here."

"For an Ideal World?"

"For a chance. For contributing to a hope. What do you want me to say? It's better than drinking myself to death? All right, it's better than drinking myself to death."

What can you say to that? In the American culture foisted on us by TV round-table discussions and slick magazines and Harvard and Notre Dame and Creation Spirituality, everyone is supposed to be happy, or at least competent. And if we are not, it is because something is wrong with us, not because something lousy happened to us. That people can actually dry up and die from lost love is a dreadful secret you will never see bandied about on billboards or brought up for discussion in country clubs.

As for me, why did I stay in touch? Why couldn't I make a complete break with the followers of Reverend Moon? There was my continued love for Christina and Patti, of course. I had managed to extract them (in my mind) from the cause to which they were attached. Isn't there, after all, something permanent in the love of individual people for one another? You can abandon a cause or a way of living, but can you really abandon—fully, entirely, with no looking back—the people to whom you have formed a living attachment?

Then there was my never-ending proclivity to cling to things long after they were relevant to my changing life. More generally, I think it is a part of human nature to cling to the strongest experiences in life, whether those experiences are happy or tragic. You can be as loyal to the memory of something awful that happened to you as to the memory of something wonderful. And in the Moonie experience, these things are mixed, or they alternate violently. How many evenings I spent staring blankly at the TV tube while I listed in my mind all the goods and evils of the Unification Church! Night after night, I would weigh one Moonie reality against another—psychological manipulation of recruits versus blissful campfire songs when a hundred people felt the love of God and the love of each other; superficial labeling of complex political realities versus the clear vision of a paradisiacal world; a multitude of arbitrary orders versus gestures of pure kindness; face to face deceptions versus the Higher Truth; slave-making obedience as opposed to saint-making obedience. How do you weigh these things with their proper weights?

Underlying these contending realities in the Unification Church itself there are permanent things that cannot be questioned. Such as the love of individual people for each other. Or the universal human need for religious expression. Or the universal human proclivity to combine in groups or tribes or nations. That instinct for combining is a part of religious expression, which is why religion and politics get so mixed up everywhere. Religion—or its lack (or its anti-type)—undergirds all social combinations. When it is lacking in the wider culture, it comes back in a fiercely concentrated way in tight little self-contained tribes.

Perhaps the manipulation of love is no crime at all when the desire to love is mixed up with the movement towards a corporate identity. Perhaps it is foolish to think that love is real only when it is supremely interested personal love or when it is supremely disinterested universal love. Or put it this way: isn't all love, even heavenly love, overwhelmingly interested in combining the lovers? If I criticize Moonie "Love-Bombing" as insincere psychological manipulation and ask rhetorically if love can be real if it does not come from myself alone, the further question arises: is love from myself alone even possible? Is love from myself possible at all if I am not somehow standing under the arch of heaven? And short of heaven, is love possible to me or to anyone else if it is not grounded in the context of a higher identity?

It is no easy thing to divide fundamental human needs from the particular way those needs are answered or betrayed in the Moonies or in any other corporate organization. When there is precious little way to fulfill fundamental needs in the contemporary wasteland of technological culture, what safeguards, what standards of comparison are there in the human psyche to defend against a cheap or brutal imitation of the real thing? How is the isolated human being to say, "this is right, that is wrong" in religion, when his most characteristic cultic activities are pushing buttons on the wall of a bank to give him cash-in-hand, or turning knobs on the TV to give him the soothing diversion of fictionalized violence? How can he judge secondary rights and wrongs when he is starved for permanent fundamentals: the need to combine in some semblance of love, the need to have purpose, the need to worship some image of God?

For months after I left the Church I would end my nightly accountings with the thought: the Moonies are no great shakes, but they are the best game in town. Then I would wake in the morning in a more rational frame of mind.

The sober reflections of daytime went something like this: an imitation is worse than nothing, especially if the imitation is actually a betrayal. If you reach down into the depths of yourself, if you borrow on all of your psychological assets and mortgage yourself to the hilt in order to purchase a pearl of great price, and that pearl turns out to be mother-of-pearl, your final state is ten times worse than when you started. And things are even trickier when that artificial pearl has a veneer of genuine pearl substance that is not worn away until long after you have sold all you own. Affectionate hugs and intimate talks are real, in and of themselves. The feeling of unity experienced in training sessions is genuine, in and of itself. The commitment to universal purpose is an honest commitment, honestly undertaken by Moonie leaders and followers. But I talked with some long term Moonies who let slip their long term feelings of loneliness and isolation. What had happened to love?

Moonie "love" is manifested first by flattery and later by carping criticism and verbal whipping. After a short honeymoon of applause for everything you do and concern for everything you think and evening bliss-outs around the campfire, you are assaulted with your own deeply fallen nature, and you must pay indemnity for yourself and for the whole human race—"Work harder! Pray harder!"—while the higher-ups multiply their demands until you give beyond your ability to give just for the sake of a kind word. No one has captured the process more succinctly than Lowel Streiker in his book *Cults*: "A religious experience that begins as regression to a blissful state of childlike innocence is step by step transformed into a compulsive, dread-filled struggle to regain constantly a sense of security and acceptance."

On one of my last days at Ashby house before my second escape, Onni came in and saw me standing in the hall, then went over to the low telephone vestibule and flipped through a pile of letters, letters to people who were no longer living at the house, that had been piling up for months. She manufactured a mood of irritation.

"Why are these letters here? They should be sent back. Why are they left here? This is a mess." Then she picked up the phone and called the post office to demand that they stop delivering letters to this address except for the names she proceeded to deliver—then she went silent, turned red in the face, began to shout into the phone—

I, who worked for the post office, tried to interject—"Onni, it doesn't work that way"—but she waved me off. She listened for a moment longer and then slammed down the phone.

"Satan! They are Satan!"—she gave me a hard look and turned away and bustled out the front door. She caught my quizzical look before she left.

Any obstacle to your tyranny is Satanic, I whispered in my mind to her departing flounce of skirts. More than once I heard the resounding gratitude of fellow Moonies—more than once—many times—it was almost a litany:

"Onni is so hard on us because she loves us so much."

Locks exuberant children in a closet for two hours. Yells at Christina, "You are stupid! You are stupid!" Humiliates tired or troubled Family members in front of a hundred of their peers. Excoriates the whole Family in late night gatherings with charges of "laziness" and "unfaithfulness" if we have not managed to sell a sufficient number of dying roses that day.

"She loves God so much! I wish I could be like her!"

Chapter Five

Rocky Mountain Dharma High

It is three years after the World Day debacle drove me out of the Moonies for the second time. I am living in Boulder, Colorado, immersed in Buddhist meditation and poetry workshops. Both of these activities are under the auspices of Naropa Institute, a Buddhist college founded by the Tibetan lama-in-exile, Chogyam Trungpa. The Institute is a cauldron of spirited creativity. It is on the leading edge of the American mind, which is seeking reality and enlightenment and, as always, ever more sophisticated adventures. It has attracted Allen Ginsberg, Ken Kesey, William Burroughs, and a number of other poets and writers from around the country—some for the annual summer extravaganzas, some as year-round residents. A long poem I wrote during my post-Moonie exile in Moraga has just been published by Lawrence Ferlinghetti in his internationally renowned *City Lights Journal*—actually an anthology—and so I have gained some respect and an entrance to the colony of literary superstars.

The swirl of parties and the defense of literary status rather overwhelmed the Buddhism; egos were inflated in a land where egos were supposed to be made small. Buddhism as a religion and a practice has the goal of destroying the "grasping and repelling self," but that self is nowhere more intent on its own survival and enhancement than in the company of the great or near-great. I was certainly not immune to the contradiction. The crowd of erstwhile beatnik poets from San Francisco and slick surreal poets from New York City attracted a bevy of literary groupies, like the teenage girls who try to gain access to the bedrooms of rock stars. I call them literary groupies because they were not out to offer their bodies to the likes of Willie Nelson or Kris Kristopherson or Mick Jagger, but the likes of Allen Ginsberg (who is bi-sexual), and Gregory Corso and—well—even me. I was in fact seduced by a young lady for no other reason than the glamour attending to my status as a published poet. Afterwards she gave me an amulet that had once belonged to a well-known West Coast Zen and nature poet, and took a memento from me to present to her next conquest. For her this bestowing of sexual favors was a sort of networking agreement with her own erotic gods, but for me it was the seal of good housekeeping in the Valhalla of poetic warriors.

It was all a heady business, and I must confess I enjoyed it immensely—me downstairs with my girl, while upstairs Gregory Corso screamed obscenities at his life-long friend Allen Ginsberg as all the lucky youths gaped in wonder. Oh it was glorious, it was a Dylan Thomas bacchanalia with exotic ladies dancing in the corridors and rock-and-roll pounding in the ears, and Aleister Crowley glowering from the bookshelf. There were parties and more parties all summer long in our student housing motel, with its glass sliding doors and sweep-around balcony and swimming pool in the courtyard below. There was little method to the madness, but there was plenty of magic and lots of pain, and a heaven of sorts for some of us, especially while the wine flowed and the band played on.

But there came a time when the glamour of hobnobbing with famous *literati* paled, and a kind of moral revulsion set in. Sex in the fast lane, vicious gossip and back-biting among the "blessed company of poets," Promethean celebrations of the self that mocked the gods of restraint and order, a literary *Weltanschauung* that glorified Gertrude Stein and Jack Kerouac and French Dadaism, a garishly surreal unrealism in life and art—all combined to breed an anxious emptiness that could no longer be filled by wine and women and song.

I took long walks around Boulder, trying to establish something solid with the trees and mountains. I read Catholic mystical treatises like *The Cloud of Unknowing* and the *Imitation of Christ*. The memory of the Unification Church crept back into my mind.

Up the hill from where I lived was a large rambling house with five or six white vans parked in the driveway, and a small sign in front saying "Collegiate Association for the Research of Principles." "Research of Principles" was a giveaway, as were the lines of shoes I could see through the broad window on one side, and in the evening as I walked past I would peer inside and sometimes see a group of young people kneeling in a circle, half-hidden under the slanting roof. I could not keep myself from returning late at night when the moon cast a mystical glow on the place, and feeling throughout my being the deep contrast between the life I was immersed in and that other life I had left behind. It was a pull from way behind the gut, as distant as the stars, wholly removed from the garden of earthly delights.

The revulsion I had begun to feel was capped by a party in William Burroughs' apartment, with Kesey and Ginsberg and Corso and a prancing transvestite, and Burroughs' young blond and blue-eyed "literary secretary" proudly informing everyone of his special position with the great author. The great author, meanwhile, walked with a cane and wore a black coat, and looked like death, and talked about "raising up the beast of the abomination." Years before he had accidently killed his wife by trying to shoot an apple off her head while doped-up on methedrine. His five-year-old son witnessed the incident. That son—now in his twenties—who called himself "Burroughs the Lesser," was also in Boulder, and we became friends for a while. Burroughs the Lesser had a transplanted liver, and a few years later he died, unwilling and unable to stop the whiskey and heroin that had cost him his first liver.

"The Beast of the Abomination" talk was not serious or intentional Satanism. There were no seances or rituals to raise the devil. It was the dregs of cynicism and heroin and homosexuality, mocking the benign Buddhism that was supposed to take you to a place beyond good and evil. We would watch the tall, pallid Burroughs the Elder tap-tapping down the sidewalk, looking like Death Incarnate. But by now I had had enough of them all.

I gravitated away from the literary superstars and towards a set of lesser lights who were interested like me in the magical and mystical and religious. These were people with less opportunity for glory and more need for truth. (But here I malign Allen Ginsberg, who did indeed become a friend for awhile and who has always been driven by the need for a religious resolution. His move to the feet of Chogyam Trungpa had drawn all the others to Boulder and Naropa Institute. By now he has become the grand old man of American poetry, and a few years ago he was lecturing at Columbia University for—reportedly—$60,000 a semester.)

But the people I grew to love and respect most were not so ready to debunk Western traditions for the sake of securing themselves in the exotic playgrounds of the East, and who even gave some thought to Christianity—though the Christianity they valued was of an unchurched, esoteric variety complete with Arthurian legends and Tarot Cards. It was an underground, poetic, individual sort of Christianity. In fact it was something of a leftover from the occult delicatessen of the sixties, without the intensity bred by the feeling that all things were at a cosmic crisis point. I was older, my friends were older, and we had all been through it before. The cosmic fire that had consumed us in the late sixties had passed over and left us to our own devices. Now was the time of re-creations and imitations, or, as I was beginning to say to some close friends, now was the time to go in another direction.

One of these friends was a lapsed Catholic trying to find his way home from the hinterlands of Asian mysticism. One evening we were drinking beer in the house he shared with another like soul, and a young woman he knew came in and talked with us about God and the Bible and something called "Twig Fellowships."

"Twig Fellowships?"—how corny! But this absurd nomenclature was based on the image of a tree, as my friend explained it: the trunk was Jesus Christ, or (organizationally) headquarters, and then there were state branches and smaller branches, and twigs on the branches—so the little groups where the Word of God was discussed and Power for Abundant Living courses were offered, were called "Twig Fellowships." I still thought it sounded unbearably cute, but the young lady was attractive, and I went along for the ride. She was studying for a Master's Degree in Music at the University of Colorado, was friendly and intelligent and charming, and intent on getting me involved in her brand of Christianity. I was all set to go. It seemed at least potentially an answer to my longings to lead a more genuinely religious life.

There was a particular area in which Caroline and I hit it off particularly well. She as a musician and I as a poet were both extremely responsive to sound—in fact, I had spent the last couple of years berating the semi-surrealist poets of my acquaintance on their ignoring the sounds and rhythms of words while they search for ever-new pictorial images and obscure insights. It was a poetry of the eye-brain rather than the ear-brain, and because of that (I kept declaiming) it was jarring and devoid of compelling beauty. Likewise in the modern music which had lost its tonality and melodic forms. Caroline and I agreed that the twelve-tone scale and atonal music introduced in this century were so grating on the nerves as to be almost diabolical. So when I later found that the Way Ministry had elaborated a theory of heavenly as versus diabolical music, I was (you might say) all ears.

Caroline lived in a modern split-level house on the outskirts of Boulder with seven or eight companions in the local "Twig Fellowship." I was a guest for dinner there on several occasions, and there I found that the organization they all belonged to was called "The Way Ministry" or "The Way International." Its founder and leader was Dr. Wierwille, an erstwhile Evangelical preacher who had struck out on his own in the 1950s and had built up his own church, advertised as a non-sectarian Biblical research society.

As it turned out, it was much more than that.

One night I sat around the kitchen table in the house with a couple of "Twiggies" and listened to a cassette tape. It was the confession of a girl who had been deprogrammed from the Way Ministry and had then spent some time traveling around the country deprogramming people from other cults. She partook in the (unsuccessful) deprogramming of a Moonie and saw his agony and identified with him and felt horrible. The Moonie later escaped and made his way back to the Unification Church, and the girl later made her way back to the Way Ministry. She said on the tape player, nearly crying with shame, that she could never do that again, never be complicit in driving a believer, in whatever belief, away from his belief.

As I listened to her, I thought she had learned something. She had learned a respect for other people that her parents and other parents who kidnapped their adult children did not feel and an acknowledgment that, if she was an adult and responsible for herself, she had to let other people be adults and responsible for themselves. Probably her maturity did not go down well with the Moonies, the Way Ministry, or her own family. She had seen (I surmised) that grasping parents and cults were both playing the same game of "you belong to me be alone," while she had discovered in herself the courage to say: here goeth I, and that other one has the right, just as I have, to walk unhampered towards his own religious discovery.

That is the way I thought listening to that young woman's plea. I no longer feel that way. Now I am certain that psychological manipulation can indeed coerce souls and enslave them. But in 1979 I was distrustful of deprogrammers, and I hated the thought that I might have been brainwashed, therefore mentally incompetent, therefore subject to legal maneuvers that could put me (albeit temporarily) under the unlimited control of parents or state-appointed guardians. Every day old people are put under similar constraints and robbed of their liberty and their fortunes. The mental incompetence formula has been abused to the extent of forcing Catholic converts back to the Protestantism of their parents, and Pentecostals back to the gray walls of mainline Protestantism. The legal formula is a disaster for human liberty and responsibility. Better "illegal" abductions, a storm of facts to counter the rote creed of the cultist, affection from brothers or sisters or old friends—then let the rest of it come out in the wash. Maybe it will be successful, maybe unsuccessful. But keep the state out of it.

The girl's sympathy for the Moonie was lost on the young man who listened to the tape with me. He had been a member of the Children of God, perhaps the most notorious and damaging of the cults, had been deprogrammed, and had spent a year or two driving around the country with a band of deprogrammers extracting Children of God and Moonies and other imprisoned souls from their respective mind-stealing jails. Now he had found the One True Church—again. His eyes lit up as he regaled me with lurid tales of his adventures as a deprogrammer, as if he missed that hectic and heroic life on the road. I asked him if perhaps he thought the girl on the tape was right about not violently messing with other people's religions, but he did not agree. He was the kind of person who always had to be right, and wherever he landed was the right place—to the exclusion of everything else and in enmity with everything else. I didn't tell him that at that moment I felt very much like a Moonie.

Another tape I heard that evening talked about the evils of the deprogrammers and incidentally boasted that the Way Ministry had achieved the status of being number five on the deprogrammers' hit list. I couldn't help privately relishing the fact that the Moonies were number one. Who were the others? At that time—the summer of 1979—they were Scientology, the International Society for Krishna Consciousness (better known as the Hare Krishnas), and the Children of God. Of the big five, three were vaguely Christian, one was vaguely Hindu, and one was science fiction. The religious or irreligious doctrine didn't seem to matter; what seemed to matter was the degree of power the group or the leader of the group had over the soul and life of the devotee.

As I talked with the Way Ministry people around the table, I kept my own counsel and indulged in comparisons. To defend against deprogramming efforts, Moonies were told to keep their minds tightly focused on Father Moon, and chant *"Out Satan, Out Satan"* silently or out loud to their tormentors. In whatever way they could, they must keep from responding to the wily arguments of the devil. They were assured that they would be deprived of food and sleep, beaten, raped (if they were women), or thrown naked into a room with a prostitute (if they were men). The same horror tales of imagined abuse preceded Way Ministry devotees into their trial with the Satanic secularists who had kidnapped them. They were given secret chants by Dr. Wierwille to bolster them against the onslaught, and of course there was the ubiquitous Way Ministry practice of speaking in tongues, for this meant that an Angel was speaking through you. How could mere mortals break through such a defense?

That evening I felt right in the middle of it again—the thrill of belonging to an outlaw group (that is, outside the pale of normal society), a twenty-four-hour-a-day religious commitment demanding your whole loyalty, a very present and manifest devil in the form of deprogrammers waiting to get you, a tribal identity, a fellowship of love—everything that was missing in the secular American landscape. Since I had been a Moonie, I was skeptical of this bunch, but I let Caroline talk me into attending the Way Ministry's version of a training session. This turned out to be a series of video lectures presented by Dr. Wierwille, and took place over a period of a couple of weeks. The cost was $100, for which you also received five or six paperback books written by Dr. Wierwille. The lectures and books talked a lot about how to "properly divide the Word of God." We used the King James Bible (Caroline presented me with a copy) with a lot of corrections based on the scholarship of Way Ministry researchers. Since the Bible is the Word of God, it must be entirely consistent with itself.

For example, the Gospel of Mark has the two thieves crucified with Jesus both taunting Him (Mark 15:32); Luke's Gospel has one of the thieves taunting Him, but the other thief rebuking the first (Luke 23:39-40). Dr. Wierwille's solution is to say that the two Gospels are referring to two different pairs of thieves, bringing the total up to four. (This despite the fact that all four Gospels say specifically that two thieves were crucified with Jesus.) There are hundreds of other ostensible inconsistencies in the Old and New Testaments—the same stories told in slightly different ways, differing numberings for the same tribes or armies, different renditions of the Hebrew invasion of Canaan, different itineraries of the life of Jesus—all brought to immaculate harmony through the profound scholarship and interpretive ability and revelations of Dr. Wierwille. Many corrections of the King James text came from the Peshitta Bibles written in ancient Syriac, purported to be the most reliable of the early texts.

I was myself of a scholarly bent of mind, and I lived right across the street from the University of Colorado, so I checked up on Dr. Wierwille's deductions by reading a number of books on Biblical criticism—not the specious "form criticism" that derives from the German rational materialism of the nineteenth century and which still dominates seminary studies (Catholic included) in the United States, but the textual criticism based on comparing the most ancient existing manuscripts. I filled my head with things like the Codex Sinaiticus and the Codex Alexandrinus and found out (among other things) that the Peshitta texts Dr. Wierwille valued so highly were as corrupt, if not more so, than the so-called "received" texts on which the King James Bible is based. The Way Ministry's textual scholarship was, to put it mildly, a sham.

What was worse was Dr. Wierwille's interpretation of Biblical texts. In I Corinthians, where the different gifts of the Holy Spirit are listed, Dr. Wierwille decides that St. Paul means that *all* the gifts of the Holy Spirit are given to *all* believers. These include the power of healing and teaching and prophesying and speaking in "divers kinds of tongues." If you have any one of these gifts, you have them all. Speaking in tongues is of course the most recognizable and, therefore, the manifest touchstone of salvation. This is the special hook of the Way Ministry: to get you to believe you can speak in tongues. If you can do that, your powers as a Son of God are virtually unlimited.

Another strange decision on Dr. Wierwille's part is to say that the Gospels apply only to Jews and not to Christians. Christians, for example, need not pay any attention to the Lord's Prayer. They need not ask God to be forgiven their trespasses: God has already forgiven them. They need not ask to be delivered from evil: God has already delivered them. The Way Ministry equation is this: only Christians are saved, and once saved, cannot lose their salvation, and the proof of being a Christian is that you have the gifts of the Holy Spirit, and the proof that you have those gifts is that you can speak in tongues. The trouble—one of many—is that Dr. Wierwille's interpretation of I Cor.12 goes against the plain sense of the text—whether that text is read in English or Syriac or Greek. He also conveniently forgets what St. Paul says immediately following: "Though I speak with the tongues of men and of angels and have not charity, I am become a sounding brass or a tinkling cymbal."

I shared my misgivings with Caroline, but went on attending the daily video and discussion sessions with her, more or less to please her, more or less out of curiosity about what would come.

On the weekend dividing the two halves of the seminar, Caroline and I went out to a ranch fifteen miles east of Boulder to partake in a Way Ministry jamboree. The ranch was owned by the parents of one of the members. The land was high and dry and rocky; the sky was bigger and clearer than it had ever been in California. We arrived in a troop of cars and pick-up trucks and motorcycles and drove up a gravelly, gully-like road to a hilly terrain that was too high for pasturage. Here we had ten or twenty unfenced acres all to ourselves.

I observed everything and everyone and compared it all with the Moonie experience at Boonville. Everything here was less regulated; the people more independent—they owned and drove their own vehicles, for example, and every once in awhile an argument would break out between a married couple or between organizers and rank-and-file members. The dictatorial set-up so characteristic of Moonie life was missing. This was almost like a normal group picnic. On Friday night we went off in various directions and bedded down in the grass in sleeping bags, and on Saturday there were three-legged races and songfests and finally a campfire hot-dog roast. It was all comparatively relaxed—there was time to walk and talk privately—but on Saturday night when a young man in a cowboy hat brought out a guitar and sang a gentle song while thirty of us sat cross-legged around the fire, I began to get chills of remembrance. Sure enough, a young woman got up from the circle and cried and said she had never known love until she met the Family.

The Family! Why does that word make a twenty-five year old man or woman cry in Boonville, California, or in Niwot, Colorado? No—I cannot credit the theory of psychological immaturity. Nor will I call into question parental shortcomings. There was something deeper here, alien to all that, incomparable. It is atavistic; it is basic; it is composed of religion and tribe. It is almost as if you could say: religion (a shared transcendental need) and tribe (a shared identity with the group) means: Family. This is something that does not call for psychological analysis of weak egos, but does call into question the weakened nuclear family and the incoherence and disarray of our society. There was a cry and a joy in that woman's heart that meant breaking into something very new and very old: God and tribe. You might even say, the God of the tribe. But this might seem to mean: a false god. I say rather that it is the true God, even when the religion is false.

I am abstracting from the particular content of a religion (or an *ersatz* religion), what is real and valid—and which always presupposes Christianity, for Christ is everywhere. The despicable crime is that every religious cult hits on it—this something real and valid—I don't think they calculate it. But it always happens when a group is brought together all intent on God—and this thing that always happens is then used to promote whatever agenda the group is on.

That is the crime—that this social and transcendent bond-happening called Family, which should exist everywhere and at all times and be a natural foundation into which God's revelation may be poured, is instead so rare in the contemporary secular wasteland that the tribal event is itself taken as proof of the unique truth of the particular theory or purpose of the cult. It is taken as proof that the leader of the cult has the full sanction of God, despite appearances to the contrary, and no matter the degree of tyranny he imposes on his followers.

There is a capacity and a need in the human soul which has been covered over, atrophied, driven out by the transformation of tribal society into cities and isolated family farms and—after how many centuries?—isolating individuals into lone agents, each with his own "philosophy of life." That communitarian capacity is wakened once again when you encounter once again a tribe with a god.

Joining the Family! How that phrase echoed in my mind as the moon dipped down and the Colorado sky went big and dark and another hot dog was thrown on the grate. My heart went out to the poignancy of these people. I so much wanted to be there with them, in all my heart, but the phrase kept going through my mind: Unification Church, Unification Church. I was in the Way Ministry circle around the campfire, but I was totally separated. Everything that went on at that picnic drove me back to the real professionals at this sort of thing—the Moonies.

I saw it as levels of scenario, levels of demanded participation, level of hook. The Moonies could get you to say, "Never have I known love until I met the Family" in two days flat.

That night when I bedded down in a sleeping bag next to Caroline I whispered in her ear: "That was pretty good, but the Moonies do it better."

Then again, in the Moonies I could never have gone off to a private spot with Caroline during a training session. Even if Father Moon were to bless us with matrimony, we would most likely then be split up to work for the Kingdom of God in different cities. The Moonies don't want you to be sexually active, despite their ostensible promotion of the family. (Children get in the way.) What the Moonies want is to turn out a pre-pubescent army whose whole purpose is to do the bidding of Our Father Who Art On Earth.

But this was not my state of mind in the summer of 1979. The state of my mind in the summer of 1979 around that campfire with those people was one of overwhelming nostalgia for the Family I had once belonged to.

The essential hook of the Way Ministry, besides a mild version of the training sessions, was to get you to think you could speak in tongues. This is how it happened. On the last day of the seminar, after all the videotapes and question-and-answer periods were done with, the three of us who were potential recruits were herded into a back room. There Paul, a smiling ruddy-faced young man, and another Way Ministry leader told us to relax and compose ourselves. We needn't wait for some mystical feeling of the presence of the Holy Spirit in order to start speaking in tongues. The Spirit was already in us, and we simply had to open our mouths and speak in the voice of the Spirit. It was easy; it was only self-consciousness and disbelief that held us back. Paul demonstrated and then gently led the three of us into the mood of the event. First one, and then the second recruit started mouthing noises that made no sense in any language on earth, and there was great relief and joy expressed all around.

Then it was my turn. I certainly did *not* feel even a hint of the presence of the Holy Spirit. But in that company, under those looks of hope and concern, I wanted to please. I knew I could make strange noises, too, and so I did.

"Gludinglemal slewitch charunti phit. Gistoblock dirridle." "Yes! Great! You've got it! Do it some more!" "Gilbit nerophat oongoodle," I said. "Maper-o-sliggle!" "Yes! Relax! Good! Let the Spirit come out!" "Ack phu de ran tin. Bedackle oraflake!" A few minutes later we were all back in the living room, receiving congratulations from the assembled company, and singing in tongues!—to a melody of (you guessed it) "You Are My Sunshine." Singing in the tongues of angels. Wow. Then somebody is commanded to interpret your angelic message. He delivers a short running speech praising God and Dr. Wierwille and the Way Ministry as the work of God and how we all must be united in purpose. The short speech lasts just about the time it took you to sing your angelic song among the blessed company of the saved. Glory be to God!

It would have been too heartbreaking for my new friends to learn what I really thought. I didn't buy it for a minute. Later I told Caroline that anyone could mouth garbledigook; that the whole experience was a ridiculous exercise in deliberate baby babble. She dropped me like the unbelieving cynic I was, and I never saw her again. But a few days before that happened she admitted that she kept up a running silent angelic speech in her mind, so as always to be in touch with God. This was common practice among Twiggies. I thought it was nuts.

The Way Ministry was easy for me to discredit—Dr. Wierwille was obviously way off base both in his Biblical scholarship and in his interpretation of Scripture. His notions about the Jews (unsaved) and about Christianity starting with the first chapter of Corinthians, I found alarming and elitist. The hook of getting you to speak in tongues was an absurdity. This is not to say that speaking in tongues is everywhere a fraud. The descent of the Holy Spirit, I am sure, does indeed happen among Christian groups. But it doesn't happen in the Way Ministry, unless it happens to a few graced souls, and in spite of the doctrine and practice of the Way Ministry.

Stop reading this for a minute, close your eyes, and intentionally mouth a string a nonsense syllables. See how easy it is? This is what goes down in the Way Ministry as speaking in the tongues of Angels. It is only in the context—in the social grouping, the tribal bonding over a two week period, the Scriptural study, the Godtalk—that you may be led to think you are engaging in anything more exalted than baby-talk.

There are other things wrong with Dr. Wierwille's cult besides the dangerous self-delusion that you are automatically saved if you are a "Christian" according to the Way's (again self-delusive) prescription. The cult is virulently anti-Catholic and anti-Semitic. There is first of all the familiar ultra-Protestant myth that the Catholic Church is the Whore of Babylon—but that shibboleth has grown feeble with age, and presumably the Church will survive it as it has survived everything to date. What is worse is that Dr. Wierwille has his followers believing that Hitler's Holocaust of the Jews never happened. He recommends two books promoting this insanity: *The Myth of the Six Million* and *The Hoax of the Twentieth Century*. Their contention is that the Holocaust was nothing more than Zionist propaganda. (Presumably all those photographs of dying, starved people and piles of bones and lime pits filled with skeletons—all these were faked. Presumably my step-father was hallucinating when he liberated concentration camps with General Patton's army in World War II and saw with his own eyes those horror-filled faces and incinerated corpses.)

What is devilish about such shameless falsification of history is that after a generation, people do indeed forget—they no longer have direct knowledge, and must get their knowledge from books, or, like me, from old soldiers' war stories. But when the old soldiers die and the books lie, how shall the truth be recovered? If the horror of the Holocaust is wiped out of consciousness, if we turn away from the knowledge, thinking it is too horrible to ever have really happened, we shall become free again to play Satan's game of "get the Jew."

Fifty years have passed since these events took place, and it is human nature to want to forget the horror. In a tribe such as Dr. Wierwille rules, isolated from the mainstream of society and information, the big lie can overwhelm verified historical knowledge: and that can be dangerous for the human race. Dr. Wierwille is not alone in resurrecting the hoary tradition of finding in the Jew the scapegoat for all the evil in the world.

Something else has been happening in this "Christian" sect that puts it far beyond the pale of legitimacy. It is engaged in weapons training (under the innocent label of "hunter safety programs"). And it has been stockpiling weapons in its facilities in Colorado.

Setting aside the moral question—why not forget about defending yourself and consider martyrdom?—it is perhaps legitimate under some conditions for a group to arm itself in defense against vigilantes or the armed forces of the State. But that would be in response to previous violent acts on the part of forces opposing the group—say, a few murders or a few hangings. But no such thing has happened to the Way Ministry, the Summit Lighthouse, Synanon, the TFP, or the Society of St. Pius X. These are five sects I know of—there may be others—that have armed themselves.

Armed themselves without reason. Neither police nor the National Guard nor the U.S. Army has made armed assaults on the above-named groups. The point to bring out here is the terrific degree of social disaffection that can make people who gather together for the sake of love or purity or heaven—can make such people clothe themselves with violent imaginings, turn their peacefulness into war, think themselves a persecuted minority *before* they have been persecuted, and take up arms against an imaginary threat from outside. It is a kind of social psychosis that ends up provoking what it fears.

On the sociological level such disaffection and paranoia illuminates the violence in contemporary American culture; on the psychological level it reveals the deep anger in the heart of the soul; on the religious level it puts the lie to any pretensions of religion.

The first (and hardest) thing you are supposed to learn in religion is that the beast is in your own heart too, and if you can't get the right balance between "them" and "us," you are falling precipitously from religion into anti-religion. How often I have talked to sectarian Catholics who have transformed altruism into enmity, love into hatred, peace into war! That is the downside to a tribal identity. The tribe (in its modern, artificial manifestations) is self-conceived as an elite remnant, with the whole outside world in the snares of the devil. With that self-serving credo informing the tribal soul, the tribe is incapable of performing that central Catholic act, the examination of conscience. Inside the tribe you are saved, outside you are damned. Traditional Catholics who should know better than anyone else the paramount importance of confession, instead become mirror images of Way Ministry devotees.

It is perhaps unfair to quote something out of context from a newspaper story. Take it for what it's worth. The *Kansas City Star* of February 8, 1982, ran a story quoting some ex-Way Ministry members, who are said to have said, "They gladly would have killed anyone, including their own parents, if Mr. Wierwille had asked."

It rings true to me, knowing what I know about the psychological control a cult can have over its members. I knew nothing about the guns or the pernicious falsification of history when I was a potential recruit. But what I *had* experienced made me think more and more about the Unification Church. The Way Ministry seemed to me to be a cheap imitation of the real thing. I could at least take the Unification Church seriously. The idea of Way Ministry people secure in their own salvation running around mouthing garbledigook all over the place struck me as sadly comical. At least in the Unification Church we weren't so hung up on our own salvation as we were about saving the world. And we had the Living Christ—if we would accept it. We had the Apocalypse in our hands. It was altogether more idealistic and more radical. Our theory was more exotic, more comprehensive, more into the nitty-gritty of the whole cosmos and the whole of history. It was a much bigger and better proposition. Compared to the Unification Church, the Way Ministry was a pathetic little fundamentalist sect, following in a long line of sectarian Bible-bangers. As for the Unification Church, it is either the Second Coming of Christ or something very much like the coming of the Anti-Christ. You have to take something like that seriously.

Well—these were my nostalgic thoughts after my taste of the Way Ministry recalled to me my Moonie experience. The campfire, the songs, the "Family"—all of it keyed my soul to that past life I had walked away from. My mind followed, expunging the fact that I didn't take the Unification Church's doctrine seriously at all.

After my rejection of the Way Ministry and Caroline's rejection of me, I ransacked the University of Colorado's library for more books on the Bible, then the Apocrypha, then the so-called Gnostic gospels which had been rejected by the early Church Councils, but which had been resurrected by New Age pundits. Then I read the theosophical writings of Madame Blavatsky and the esoteric astrology of Alice Bailey. I attended poetry workshops at Naropa Institute, went up to Marpa House to meditate Buddhist-style, and on several occasions drove up to the Rocky Mountain Dharma Center for week-long meditations. I published some lousy poems in tiny journals floating around the Buddhist Sangha (society of devotees) in Boulder. It was a holding pattern. I identified with none of these activities or theories or accomplishments wholeheartedly.

Meanwhile half of me wanted to return to the Unification Church, and half of me mistrusted *any* religious theory or organization less than two thousand years old. I was as disgusted with latter-day re-workings of the original Christian message as I was with what happened to Eastern religious traditions once they got swallowed up in the all-consuming American psyche.

And yet I could not help consuming everything religious in hopes of finding something I could digest. One morning I thought Buddhism was the best bet, because it had no doctrine to believe, but was essentially a practice, which, I thought, allowed me access to whatever ultimate reality there was. Of course, I was wrong about that. During meditation one tries to rid one's mind of all concepts, ideas, and the background buzz of subliminal thought that clogs the passages of reality. But the religion of Buddhism is certainly a doctrine as well as a practice. For example, Buddhism says that the human soul or self does not really exist. We are "bundles" of traits, desires, imaginary selves who exist through one incarnation after another, the goal being to dissolve that "bundle" and become one with Reality—in some life. Buddhism cannot be collapsed into Christianity, much as people try.

Having been burned by the disordered imaginings of latter-day "Christians," I began to hear the litany in my mind: "If you are going to be a Christian, you have to be a Catholic." The Catholic Church was always there, and always had been there. It was always in a corner of my mind as the religion of last resort, after everything else had fallen apart. It had always been there in history as a bastion against slippery philosophies and do-it-yourself religions—or so G.K. Chesterton informed me in his brilliant and seductive apologias.

From my viewpoint on the mountains of the East, far outside all the Christianities, it was simply obvious to me that the Church of Jesus Christ is the Catholic Church. The litany in my mind was nothing mystical, but only the recognition of a fact. I still have trouble seeing how anyone could convert to one of these side-line Protestant sects that were born in the minds of troubled men fifteen centuries after Christ had established His Church. Every Christianity besides Catholicism is a split-off from Catholicism.

That fact alone was enough for me to know that the only possible genuine article is the Catholic Church.

But a lot of people have no sense of history, a lot of people simply stay in the Church they were born into, and a lot of people think it's no big deal to slide out from under the authority of the Church when they aren't getting an emotional jolt every three minutes.

If on the one hand the Catholic Church was a rather vague touchstone, solid but distant, on the other hand it was becoming more persistent as a notion in my mind. To really join it would be an ultimately radical move—it was certainly not "New Age," like all the other religious alternatives swimming around in my mind. It went deeply against the grain. But I had become royally sick of new and evermore new things, as if the leading edge of the human race must create its own reality moment by moment. Even though Buddhism was ancient, it was new for *us*, and therefore exotic, attractive, and "hip." To become a Catholic, on the other hand, would be an utterly uncool thing to do. In itself, Catholicism might mean the heart of the mystery; but in Boulder society, in the crowd I ran with, to announce that you were seriously considering the Catholic Church was to elicit looks of troubled condescension or shocked disdain, as if you had vomited up your supper on the bright tablecloth of spiritual delights. It meant going backwards, to authority, to "patriarchy," to heresy-hunts and Inquisitions, before the great liberation. It made my friends (some of them) sick to their stomachs to hear about it. But I was beginning to think that it meant growing up.

How? Well, the other paths and ways and waysides were all a part of a perpetual youth, all a part of the great romantic adventure, all expressions of anti-social rebellion. No matter the sincerity of the religious yearning, it all took place within the framework of myself as a lone player in the fields of the Lord. The Catholic Church meant the realities of working and marriage and families and the social establishment. The Church was as big as the world—bigger, of course, when you consider its Founder. In some respects, it *was* the world, and perhaps the world has too much invaded it (but that's another story). It confronts the adult world straight on, deals with it, is fully in the world but—in its essence—is not of the world. So for me to enter the Church meant putting away childish things. And I knew it meant not insisting on being sated every moment with spiritual satisfactions. Growing up means you can't forever be drinking from the teat of the Great Cow hovering over your crib. It also means you realize you're not going to change the whole world, no matter how fierce and strong your convictions. It means limits, and it means examining your conscience and realizing you may be responsible for some of the things that happen to other people for good and for evil. It means not ascribing the worst motives to people who disagree with you.

It is difficult to explain this conception of the Church. Think of a childish baseball player. If the pitching coach is incompetent, or the pitcher throws spitters, or the ballplayer even under the best conditions can only bat .200, he carps, he complains, he says "I won't play." He looks around for another team: maybe things will be better in a new town.

But when the ball game is the whole of life, he stands in there and bats. He works on his batting stroke. He runs out every ground ball. It all has to do with the knowledge (usually subliminal in my soul) that the Catholic Church underlies and overshadows everything on this earth.

Oh, there was something real in Buddhism too. Several times in the three years I spent in Boulder I trekked up to the Rocky Mountain Dharma Center, fifty miles north, 12,000 feet up in the sky. These were week-long retreats, when we meditated all day long in the central hall while the cold snow fell outside. At night we would walk out a quarter or half a mile to the small cabins dotting the hills, where we slept half the night until the fire went out and the cold chilled our bones. Sometimes on these long treks through the deep snow my emotions would dry to a point, my mind would open to a place without content, and emotion and thought became as if one thing. And I would touch a place in my being released from the self, where there was no fear of life or death.

It was, I think, a genuine taste of the infinite, and it is something (I am sure) that the Buddhist sages had. But was there any love in it? It seemed divorced from human beings, or it seemed to enfold all human beings within a huge self that had no limits since it had no fears or desires. There was something, I think, that could become love, but a kind of love that would be impersonal, given equally to all, with no desire in it. A patrician sort of love. How close this is to the Christian concept of *agape* I do not know.

Back in the meditation hall we would end the day's sitting meditation with a series of chants, one of which went "Cut the aorta of the distorter of the teachings." I was stunned by the violence of the image, and began to think that Eastern religion had its devils too. In the corner of every (Tibetan) Buddhist mediation hall there is a fierce-looking little black idol, who is there perhaps to remind the Buddhist practitioner not to become too smug. If so, he didn't have much salutary effect, because if there is one overriding characteristic of Boulder Buddhists, it is their intellectual snobbery. Buddhism is for the "New Age" American the hippest of all religions. It draws the smartest people to it, those who are happy to hear that "concepts" can only get in the way of enlightenment. I remember lounging in the outer hall with my compatriots after a day's meditation, while we massaged our sore legs and smoked Galoises and Viceroys, and making the ironic comment to the dark-haired woman across from me: "If Viceroys are the thinking man's cigarette, Buddhism is the thinking man's religion." Straightened out, this comment meant that Buddhism is a religion for people who have thought too much and are worn out with thinking. It is a very popular religion among the post-existentialist crowd, those who have read too much Nietzsche and Sartre and Camus.

Buddhism tries to overcome that last and most profound dualism, the dualism of good and evil. The "crazy wisdom" of Buddhism says that every action born of desire for good or for evil breeds its opposite in the Great Cosmic Equivalence; moral action is, therefore, futile. This notion translated itself into slogans like "idiot compassion," producing ill-mannered behavior and a disdain for acts of kindness. Boulder Buddhists, like all sectarians, played Follow the Leader, and since Chogyam Trungpa was an alcoholic and a philanderer, there was much drinking and much adultery in the local Buddhist Sangha. The road to enlightenment looked a lot like the road to utterly selfish and unrestrained behavior. But it was "sophisticated." Trungpa died a few years ago of a sudden massive failure of his internal organs. Read: death by acute alcoholism. His second in command, an American, showed up one morning at the Boulder Alcoholic Treatment Center for a seven day dry-out.

My intermittent flirtation with Buddhism was all but over by the summer of 1980, while the thin thread that was drawing me to Catholicism grew stronger. I kept thinking that Catholicism overarched everything, so that every other religion or sect was a chopped-down piece of it. After my dalliance with Caroline and with Dr. Wierwille's sordid burlesque of Christianity I was more and more on the search for legitimacy, and that meant the biggest and the oldest. It meant something as far removed from sectarianism and do-it-yourself religion as I could find. It meant something that had an ancient and intact teaching authority. Legitimacy, of course, meant much more than that, and one thing it meant was the Virgin Mary.

I began to send myself to sleep at night by reciting the Rosary in my mind. I would walk down to Boulder Creek in the evening and stop and be still and send a mental prayer to Mary and remember the prayer I prayed on the hilltop in California back in 1973. The threads were coming together.

I read Thomas Merton's *The Seven Story Mountain*—for the third time. I read G.K. Chesterton's *Orthodoxy*, *The Thing*, and *The Everlasting Man*. I read Merton's *The Waters of Siloe* and *The Sign of Jonas*, and then five or six books on Vatican II, and then seven or eight books on the Marian apparitions. I read about Catherine Laboure, and Lourdes, and La Salette, and Fatima, and I learned for the first time that there are uncorrupted bodies of saints in European cathedrals. I realized there was a whole world that had been expunged from Protestant or post-Protestant secular histories. It was just after I read a biography of St. Joan of Arc that I had a peculiar and exalting dream, one that I shall never forget.

I was in a drear and gray landscape, perhaps in Ireland or in Normandy. Before me was the crumbling facade of a stone chapel, and behind it the half-destroyed rubble of a stone monastery. This was all very dim and dark, and I was bodiless, floating somewhat above the ground, enjoying (or enduring) a bird's eye view. The mood was lugubrious and then desolate, and all of a sudden, a slight change in perspective showed me the reason: I was face to face with the corpse of Joan of Arc, hanging from a gibbet. My bodiless spirit could not help moving right up close to that dead white face, as if I were a camera moving near to get the angle of it right. This was against my will, and I certainly did not like what I was forced to see. It was over in a second, but the scene disappeared leaving a chill in my heart as if the Church were dead and the witches had won.

Suddenly another scene appeared, all bright and green and pastoral and boundlessly beautiful, and I found myself standing beside a richly colored light brown path bounded by a row of emerald cypresses. It was like a new and richer earth, or a surprising kind of heaven. And walking down the path towards me was Joan of Arc herself, a young, plump, peasant girl with a laced bodice, buoyant, serene, full of life, full of love. She drew near and looked at me with startled joy. "I never expected to see you here," she said, and as I woke up I heard her say something else which I strained to catch. I finally settled on, "I thought you would be with Brian Prendergast," but that was not right. It was something more like, "I thought you would be with Uther Pendragon"—in other words, lost in the deceptive magic of middle earth instead of being there with her in the bright woods of heaven.

This interpretation made sense to me, since I had been messing around with syncretistic mixtures of Eastern and Western religion á la Blavatsky, with Tarot Cards and with poetic excursions into the myths of Germany and Iceland—though at this time in my life I took none of it as more than food for poetry. Still, there was all that delving into everything magical and mystical, a legacy from the sixties in San Francisco.

A few weeks later I dreamt that the Pope had been shot and killed. (Six months later he was shot, but not killed.) And one morning in the midst of struggling with a poem full of horses and chapels and fields of coriander, I paused and wrote: "All roads lead to Rome or all roads lead to myself."

So why didn't I take steps right then to enter the Catholic Church? I did, but they were not very forceful steps. Let us say that I was coming from such an inward and bookish place that my first contacts with the "Church External" were necessarily disappointing.

The one time I went to Mass with my lapsed Catholic friend (on my urging) there were about twenty of us in a modern-looking church that could have held 200. A troubled priest, wobbly on his legs, looked out over the sparse congregation and said, as if to himself: "Maybe we'll have to lose a whole generation." It was the Solemnity of the Assumption of Mary.

My friend was enthusiastic about the books of Teilhard de Chardin. I took a look at one, but stopped reading after a few pages. It seemed to be a jumble of mystical evolutionism that had nothing to do with either Christianity or with science. Even as poetry, it was tripe. My opinion on this favorite son of the new Jesuits has not changed. If I had known of his popularity in the academic towers of the Church today, I would have stayed away even longer than I did. At the time I didn't even realize Teilhard was supposedly a Catholic writer.

God continued to work on me. I would sit in stalls in public rest rooms and pick out crosses from the black and white hatched tile floor. I would walk alone into a woody area of town after reading a passage from *The Cloud of Unknowing* and feel an emotion that was rare, but warmer than what I had experienced at the Rocky Mountain Dharma Center. Catholic mysticism seemed a touch more personal than the Buddhist brand. The idea that Love is the center and source of all things, and Love is a Person—this was indeed a warmer idea than the mysticism sluicing into America from the cold hills of Tibet.

Finally, I had to see a priest. I made a little list of the things that I wanted to ask about, things like the Trinity, the Godhead of Jesus Christ, and the eternity of Hell. Just up the block from my apartment was a Catholic center attached to the University of Colorado. I walked past it three or four times, then turned and walked in. A crucifix was on the wall by the door. It gave me courage. A youngish nun sat behind a desk. I mumbled something about being interested in the Catholic Church, reached into my back pocket for my little list, and started off with a question about the Trinity. The nun smiled. She was friendly and bubbly, and interrupted me to talk about "cultural Catholicism," and "pluralism," and how I shouldn't worry too much about theology—"there have been many new developments." I was taken aback, just a little, and said I thought I should speak to a priest. She told me about the exciting things happening in Latin America. I wasn't much interested in the social end of things, so I asked again to see a priest.

Ten minutes later I was upstairs, sitting across from a young, harried man, in shirt sleeves and (maybe) a Roman collar. The first thing he said, after he got off the phone, was, "Why did she send you to see me? Huh. Why did she send you to me?"

I said something like I had asked to see a priest because I was interested in becoming a Catholic. I pulled out my dog-eared list once again. As I nervously rattled off a question (maybe about the

Trinity, maybe about hell), he held up his hands, stopped me, and stared at me with what seemed at that moment to be a look of suspicion. I realized I was dressed in Levis and my hair was a bit long. Didn't he take me seriously? Finally he pointed to two books on the shelf. One was *Christ Among Us*, by Anthony Wilhelm. The other was a smaller paperback with a green and white cover I can't remember the name of. He reached for the books, handed them over, and said, "Be sure to bring these back." Again he shot me a strange look as if I were some kind of inquisitor, harassing this overworked servant of the Lord. More likely, he thought I was an irresponsible hippie who would steal his books. By that time I was angry.

The whole impression I got from that interview was that I was imposing on the precious time of this man, bringing some trivial problem to him that could better be handled by the nun downstairs, or by a book. It was quite a let-down.

When I read the books, I was disheartened more profoundly. All I remember is one particular passage in *Christ Among Us* where the authenticity of the Resurrection of Christ was debated, in small print—several viewpoints were presented. At the time, I was shocked. Now I would just say that it had no place in a catechism, which is supposed to present the Faith unambiguously to young Catholics and to potential converts. The other book, I think authored by Richard Chilson, was worse. Both books seemed to slide around the idea of miracle, whereas it was the miracles that had attracted me to the Church in the first place: the miracle of the sun at Fatima, the miracle of the healing waters of Lourdes, the miracles performed by Jesus, the miracle of the Resurrection, the miracle of the Incarnation, the miracle of the Mass. The whole Faith hangs on miracle—the irruption into the cosmos of something greater than the cosmos. I took the books back a few days later, said thank you (to the nun, not the priest), and left.

A week later I told myself to try again. On up the hill from the Catholic center was a large new Catholic building, part of a theological complex at the University. The inside was richly appointed and dark. I had an interview with the resident theologian. I asked about the doctrines of the Church. He pointed to a book behind him in the bookcase, and told me everything I wanted to know was in that book. It was very thick, yellow-jacketed, and on the cover was the title *On Being a Christian*. Then the theologian just peered at me. He had nothing more to say. I had nothing more to say. I left.

I hadn't asked to borrow the book. It was by Hans Küng, and I had already read a few heretical, shallow books by that arrogant gentleman.

What was the matter with these people? I had been treated civilly only by the nun, and she disturbed me by her innuendos about the "cultural relativity" of the new Church. I was simply put off, by the priest, the theologian, and the catechetical books. Neither priest nor theologian had shown the slightest interest in having me enter the Catholic Church. I mouthed silent imprecations at these fools as I crawled home.

Disheartened, I looked around for something that at least was still in touch with miracle and mystery. I read some theosophy again: at least these people had faith in the supernatural. Madame Blavatsky had apparently gotten in touch with a couple of spirits from Tibet named El Morya and Koot-humi, who were interested in merging the religions of the East and West under a higher synthesis. From that beginning back in the late nineteenth century, a hundred derivative groups have formed, among them the "I AM" movement in the 1930s and the present-day Summit Lighthouse, also called The Church Universal and Triumphant. All of these sects have in common the notion of a Great White Brotherhood (the "white" referring not to race but to spiritual purity). This brotherhood is composed of high spiritual beings from all the religions who hang out together in the empyrean and do what they can to elevate the spiritual level of mankind. Jesus Christ is among them, and so is Siddhartha Buddha. So is Krishna and Hercules and Homer and an eighteenth century French alchemist named Saint-Germain. Saint-Germain is the spiritual major-domo of the group calling itself The Church Universal and Triumphant. Recently this sect moved its headquarters from Pasadena, California, to Montana, where it has built a huge underground bomb shelter as it waits anxiously for the Apocalypse.

I had some dealings with these folks back in 1977, before I moved to Boulder. I had been taking home some nixies from the post office—junk mail that couldn't be delivered or returned. I kept some which looked interesting. These were pamphlets published by the Summit Lighthouse and contained a lot of intriguing speculation about the spirit world. There was talk about different colored spiritual rays that covered the earth in different eras, about the Archangel

Michael and the Virgin Mary, about Saint-Germain and El Morya and decrees. The decrees were statements supposedly with the force of fiat, suitable to our exalted status as human beings. You say it, and it is so, or it becomes so. I started saying the decrees alone in my apartment. Most of them started with an emphatic "I AM"—as in "I AM A SON OF GOD." I ordered several books from the group, and read about Elizabeth Clare Prophet and Mark Prophet (he had recently died). Elizabeth Clare Prophet constantly received messages from the Brotherhood, and was possessed by these entities as she spoke them. Sometimes even God the Father spoke through her. (On these occasions her voice was appropriately low and deep and gruff.)

It's not as if I believed all these things. I was just interested in delving into the spiritual dimension, and this elaborate mystical system seemed a good enough entrance. It allowed me to keep my hand in, so to speak, after my dismal departure from the world of Sun Myung Moon.

In the Spring of 1977, I decided to quit the post office and spend a couple of months at Summit University in Pasadena before heading out to Colorado for poetry and Buddhism. I plunked down $1000 for tuition and hopped in my little red car and headed south. I remember only a few things about that disastrous time. First, Mrs. Prophet put all us newcomers on an apple juice fast for five days. No solid food at all. The first book we were supposed to read had a picture on the front cover depicting early Christians preparing to give themselves enemas with a huge gourd. We also were supposed to cleanse our innards nightly with a colonic (a kind of super enema). I ducked that obligation. In the mornings we drank apple juice in a large hall while the Rosary played over a loudspeaker. Then we went to an auditorium where we heard Mrs. Prophet, sitting on a throne in front, speak in the voice of St. Michael the Archangel. Afterwards we chanted the decrees. But the chanting was ten times as fast as I had done it on my own—so fast that the words slid into a high-pitched buzz. It was disconcerting. After three days I was weak and hungry and dry (apple juice is astringent and not much help for thirst).

On the fourth morning I walked out on the lawn in front of our dorm and saw ten or fifteen people of all sexes and ages prancing barefoot on the grass. I asked one elderly gentleman what he was doing. He told me that the grass contained protein, which came in through the soles of the feet and fed the body in a pure and spiritual manner.

That and the apple juice fast and the buzz-saw decrees finally got to me. I had had enough. I walked over to the administration building and told them I was gong home and please give me my money back. They tried to talk me out of it. I was missing the chance of a lifetime, etc, etc. I said the decrees were chanted so fast they put me in a trance. They said give it a chance. I said it was eerie and didn't seem spiritual at all. I said I didn't cotton to five days with nothing but apple juice. I was already faint and giddy. They said I was turning my back on God. I said the people who thought they could receive protein through the soles of their feet were fanatics. They said some people got carried away and went to extremes, not to worry. I said good-bye, and please return my money. They said they would send a check.

Later that day, as I was packing to leave, one of the leaders of the Summit Lighthouse knocked on the door and came in. He said he had been told I had said they were all a bunch of fanatics. I said that's not true, what I said was, the group of people rubbing their bare feet on the grass to soak up protein were fanatics. He didn't hear me. He said, what's wrong with being a fanatic for God?—all really religious people were fanatics. I said, not like these folks. He got angry. He said you are bound by solemn agreement not to reveal anything about your experience here, remember that. I said if you don't stop threatening me I *will* tell the world about what I saw here. He threatened me again, and stormed out. So I'm telling the world.

I drove off and stopped for gas and a candy bar. I could barely pull the plunger on the candy machine. I could barely choke down the candy bar, I was so weak and famished. I drove back to Moraga, weak, hungry, thirsty, angry, disillusioned, and indignant. My car's engine seized up just as I was getting home. The new engine cost $450. I had to write several threatening letters to Summit University before I received a partial return on my tuition, two months later.

Thus endeth the sad tale of my run-in with Elizabeth Clare Prophet and the Church Universal and Triumphant.

Chapter Six

Moonie Reprise 1980

Why I delved into Madame Blavatsky and the other original theosophists three years after my little nightmare in Pasadena I do not know. Maybe I simply wanted to look into the historical and intellectual foundations of Elizabeth Clare's feverish reworking of the old guard mystical syncretists. In any case, I soon dropped the study and returned to Sir Frederic Kenyon's works on the ancient Biblical manuscripts as an antidote to the Way Ministry and to Chesterton as an antidote to "culturally relative" Catholicism.

I was still smarting over my cold receptions by the priest and the theologian, though longings for the Church reverberated in my mind. I thought long and hard about the Moonies, too. I had a dream.

I was in a tunnel system underneath Manhattan. All the subways were gone, and the tunnels were muddy-brown, depressed, unhappy, with rounded walls and an earth-like feeling. The muddy color turned gray and then black, as I scrambled along, looking for a way out. I was trying to get to the entrance of the bus station, so I could get above ground and out into the city. Finally I made it to the glass doors of the Port Authority Bus Terminal. I went through the doors and suddenly I was on the sidewalk. Everything was now clear and bright. Across the street was a large building, and on the face of the building was a brightly colored sign in the shape of a rainbow. It went in a huge curve over the whole front of the building. It had a pure white background with brilliant red letters. The letters spelled out U N I F I C A T I O N   C H U R C H.

Suddenly I was across the street peering at a brownish decrepit area next to the entrance of a bookstore. There was a small framed area on the face of the building where posters and announcements were displayed. All I could see on the grimy facade was a little sign in dirty white letters that said: The Great White Brotherhood. It was a neglected little corner of the building, as if in a back street tenement, unimportant, out of synch, out of date. Up above I knew was the overarching brilliant sign of the Unification Church, and I knew the great building belonged to it. I opened a little door and walked into the bookstore. It was not a bookstore after all, but a reception area, and a young woman was sitting at the desk. She was wearing a misty, flowing, turquoise-colored dress. I walked past her and around the corner into a large hall, filled with gentle people all dressed in blue-green flowing robes, all smiling with a secure warmth. I was delighted by the light blue-green clothes everyone was wearing, casting a mild silver-blue over the whole atmosphere. It was all a sparkling blue, tinged with the gentlest green. It was a reception of some kind; everyone smiled and welcomed me; everything was light and bright and filled with a most peaceful harmony. As I walked through, I knew that I was to meet the woman who would be my wife. Yes, there she was! It was her! We looked at each other with that deep eternal grace which is the only genuine love. We were together . . . forever . . . at last.

When I woke I was gloriously happy for a moment, then angry. Another terrific dream, promising heaven, directing me back to the tuna-fishing arms of Father Moon. It seemed like the only way to get the Unification Church out of my system was to join it again.

I temporized. I prayed. Two Mormons came to the door, clean-cut, offering the way of the saints of the latter days, and I nearly cried with frustration. A malevolent God was assaulting me with a thousand religious alternatives. Downtown I passed a Divine Light Mission temple, devoted to a fat teenage God from India whose mother was suing him for a piece of the action. On the corner a band of born-again Christians assaulted me. I brutally asked them if God had reserved hell for the billions of people who had never seen a Bible. I walked into a new coffee shop a block away, where a young man in a suit (and matching socks) welcomed me and pointed to a blackboard where he had just written, "You are saved by faith alone, not works." Later he grabbed me by the arm as I was edging out the door, and we prayed for me to accept Jesus as my Lord and Savior. I mumbled hallelujah and stumbled out into the street, unreborn. A few days later I visited a Pentecostal church on the outskirts of Boulder. After we'd praised Jesus a hundred times and sung rip-roaring spiritual songs with our arms waving in the air and our butts waving in the aisles, the young minister's vampish young wife introduced herself to me. She told me that when her husband had first gotten overshadowed by the Holy Spirit, she thought he had been possessed by a demon, his eyes were so wild. But now of course she knew better. I wondered. A block away I knew my former girl friend was going gobble-gobble and prophesying to beat hell at the Way Ministry house.

Enough! I removed myself from the fierce clutches of the saved, eschewed all companionship, and was visited one night by a nice Indian woman selling tickets to a singing performance by a group called "Sunburst." Her manner was genteel, her age was about thirty, her eyes were dark and friendly, and the brochure she gave me showed a red splay of sun on a white background. I had seen the same logo displayed at Moonie headquarters in San Francisco seven years ago.

The next day I called San Francisco and asked for Christina. She was in New York City. I called New York. I said to Christina, "I want to come back."

She said, "Come back."

How was it that I forgot the zombies croaking "Happy World Day," seemingly brain-dead and incapable of anything other than stylized talk? How did I forget the glib insincerity of "love bombing," the rose thorns stuck in my fingers, the exhaustion of mind and body, the enslavement of the soul, the wealthy Dursts sitting on gilded chairs while we slammed our heads to the floor in obeisance to an absolute dictator? All of it was subsumed beneath an overriding purpose. I would marry Christina and run the world with her. Or something. Something instead of nothing.

I promised myself I would be a good Moonie. Total commitment to total theocracy. No more infinity of inconclusive deliberations. God called. God's champion called.

I got off the plane at Kennedy Airport on August 1, 1980, and in the waiting crowd was a girl with a sign hung around her neck with my name on it. Another thoughtful gesture from Christina—I would be driven straight from the airport to the waiting arms of the Family.

My escort turned out to be a coterie of three young Moonies. They took me in hand and walked me to the van, and as we drove through this behemoth of cities, I told them about my long-ago experience in Oakland, thrilling them with names—Onni, Dr. Durst, Boonville, Dana Street. They were awed that Dr. Durst had been my team leader in my first training session and that Christina was my spiritual mother. I felt like a prodigal son, returning after twenty years in the wilderness, only to find the kids grown up and a new generation of enthusiastic children running out the gates to welcome me home. It hadn't been that long, of course. Just three years previously I had said farewell to Christina over coffee in the (Moonie-owned) Aladdin delicatessen in Berkeley, a couple of days before I left town for Boulder and Buddhism.

I learned from the young Moonies that Dr. Durst had just been made president of the Unification Church in America—which meant that Onni was the real head. This elevation represented Father Moon's belated recognition of her fantastic success in laying the Material Foundation. As far as I could judge, the Oakland Family had in the past eight years brought in more money and members than all the other American Families combined. Christina was in New York to prepare suitable quarters for the Dursts and to run interference with the New York City Moonie establishment. I found out later that the Oakland Family was resented by many other local Families, one reason being the propensity for flower-selling teams sent out from Oakland to invade the territory of other cities and in effect compete for sales. The Oakland Mobile Fund-raising Teams had earned the nickname of "the Oakland Raiders." Onni ran roughshod over other sections of the Family; there was no coordination. Two blocks away from the Hearst Street house was a Unification Church house on Euclid Street in north Berkeley that had been in operation since before Onni hit town. To us in the Oakland Family it was as if the Euclid Street Family did not exist.

It turned out I arrived in New York City only a few weeks after the Dursts and Christina and Nadine and Sherry and a few others of the Oakland Family had arrived. I landed right in the middle of a sweeping organizational change.

We pulled up in front of Unification Church headquarters—recently the New Yorker Hotel. When I walked in I had to state my business to a security guard manning a desk just inside. What had been the hotel lobby was huge and high and bare of furniture or decoration. It reminded me somehow of a Mexican railway station. In Mexico the government owns the railways and has built palatial granite stations with great columns and polished stone floors. But huddled next to the columns or in little groups around the splendid expanse of polished granite are families with squalling children and paper sacks and cardboard suitcases and caged chickens.

The great entrance hall of the New Yorker Hotel looked something like that—an inappropriately palatial way station for dispossessed travelers. Hundreds of suitcases and cardboard boxes full of clothes and books were stacked here and there around the floor—but that was all. The space was too large and impersonal and unsettled; there was nothing warm or aesthetic or secure under that huge high ceiling. It looked so little like a home that I felt like running back out into the street.

Just then Christina came bounding downstairs and gave me a quick warm welcome. She was a little older, a little more tired around the eyes, but she had that same indomitable presence. After we hugged for a moment she barked a few orders to some Moonies near the desk, and then we went upstairs to a large office with a couch and chairs and paper strewn around the floor. She complained about the living quarters that the New York Family had prepared for the Dursts—"totally inadequate"—and in a moment she was on the phone arranging for the delivery of a new sofa for Onni. She put me in the hands of a fawning Englishman who led me upstairs and down some corridors until we found a vacant room for me. Then he disappeared.

It is hard for me to get the sense of how I felt during my two or three day stay at the New Yorker Hotel. Except for a lunch date with Christina, I had precious little human contact. I was more or less lost in the shuffle; I was not assigned to any group or work assignment; I wandered about on my own, looking for some way to fit in. I suppose what I want to say is that Moonie life is so much a matter of Following Center and twenty-four-hour-a-day assignments for everyone that if you are in the milieu, but unassigned, you feel totally left out. No one has time to talk to you.

And I wanted to talk to everyone. I was fresh from a five-year separation; I wanted to grab everyone by the lapels and say, "How is it? How is it going for you? What is going on?" On that first night I ran into Nick—who had run the Gardening Company I worked with back in 1973, and who was always working out new strategies to win dodge ball games on the way up to Boonville training sessions. I had always liked him—he was a quiet, unassuming giant of a man—and when we shook hands after not seeing each other for five years, I asked him how those years had been for him.

"Lonely," he said and disappeared on some errand or other. At least he had said the realest thing I heard during my stay a t the New Yorker Hotel.

Christina had no time to talk; Nick had no time to talk; and I remembered what I had forgotten: there was just no time for personal conversation in the Family—and, I thought (fresh from five years of extremely individualistic living)—the long-term Moonies had simply forgotten how to talk personally. There had been no rebuff of me—there was nothing personal in it—and that was what was wrong. It hit me bodily that "normal" people who had been friends and who ran into each other after a period of time *found* the time to become reacquainted, to reestablish the human bond, if only for five minutes or so—but here, that essential social custom went unpracticed. For me, newly arrived from the outside world, it was unnerving.

That night or another night I wandered down to the kitchen in the basement, in search of some food, feeling pretty out of synch. The hotel was being repainted and refurbished, and as I wandered down one staircase and up another, it seemed like I was walking through an unsettled dreamscape. It was close to midnight when I found the kitchen. It was a mess. Dirty dishes all over the place, leftover food slopped on the stone floor around open drains, open cans of flour and honey and margarine perched precariously on rough wood shelves, huge metal bowls and iron kettles crusted with burnton food stacked here and there around the floor. A lone Moonie stood over a metal sink, wielding a spray nozzle, a mountain of dirty dishes next to him on the counter. At a table in another corner three teen-age Puerto Rican girls were giggling and eating melting icecream.

Standing off to one side, looking at it all, I was suddenly overcome with that huge impulse to "give it up"—to give myself over to "it." It is indescribable. It was more than just losing the faculty of critical judgment. It was entering fully into the dreamscape, a place where everything was sucked into the karmic well of Mr. Moon. It was to lose a pretty deep part of what made up my personality, to be replaced by—what?—the "public man" fostered by the Divine Principle? I didn't know. It was not at all like my mystical moment in the San Francisco headquarters in 1973. It was scary. It seemed so *inviting* to let myself drop into a place where there was no responsibility, no protest, and perhaps no love.

And perhaps no self. As I say, it is indescribable. I do believe something *wrong* was happening to me in the kitchen that night. And I do not believe it was what psychiatrists call a "depersonalization reaction." In my undergraduate studies I read about such things. They are always preceded by a high state of anxiety. There was no anxiety in this experience. There was no anxiety preceding it and no anxiety after it. There was rather a seductive calm associated with it.

What was it then?—if it was anything more than a moment's disorientation? It was not joyous—I can only call up images of an ant-life, a group mind, an *increase* of self-confidence at the *expense* of separate existence. How can self-confidence increase if your self disappears? It is your separate self that disappears, or is buried, only to pop up on occasion with responses like, "I'm lonely." It is the tribal "self" that becomes your self. That is what gives you the foundation for an enlarged "self-confidence." Having that tribal self, however, means that as the tribe goes, so you go—to Guyana (Jonestown, 1978) or to loosening the wheel lug nuts on the cars of enemies (Society of St. Pius X, 1993).

I must say that I have had extraordinary mental experiences within the fold of the Unification Church that I have not had anywhere else—good, bad, strange—but always calling into question what a human being is, not just calling into question what I am. There is always something general as well as personal in it. Moonie brainwashing can be compared to other cult brainwashing, but as an extreme or as a standard by which all the other cults are compared. In fact all the anti-cult books pick up on certain Moonie practices and even Moonie slogans, like "Love Bombing," which is just a fortuitous phrase from the unsubtle mind of our dear Onni. Or it might have come out of one of our "rah rah" slogans made up for a dodge ball game. I seem to remember the war cry: "Bomb them with love!" as our team's Center Man swung back the dodge ball and prepared to demolish the opposition on an afternoon in Boonville.

The Moonies are the standard, all right, and not only as a cult, but as an influential world-wide religio-political organization. Right-wing Japanese industrialists fund real estate ventures for Mr. Moon. The Unification Church publishes a daily newspaper in Washington, D.C.—the *Washington Times*. Mr. Moon even has sociologists eating out of his hand, writing learned monographs on group interaction and peer pressure while Mr. Moon laughs all the way to the bank. He is eminently respectable with a certain brand of Catholics who share his views on Communism and look no further. He wines and dines physicists at all-expense-paid forums and pays the way of reporters to cover the front lines in the Far East. He has Latin American diplomats in his back pocket and, sad to say, a number of academic metaphysicians who can see no evil in anything called religious, who send their sons and daughters to his international religious festivals, and who ignore the fact that these events are funded on the backs of slaves selling flowers in a Michigan blizzard.

But does it matter that so many rank-and-file Moonies are slaves under psychological coercion? Does that make a whole lot of difference when Mr. Moon is attacking the world on all levels, co-opting the rich and powerful, the intellectual pundits, and even whole governments if he can? When the influence is so broad and so pervasive (and these days, so unreported), what matter if in the guts of the Family some strange and troubling things are happening to people?

The answer is that it makes a whole lot of difference. Suppose Mr. Moon and the Unification Church were to beat this monster called atheistic Communism? And take over the remaining countries of the world? What kind of heaven on earth is envisioned? Once you see through the terminology of "subject-object," you find that it translates into internal dictatorship from top to bottom. There is no provision for an equality of persons, even in the eyes of God. In every aspect of life, everyone is above someone and below someone else. It is a perpetual army. In this heaven on earth there is no redress of grievances (grievances are Satanic), and no independent court of appeal (how can there be an appeal from God?).

Far from being a temporary expedient made necessary by the danger the world is in, the little society of totalitarians called Moonies would become a world society ruled totally by a God on earth who eats every new meal from brand new plates. In the final analysis there is no division of means and ends here, despite vague slogans of paradisiacal love. The Moonies would make the whole world into one gigantic training session—training for unquestioning obedience. It is identical to certain organized Nazi and Communist experimental efforts to engender automatic obedience among troops and among cadres, programs which had some success in the recent past.

Perhaps that little fantasy in the kitchen—in the guts of the Family—was a semi-conscious preview of the brave new world of Mr. Moon. I had thought along these lines before I came to New York. My answer to these fears was something like: better an active life under obedience (and for the sake of God) than life in an utterly indifferent society that doesn't give a damn about me at all. But here, in New York, having decided to come back, I could not countenance such a dark realization. Here there was no room for cruel analyses of myself or the Family or what we were all about. I wanted to get back to the joy of it, the hope for the Kingdom of Love, the dedication, and the people I missed.

A day or so later Christina put me on the van for Camp New Hope and a twenty-one day training session. We drove up in the evening, about a hundred miles into the Catskills. It was dark when we got to the place, and we drove through two wooden gates, down a dirt road for a hundred yards, and pulled up in front of a ramshackle main building.

Camp New Hope was a former Boy Scout camp, dilapidated and dotted with small green-painted bunkhouses. There were three or four larger wooden buildings in the central area, and spread out around the grounds, under trees, were ten or twelve picnic tables. These would serve as gathering places for trinity meetings and meals. Each trinity established territorial rights over its own picnic table and kept it for a week at a time until the arrangement was altered for the weekend seminars. It was details like this that fostered an ever-tightening group unity.

About a quarter mile down a path through the woods was a small lake with a stony beach where we had campfires and picnics and sometimes went swimming—with our clothes on. (Bare flesh might excite Satanic impulses.) Back in the main area a large kitchen and dining hall were in one building, and nearby was the staff house. On the other side was a string of five small bunkhouses, and up near the staff house was a larger dormitory. About a hundred yards away was a fairly large enclosed theater with a long low stage where we held our Saturday night musical performances. Around the perimeter of the property was a woven-wire fence. At night Moonie security guards would make their rounds of the place and look out for trouble from the outside.

Was this necessary? It was. Dr. Durst came up to the camp to give the introductory lectures of the weekend training session, and in the midst of the Saturday morning lecture, while heavenly children and their guests sat on long wood benches in the dining hall listening with rapt attention, he broke into an indignant diatribe against the bestial persecutors of religion. What was wrong? Something out of the ordinary, I thought. Then he said: "Just last night, some maniacs burnt down one of the buildings on our property."

It was in the news. It turned out that some local hooligans had indeed torched an outlying shack, well away from the populated area of the camp. The sheriff was investigating.

This was on the second day of my residence—it provided a thrill to start things off. But nothing else like that happened while I was there.

A twenty-one day training session is not as hectic or exciting as a two day one. The weekends are of course the same—since they comprise the two-day session. On weekends several vans loaded with potential recruits would arrive and temporarily double our population. But after they left on Sunday evening—minus some new recruits—we had the place to ourselves. It is amazing how quickly I became a resident of Camp New Hope, even to the extent of resenting the weekend intrusions on our peaceful life. Our daily schedule began with the usual calisthenics, then breakfast with our group, then work assignments. There was plenty to do. All the buildings were being repainted, new shelving was going up in the walk-in pantry, ditches had to be dug for drainage pipes, and the whole place had to be insulated for winter. This was in addition to the usual latrine and kitchen and house-cleaning duties. We worked in small groups of three or four, with a Center Man. (Often the Center Man was a woman.) This usually resulted in an arbitrary and overly-bossed situation since most of the jobs were simple enough to figure out for yourself. But Following Center was the theory, and so it was put into practice in the most absurd situations. Of course, I complained—and then we would stop work and hold hands in prayer, assuring Heavenly Father that we would do our best for unity and "Heavenly Purpose."

At lunch time we would gather together with our trinities and make up a song to sing to the assembled company afterwards. There was tension in that for me—but not at all like the terror I had known at Dana Street. Seven years had built up some social confidence in me. We would cut-up at lunch too, squirt each other with water from the garden hose or otherwise engage in high-jinks. The idea was to get you to feel less and less inhibited about acting like a child. This was the pattern. First a renewal of childlike delight, then later on the grim realization of sin and indemnity, crucially serious purpose, and the constant pervasive enmity of Satan.

But lunch time at Camp New Hope was great fun. There were three or four Australian girls living on the land and perhaps fifteen English Moonies. The Australians in particular were zany and given to practical jokes. In the afternoon we had an hour for private meditation—actually this hour was more often spent in taking care of personal things like writing letters or doing laundry or buying toothpaste or notebooks. Then there would be another hour or two of work, a lecture, dinner around a picnic table with our trinity, often entertainment at night, maybe another lecture, then to bed. We slept well at Camp New Hope, seven or eight hours a night.

The ambiance of this camp was more friendly and independent than I had remembered from before in California. In the morning I would wake up and walk out to the woods and see five or six teenage blacks playing basketball on the court next to the drained swimming pool. Such independent activity would be unheard of in Boonville. I got the idea that these kids were glad to get out of the ghetto and spend a few days in a rural area and were playing along with these freaky God-people just for the chance to take a vacation from city life. There were about fifteen Hispanics who had their own Spanish-speaking Divine Principle lecturer. They would be sitting, polite and attentive, around one of the picnic tables as I passed by and said hello in the afternoon. The girl who gave the lectures (in Spanish) was blond and pretty and very serious. One day she got a bee sting that made her hand swell up, but she refused to stop lecturing for such a minor incident. In any case, it would serve her well as an indemnity; perhaps it would restore one of her ancestors in the spirit world.

The English were serious and properly Moonie-like when talking to an American, but I noticed that among themselves they would often revert to quick wit and clever insults. A Sussex aristocrat would pick on a slow-thinking Yorkshireman; the Australian girls would flirt with the English boys and make them blush.

There was a lot of diversity of class and race and nation, but a lot of friendliness too. I was assigned to Joshua's trinity. He had been the camp director until Onni and Christina arrived on the scene; now he was in the process of being shunted aside while Sherry (an Oakland Family Moonie) took over. Joshua and I became friends. He told me about how he had met Dr. Durst in California and thought of him as a mentor and father figure. I told him about my living in Dr. Durst's house in Piedmont and seeing him getting up in the morning from his sleeping bag on the floor next to mine, and bending over and praying with his head to the floor. (I didn't tell him about Durst the pontiff, holding court in the plush mansion hidden in the Berkeley hills.)

Joshua had been a songwriter and guitarist before meeting the Family. His talents came in good stead, since Moonie recruitment is keyed around music and group performance. He was easily competent, but did not rule with a heavy hand. It seemed to me that he didn't rule at all. He never gave me an order. He treated me with deference and respect, and I returned the favor.

On the first weekend I ran into the Indian woman who had visited me in Boulder to sell tickets to "Sunburst." (Everything conspires.) She was in my trinity for two weeks. I met Ricky, our car fix-it man during my first summer at Dana Street house. He had some gray in his hair and was more considerate than ever. He had his own trinity now. I met Annie, who in 1973 had been torturously shy and depressed. We had sold flowers together in Berkeley. (You never saw two people less fit to be salesmen.) Now she was quietly strong, comforting to be around—and one of the best dodge ball players in the camp. Her self-confidence had grown magnificently in the seven years she had been with the Moonies.

You could give three contradictory accounts of Annie's personal growth: (1) With or without the Moonies she would have matured. She was a tough girl underneath the shyness, and that would have come out over the years.

(2) The intense socialization process the Moonies offered was the best thing that could have happened to her. It gave her the ego-strength she had missed out on, growing up as she (probably) did in a dysfunctional family.

(3) She was "perfectly possessed" by the genie of the cult. That tribal identity had consumed her and then reflected back on her to give her the appearance of having a strong inner character. But take her out of the Moonies and she would shatter like a glass doll dropped on the sidewalk.

Take your choice.

A humble young Canadian man was assigned to be my spiritual friend. He would accompany me to lectures, ask me how I was doing, be sympathetic when I complained, run errands for me. I accepted this service as my due. I thought of myself as an elder statesman returned from foreign lands. I knew of course that he was under orders to be my "love bomber," but I didn't mind at all. Actually I never thought about it. He was a pleasant companion, and we talked genuinely to one another. I missed him when he was gone.

It happened overnight; no good-byes; he was simply assigned elsewhere. I was a little angry.

On Friday it was announced that we must all prepare for "Friday night entertainment" which would take place during a communal dinner in the huge dining hall. (Ordinarily we ate all our meals with our own trinities at the variously dispersed picnic tables.) Each of us, I was told, would be called upon to contribute something. I knew that not everyone in the camp would have time to entertain, but I saw the event as an opportunity to test my stage presence, and, perhaps, to actually contribute something from myself to the Family. I talked it over with Joshua and decided to read part of the poem I had published in the *City Lights Journal* two years before.

The dining hall was decorated with freshly painted artwork for the occasion. There were streamers and Chinese lanterns and a long low table about a foot and a half off the floor, piled high with food and plates and silverware, and about a hundred Moonies sitting on the floor three-deep around the table. The people nearest the table piled plates with salad and a rice dish and corn bread and passed them back to those sitting behind. Everyone was jammed together in customary Moonie fashion. While we ate, one person after another stood up and delivered an unrehearsed testimonial, or even a mild complaint, which was answered with kindness by Joshua or another staff member sitting at the head of the table. After dinner a Jewish girl from New York City got up and gave a fair rendition of a song and dance from "My Fair Lady." Then it was my turn. Here is the poem I read.

> I think of commonwealth, or commonweal
> As a center, round which the family of man
> Revolves: a mist of human things
> And more than human: love, emotion
> Are previous to man, wider and deeper
> Than the far black reach of space
> That spawned the stars that spawned us.
> And I love to think of a face I dreamed
> Some nights ago; a woman's face,
> A face I know—but in expression
> Cleared of pain, luminous, expectant.
> In our good dreams we visit
> That place where beauty is.
> It is a center, and a commonweal,
> Its presence sensed in particular
> Single gesture. I think of gold
> Beaten to a form, human or divine
> Or the sparkling gold upon a river:
> Images of grace, particular and real.
> Time streams out the history of man
> One hundred or one thousand years
> Into the center of the commonweal.
> That which is most ideal is most real.

I thought the poem had something to do with our Unification Church goals and experience—ideally speaking. It went over pretty well (but then, everything goes over well to a Moonie audience). I was exhilarated.

The next day was my birthday; I had mentioned it in passing to someone, I forget who. Low and behold, at dinner a surprise birthday party came my way, complete with songs and a cake and ice cream. I was deeply moved; I ran around trying to find out who had been so thoughtful, who had arranged it all at a moment's notice; I thanked everyone; I almost cried with happiness. My antics embarrassed the hell out of my English trinity partner, a reserved young gentleman who had given up a career with the British Foreign Office to become a Moonie. After I blew out the candles on the cake, my trinity sang:

> We love you Tommy, oh yes we do
> We don't love anyone, as much as you
> When you're not with us, we're blue
> Oh Tommy, we love you.

I was thirty-eight years old. (But that was all right. My trinity was composed of nine people from age twenty-two to age forty-five. The forty-five year old was a "Home Church" Moonie mother. Her sixteen-year-old son was with us in another trinity. He was a second generation Moonie, full of the knowledge and wisdom sixteen-year-olds exhibit everywhere.)

A couple of days later, I used the afternoon meditation hour to walk with a young lady I had met down to the lake and back. She had been a Moonie for about four months. She made the comment out of nowhere: "You are a good Moonie." I looked at her quizzically.

"Why do you say that?" She said she had overheard me talking with a new Moonie during the training session. He had sidled up to me and complained about having to hear the same lectures over and over again. What was the point? I had said (without thinking):

"Oh, I don't know. I find that the more I hear the lectures, the more I get out of them. Each time I hear them I seem to pick up something I missed before."

The fact is, I believed that when I said it. I wasn't giving a deliberate, calculated, "good Moonie" answer. Without realizing it, I had become pretty hooked into the proceedings. Joshua was my friend (without a hint of the silly Center Man business); I had given something from my heart to the Family when I read my poem; I had time to sneak off on a sunny afternoon and talk to a pleasant young woman who liked me. I felt like my integrity could go hand-in-hand with being a Moonie; I was positive; I was happy.

On Saturday Christina came up to the camp and I joined her trinity for the weekend training session. Early in the morning she grabbed hold of my arm and told me to hurry and secure the best picnic table for our group—"one out under the trees." I hurried out and found notes already in place on each table: "Reserved for Joshua's Trinity; Reserved for Ricky's Trinity...." In confusion I decided to take Joshua's note off and replace it with Christina's. Then I waited for his group to appear and apologetically told him that Christina wanted one of the tables under the trees. Joshua made no protest all, but went off to find another location for his group. Christina's desires took precedence, and I was off the hook.

There are deep incongruities in Moonie-land. The territory is not so easily characterized. In our trinity that weekend was an attractive woman, about twenty-eight, blond, looking nothing like a Moonie. Her eyes were clear and direct, her clothes were expensive, in the best taste, perfectly matched to her coloring and form. This was a woman able to choose a wardrobe that would gently accentuate the beauty nature had given her. She was as far from being an anxious and idealistic God-seeker as it is possible to imagine. By style, by gesture, by manner, she was absolutely fit to dwell in the world as it is and in its most powerful places. You could see her as a jet-setter, eating brunch in a Paris bistro, or in the company of a scion of the Kennedy family having dinner at the Top of the Mark in San Francisco. She was as self-confident and "born to the manner" as any woman I have ever seen. Yet she talked as if unaware of her superior station—calmly, unpretentiously, without a hint of noblesse oblige—and that added to her charm. Even Christina was a little intimidated by her. I of course fell in love immediately. She was the kind of woman who made you sit up and do your best.

Obviously, she was someone from *their* world, not ours—someone from the wealthy and influential class of people for whom the world was made. Christina had somehow managed to cajole her into coming to a Moonie training session. Of course, she would be untouched by the experience; she would instantly see the silliness of the whole venture (doing the hokey-pokey in a big circle with a bunch of long-hairs and bug-eyed staff members, playing dodge ball while shouting at the top of your lungs, "Heavenly Generals, Strike with Truth!")—and afterwards disdainfully take herself back to the world of sophistication and power.

Now think of this woman sitting at a picnic table in a bedraggled former Boy Scout camp in the Catskill Mountains in upstate New

York. Imagine her squeezed in between a pasty-faced young woman with tired eyes and denim pants and tennis shoes, on one side, and a thin, hunched-over, nervous, erstwhile graduate student on the other side. Think of me, directly across from her, sitting up straight, making myself act cool, timidly engaging her in conversation, as we ate our breakfast of porridge and toast and coffee. It turned out she was a journalist for a New York City daily newspaper. But that was a temporary assignment.

"What are you planning to do next?" I asked. I imagined her as an anchorperson on a TV news show or hosting parties in Georgetown, D.C., for foreign diplomats and U.S. Senators. She looked at me with those clear, calm, grey-blue eyes and said matter-of-factly:

"I don't know. I'll have to ask my Center Man."

Center Man! She was a Moonie! What an incongruity! So you didn't have to be a loser to be a Moonie! You didn't have to be a screw-up, a care-worn, anxiety-ridden seeker after God. There was room in our house for upscale people, for serious glamour and power in the world's way. I was jealous, thrilled, and nonplused all at the same time.

(The newspaper she worked for was the Moonie-owned *New York Tribune*. "Journalist" probably meant "lobbyist." Later I learned about the "PR sisters," the sexiest, most attractive Moonie women, whose role it was to "restore" politicians and wealthy businessmen. As late as 1979 a couple of them worked on the staffs of U.S. Representatives, including that of Speaker of the House Carl Albert. The PR sisters were exempt from the body- and-soul-wrenching schedule of most Moonies; they tended to be queenly and arrogant, making life miserable for the less attractive rank-and-file Moonie sisters who waited on them hand and foot. This exquisite-looking woman sitting across from me—eating porridge from a plastic dish—probably did host parties for U.S. Senators and foreign diplomats.)

And this is what I think now: that woman was totally owned and totally self-confident.

On Friday nights after dinner and entertainment the whole camp walked out to the theater for ice cream and cake and a movie.

During my stay we saw *Brother Sun, Sister Moon* (a sensitive biography of St. Francis of Assisi), the musical *Oliver*, and *The Guns of Navarone*. Joshua explained to me that *The Guns of Navarone* was one of Father's favorite movies. It showed what a few courageous men could do in the face of enormous odds.

The Friday night movies were a special joy on top of the excitement of Friday night dinner entertainment. On one particular Friday night, after the movie was over, after the lights were turned back on, we all stood and held hands and sang, swaying shoulder to shoulder. The song went like this:

> I'll never leave you anymore
> For I have seen, in your bright eyes
> A river of love, a heart of gold
> A peaceful mind, a hand to hold.

It was my favorite Family song. It pushed me all the way into the center of joy, where there was nothing but love and beauty and truth. Beside me stood a young Irish woman with rosy cheeks and unconsciously vibrant sexuality. We glanced at each other with what seemed to me to be the same emotion I had experienced in my blue-green Moonie dream, where I met the woman who was to be my wife. But here it was live and, if possible, even more elevated. It was beyond myself or herself; it included everyone.

I was in it again—a place of perpetual wonder—such a place as human beings rarely enter outside of dreams or outside of death.

Moonie life is such that I never saw the woman again. I didn't even know if she was a Moonie or only a guest. By the next day she had disappeared, either to pursue her American vacation elsewhere or to pursue her Moonie life elsewhere. Things went downhill fast for me after that ecstatic moment following the movie. The first disturbing note in my halcyon existence occurred a couple of days later when I saw Ricky walking around with a hideous grin on his face. He looked like a sad-eyed clown with a painted-on smile. The effect was so contradictory, the grin so harshly held in place, that I asked him sarcastically what was so funny.

So he told me about "smile conditions." He had been unaccountably depressed for a while and had gone to Sherry (the new camp director) for help or advice. She had imposed on him the Moonies' customary treatment for bouts of unhappiness. He was ordered to keep a smile on his face every waking moment for a week. This was to be his indemnity for failing to follow Father Moon with constant joy and thanksgiving.

I told him that "smile conditions" sounded like plain cruelty to me, and anyway, his smile looked so obviously phony that it would turn off any potential recruits who saw it. He nearly let the smile drop from his suffering face when I said that, but he was a good Moonie, he knew how to Follow Center, and the rictus-grin stayed intact.

The second disturbing thing—another note of cruelty—happened on a Sunday evening at the end of a training session, when I spotted a slightly-crippled young man sitting forlornly on the steps of the staff house. I walked over and talked with him, and asked him how he liked the weekend.

He said, "OK," without enthusiasm, and then looked at me with a hurt expression and said, "I really loved the experience, and I wanted to join this group. But a staff member just now told me that because of my, ah, infirmity, I wouldn't be of value to the Family, that I'd be a burden for the others . . . she said she was sure I'd understand."

I exploded with angry sympathy for the boy. He had probably been rejected over and over again in his short life, and here he had been surrounded with love and thought he had found a home. Love. Hah. "That is crap!" I said. "Sometimes I hate how this 'Family' operates."

I forget what else I said, but I stayed angry, and later I checked out the story with Christina. She confirmed it, and said something about "Higher Purpose."

But I wasn't listening. I said, "Right, Higher Purpose"—with all the sarcasm I could muster and walked away disgusted. Then I remembered the children scrabbling around in the dust in the barnyard at Boonville. They were a burden to the Family, too. Kids and cripples. And who else was on the Unification Church blacklist? The too young, the too old, the infirm, the blind—anyone without the strength or ability to advance the Material Foundation. I realized that the elderly couple from the neighborhood who ate dinner with us every Friday night were the recipients of Moonie love for one reason only: public relations.

After two weeks at Camp New Hope I began to realize that what held my loyalty were the land, the tribe, and friendships with particular people, and not the Divine Principle or Sun Myung Moon. Life on the land was good; life in New York City would not be so good. I knew that soon my arcadian existence would have to give way to selling flowers or doing something equally distasteful in the ugly, noisy, concrete canyons of the city. I didn't like the idea. I remembered the exhausted Moonie veterans with artificial smiles sleep-walking around the corridors of the New Yorker Hotel, and I realized that the spirit of the whole Family was carried by exuberant newcomers—who would soon be physically and psychically worn to a frazzle by sleeplessness and the burden of Indemnity.

The more attached I grew to the land—the paths running through the woods, the lake, the bees and wildflowers, the trees and sky—the less I liked the idea of giving it up and joining the "bed at 2:00 and up at 5:00" crowd of urban Moonie souls.

A few days into my third week, during meditation period, I wandered over to the guardhouse by the gate to say hello to our protectors. There were three of them, hefty young men, and they seemed a little surprised and suspicious when I entered their domain. But after I mentioned the magic name of Christina they stood at ease, and we talked a little about security problems in Boonville and the recent shack-burning incident here—and then I noticed on the back wall a poster that disturbed me greatly. It was an advertisement for Synanon, and I knew something about Synanon. I asked why the poster was there and said something to the effect that Synanon was *not* an appropriate group for us to have anything to do with.

One of the young men answered lightly, "We have a lot in common with them, you know . . . we've been helping each other out . . . ."

I was shocked. I mumbled, "If you sleep in the same bed with snakes, you're liable to get bit," and I beat a hasty retreat.

To understand my distress you have to understand something about Synanon. Founded in 1958 by an ex-alcoholic named Charles E. Dederich, it began as a drug treatment program. Its method of treatment was a severe form of the encounter group, in which a circle of people bared their souls and verbally ripped each other to shreds. This activity became known as the "Synanon Game," with Dederich as its theoretician and master of ceremonies. Every member of Synanon was required to play the "game" at least once a week.

A description follows:

> "Above all, the Game is irreverent. In it, everything is taken seriously, yet nothing matters at all: all dichotomies are exaggerated and all differences resolved; behavior is criticized; every act is a mistake; good and evil are confused; both righteousness and venality are condemned; any point of view can be taken with absolute conviction and all points of view can be sham. There are no sacred cows in the Synanon Game. Most of all, the players spoof themselves. People have irreverent thoughts which they are encouraged to express in the Synanon Game. The process brings renewal. Irreverence is the mode."

This description is taken word for word from a Synanon pamphlet. It is a description of something calculated to destroy rationality and all capacity for judgment. Note that "any point of view can be taken," and acted out without regard to what the person really thinks. Comparison and contrast are the tools of reason, but these tools are deliberately smashed. The impressed message is that all reasoning is futile, and all opinions are a sham. Nothing is real and nothing is true. "Irreverence is the mode"—nothing is sacred, nothing is worthy of approval, nothing is good ("good and evil are confused"). No constructive emotions or thoughts are allowed to live; everything is torn down and thrown into a witch's brew *where words have no relation to reality*. What is left then, but a group of soupy souls utterly dependent on its leader and trained only for destruction?

The Synanon Game may bear a superficial resemblance to Zen Buddhism—"get rid of concepts"—but the end of the journey is not a panoramic soul enlarged towards compassion, but an ego mashed and made monstrous, squeezed off from the ground of moral being. The techniques of survival and attack developed in the Game made players adept at haranguing outsiders with no regard for honesty or truth or the implicit rules of debate. Lies, statements completely off the point, irrelevant counter-charges, sophisticated brow-beating—all these were used by Synanon members in public hearings and grand jury investigations and dealings with the press.

From its beginnings in Santa Monica and San Francisco, Synanon moved to a ranch in Marin County (just north of San Francisco) in

1964. In 1968 Dederich changed it from a temporary treatment center to a permanent community. By 1975 the group was deeply involved in martial arts and weapons training and had purchased a large supply of guns—including military weapons—and ammunition. Violence was added to the Synanon Game. Critics of Synanon were brutally beaten, as well as dissenters within the group. Abuse of children was rampant; recaptured runaways were beaten and tortured.

By 1977, there were 1400 members in California, and in 1979, centers were flourishing in Detroit, Los Angeles, New York City, Chicago, Malaysia, the Philippines, and West Germany. In 1978, the group purchased a former resort hotel in the Catskill mountains, right down the block, so to speak, from Camp New Hope.

In 1977 Dederich ordered vasectomies for all the men, abortions for all pregnant women, divorce for all married couples, and a transfer of sexual partners for all, married or not. Charts of sexual prowess were chalked up on a blackboard, and this too became a part of the Game. The internal and external violence increased, and the whole sordid mess came to light in the next year when an attorney who had criticized the group was bitten and nearly killed by a rattlesnake placed in his mailbox by Synanon members. The story received national attention, and this is how I knew about Synanon and why I was shocked to see the group given a seal of approval by the Moonie guards at Camp New Hope.

Later I found out a little more about the Synanon-Moonie connection. In the late 1970s, Synanon had tried to form a defensive coalition with some other "religious organizations," including Scientology, the Peoples' Temple (of Jonestown fame), and the Unification Church. The Unification Church, having felt the brunt of criticism for its utter lack of involvement in charitable works, started "Project Volunteer" in San Francisco. Its director was Jeremiah Schnee (who had been my Center Man in the Oakland Family in 1973). Project Volunteer, it turned out, received surplus food and clothing from Synanon and distributed it to the poor with much fanfare in Oakland and San Francisco. Synanon's leader Charles Dederich later terminated the agreement, charging that the Unification Church was taking advantage.

He had a point. I remember Dr. Durst on local television (in 1977 or 1978) excoriating the critics of the Unification Church, and in defense of the Church's religious validity, pointing to the vast charitable efforts it was undertaking. Project Volunteer (he claimed) showed that the Unification Church was expending huge amounts of time and money in helping the unfortunate. What he didn't say was that the Family was merely redistributing food and supplies received from Synanon. Project Volunteer amounted to little more than another piece of deceptive PR.

The Moonie-Synanon alliance I found out about later; at the time I only knew about the guns and beatings and snake attack. I walked away from the guardhouse knowing these things and knowing that the Moonie guards knew about them, too, and didn't care. Or perhaps the paranoia in the Family had grown so pervasive that nothing reported by the "outside world" was believed. Or maybe the Moonie faithful had been deliberately kept in ignorance of the Synanon debacle. The trouble was, any one of these three explanations put the Family in a pretty bad light, and things got sticky for me from then on. I began to wonder what would happen to *us* if *we* got swallowed up in persecution mania. Could there come a day when we would arm ourselves, with all the trouble that would bring in terms of internal policing as well as external enmity?—not to mention the severing of our connection to God.

The Synanon poster in the guardhouse became an immediate symbol of darkness for me. It was as if I'd walked into a police station in Berkeley and seen a picture of Adolf Hitler on the wall.

That Friday night, after the movie, I walked and talked with the young woman who thought of me as a "good Moonie." She was a Christian—a Baptist I think—and she had been having some difficulty with Mr. Moon's interpretation of the Bible. We had a fairly intimate conversation, and as we walked back from the lakeside in the dark there was a moment when we even held hands. Back in the main camp area, we stopped by one of the picnic tables and continued our conversation. I was careful not to be critical of the Family— to that extent I was a "good Moonie." I didn't want to disturb her with the dark ideas I was piecing together from the intimations of cruelty and violence and paranoia I had noted. We talked instead about our pasts and our hopes for the future, both intent on grabbing onto a personal and positive and courteous contact within the rote structure of Moonie life.

Suddenly a husky young man in a blue jumpsuit walked over and told us we weren't allowed to be together at night. He was a guard and had been patrolling the fence around the perimeter of the camp. I told him to hang loose, that we were just talking—but he insisted. I was affronted. I was insulted. I angrily told him to mind his own business; I told him that his job was to protect us from outsiders, and not from ourselves; I told him about Christina and Dr. Durst and how I went way back with the Family; I told him to run along and leave us alone—and all the time I felt ridiculous and shamed in front of the young woman. Here I was, a man thirty-eight years old, being told I couldn't share a few words with a woman I liked—being told by a twenty-year-old boy. Nothing availed. The guard persisted until he had his way, and the young woman and I slipped off to our separate sleeping quarters—both of us, I think, feeling like fools.

Saturday morning was fresh and new. Four busloads of people arrived; Center Men rushed around calling off names and dividing people into groups. The sun shone brightly on a huge circle of young people doing the hokey-pokey. We all exercised our mouths by saying "A-E-I-O-U and sometimes, Y" all together. Then we all ran out to the picnic tables for breakfast and songs and introductions. The introductions were the start of the "getting to know you, getting you to reveal your soul" program. "Do you ever find yourself getting mad at all the lies and hypocrisy in the world? Did you ever wish for an ideal world? You are planning to be a psychologist? That's great! It's so sad your father is an alcoholic. Were you really happy when you were doing all that sleeping around? Everybody gets lonely. We are just a bunch of people who got together to end sorrow and build happiness. How? Wait and see!" Etc., etc., etc.

At 10:00 a.m. we all crowded into the theater for the morning lecture. Everything was as I had remembered from before—a couple of fast songs to warm things up, spiritual parents smiling and cajoling their recruits into high spirits, the benches creaking with heavenly children jumping up and plopping down, just as they had done a hundred times before—in Camp New Hope, in Boonville, in the Dana Street house. An English Moonie gave the same lecture I had heard a hundred times before, the same twitches, the same gestures, the same jokes—

All of a sudden, I saw the lecturer shrug his shoulders in exactly the same way he had yesterday and the day before, in exactly the same place in the lecture, and exactly the same response from the audience—

It was weird. It was a freeze-frame. Was the lecturer alive or was he a robot? Was he an android? Were we all androids? Programmed to forever repeat the same stimulus-response, stimulus-response, stimulus-response? The lecturer at that moment became a stick figure, the laughter of the audience right on cue—I knew exactly when it was coming—even the veteran Family members standing up in the back of the hall to keep from falling asleep and being pummeled by their comrades in a futile attempt to stun them into a sliver of awareness—I had seen the same thing a hundred times before, and it seemed like I would see it a hundred times again, exactly the same thing, the same words, the same gestures, the same choreography down to the smallest details. For a moment I thought that there were no real people in the hall; only the likenesses of human beings, programmed to do the same thing again and again and again.

It was only a flash sensation, but I withdrew from the whole play as if burned by the touch of hell. Hell is not fire and brimstone, nor is it the extreme of loneliness, nor is it fear. It is the death of spontaneity and surprise. It is a tape playing the same joyless song over and over again unto infinity.

Of course, this was not an objective observation. It was a mood. But it was a profound enough mood to tell me that something deathlike was going on in the higher levels of the Moonie hook.

"I am your brain. What I wish must be your wish." This is what Sun Myung Moon had told us. Hyperbole? In that moment of horror it did seem like there was only one brain—and a thousand or a million bodies just going through the motions. In my mind, I transformed that scenario in Camp New Hope to the whole world, to a billion puppets dancing to the tune of the devil in a toxic cosmos. It is the cosmos Nietzsche called "the eternal return"—the notion that everything that happened in the past, everything that is happening now, and everything that is to happen will happen again just like it did before, again and again endlessly—and it drove Nietzsche mad. It is the philosophy the most penetrating intellects are driven to when they can see nothing higher than the God of Time. Cronus is Satan.

That momentary horror—how best to describe it? If you have ever dreamed, say as a child of twelve, of not being able to get away, while a beautiful person slowly turns into a hideous monster—you may begin to get a sense of it; of being locked into a place you first were delirious to get to and then realize—too late—it is the place where all love ends.

It took only that 21-day training session at Camp New Hope for me to realize I was not fit to be a heavenly child—that is, a mistrusted child (told what to do by a Moonie guard), an isolated religionist with a persecution complex (the shack burnt down by pranksters, blown all out of proportion), a yea-saying robot (acting enthusiastic responses whenever our masters gave the cue), a voluntary slave burdened with the sins of the ages. The quasi-mystical experiences I had undergone—the ant-brain mood in the kitchen of the New Yorker Hotel; the profound joy staring into the eyes of an attractive Irish woman after a Friday night movie; the touch of horror during a Saturday morning lecture—these had come to me I think because I made myself deliberately as psychologically wide open as possible. I wanted God to send me all the way into the heart of Moonie life or all the way out of it. That had been my intention before I ever arrived in New York City.

Now I knew I could not continue to be a Moonie. The land, the tribe, the particular friendships with profoundly good people—all that would have to go.

Profoundly good people? Yes, some of them. In the way they gave their whole effort and life and being to the cause of a heaven on earth, for the sake not only of happiness for themselves, but for all people everywhere.

As to the tribe—certainly the gaining of a tribal identity is a profoundly strengthening experience. I am sure that nine-tenths of the frustration felt by individuals in the modern world is due to the death of a tribal culture, in which everyone believes the same fundamental things, and everyone is related by blood or by friendship or both.

I suppose there are various mansions in hell. One is what sociologists call "social anomie," a psychic drifting, ungrounded by place and position and customary obligations and rewards in something corresponding to a tribe. Another is *too perfect* placement in a tribe, where spontaneous action and thought is killed, and judgment, conscience, and love are drained away. The first extreme has in our society bred random violence, drug dependency, hopelessness, multiple sexual partners in a futile search for love (love among psychic drifters provides security for no one), gender dysfunction, and all the other social ills we experience in a world that has lost even the leftover moral guidelines of a vanished Christian culture. That larger, looser Christian tribe was still a tribe. Now it is gone. To fill the vacuum, little tribes spring up, too tightly woven, too harsh on human liberty, too demanding on the human soul. The psychic drifter is plunged from the first hellish mansion straight into the second. The new found "Family" becomes an ogre.

I stayed at Camp New Hope another week, talking with Joshua (and finding no sign of robotization in him), working and singing and going along with camp life, but inwardly withdrawn. Joshua said he thought I was getting a little bored with things, and maybe it was time for me to go back to the city and get involved with the next stage, the real nitty-gritty of Moonie life. I agreed.

Back at the New Yorker Hotel, I snuck up to my old room on the fourth floor and found my suit jacket still hanging on the hook where I had left it, and I checked to make sure that my carefully secreted $300 was still in the inside pocket. That night I slept in, so as to avoid the early morning prayers and assignments and whatever else Christina had in store for me. Later I slipped out of the hotel, and that afternoon I was on a plane to San Francisco, smoking cigarettes and drinking bonded whiskey and watching the pink clouds roll away underneath me. I thought about my lovely Irish woman. Perhaps we would meet again in another life, after God straightened out the universe to my liking.

Chapter Seven

Coming Home

On the plane back to San Francisco, fresh from Moonie-land, something clicked in. Quietly, suddenly, I realized I was at a time of life where it was do or die. That meant going back to college (I had dropped out seventeen years ago) and going as far as I could in the scholarly profession.

It took a while to put the plan into operation. There were hitches. Looking for an apartment, I ran into a Korean real estate manager who (it turned out) had been a Moonie. A few months after I had settled in, I found out Christina was back in town. The Moonie "thing" was still in my head, I suppose—why else would I call her up? She was now heading up the Moonie house on Washington Street. I walked over for dinner one evening and had to work my way past a small group of vociferous ECLIPSE folks, brandishing signs picturing the Rev. Moon, spiced up with a few quotes from "Master Speaks." They were the kind of quotes that had blown the lid off for me on a gut-tearing night back in the summer of 1973. Quotes like this:

> When the world is against us, then they are going to get the punishment . . . . Every people or every organization that goes against the Unification Church will gradually come down and die. Many people will die—those who go against our movement.

Inside, a Moonie at the reception desk was collecting a dollar from each dinner guest. I was witness to a grimy little San Francisco scene. A scruffy young long-haired man, with soiled clothes and soiled face, was complaining loudly about having to pay a dollar for dinner. He was a street person, obviously, and he claimed he had been told where to get a free meal. He screamed about false advertising and how he would go to the authorities because this city had laws against such mendacity—someone inviting you to a place for a free meal and then charging you for it. He was working himself up to a fierce display of righteous indignation as only California down-and-outers can. He had his rights, you know. My sympathy for his basement-level poverty disappeared as he went on proclaiming his victim status. (I had been about to give him a dollar.)

The receptionist couldn't handle the situation. She put in a panic call for Christina. Christina came downstairs and hustled the man-boy out the door. Then she saw me and gathered me into her world. We went upstairs. I asked about Jeffy and Michelle, who had been deprogrammed in 1976, and David. David had left the Moonies around the same time, on his own. Jeffy was now "Satanic," traveling around the country speaking loud and long about the inner workings of the Unification Church.

Who was left, out of that original bunch of leaders?—only Christina and Noah (now in charge of Boonville) and Jeremiah (my old Center Man). Christina was finally beginning to look a little strained around the eyes. I felt, with all those people gone, that a large part of the soul had been ripped out of the Family. Why were they charging for dinner now? Material Foundation. Christina was giving me stock, tired answers.

A few days later we went for lunch at a (Moonie-owned) restaurant near North Beach. She hadn't told me it was a Moonie business, but I knew right away—too many waiters were standing around, pale and limp and sleepy, peering over at our table for a sign from Christina that would make them jump to attention and bring us another cup of coffee.

I said, "This is a Moonie place, isn't it? Why didn't you tell me? It's not that I would have minded, Christina, but you just said it was a nice, organic food restaurant. Why dissemble over a little thing like that? You don't have to con me."

She looked a little sad and a little hurt. We talked about us then and got onto the subject of marriage. She told me she had been "matched" in a special blessing to Allan Sayer.

"But Christina—"

"Allan has been faithful all along, always a responsible heavenly child. He is a best Moonie." (A best Moonie? It was a cute corruption of the language picked up from Onni. People were always saying things like: you are a best heavenly child.)

A little later we were walking outside on the way to her car. It seemed that she had to explain herself further. "I have finally realized what it is to be humble to Heavenly Father. Now I am really learning how to serve God." She nodded her head in a ritual manner, affirming her thought. She looked unhappy, and I was unhappy for her. At that moment I knew it was all over for me and for her: she had become a good Moonie. The old strong spirit was gone. The strength remained, but not the spirit. Allan had joined a little after I had, back in 1973. We mad-cap types had joked about his . . . stuffiness. The bland Sayer, perfect company man, matched with the vivacious Christina—you would have to know these two people to see how frightfully wrong this marriage would be.

It was all over for me anyway. I had no intention of getting back with the Family. But I still liked the idea of me and Christina as confidantes, and I still fantasized about her. Now that last bubble was popped.

Christina phoned me a few weeks later and said I should attend a conference at the Sir Francis Drake Hotel downtown on Union Square. It was to be a forum for discussing the growing attack on religious freedom fomented by faith-breaking psychologists and their allies in the judiciary. It would be hosted by the Unification Church in a joint venture with various other Christian denominations. It would be enlightening, she said. I went.

I can only recall three organizations out of the five or six co-hosting the conference. These were the Moonies, the Scientologists, and a Protestant bunch, probably autonomous Baptists. Entering the palatial front doors, walking up the steps from the huge foyer, presenting myself at the reception desk on the mezzanine, I looked and saw strange types of the human race. A Scientologist woman was manning the desk, registering people. She, and her compatriots, were cold, distant, superior, hard-eyed. All of them seemed intent on displaying their unemotional elite status—they were, after all, super-human Theta beings. Their eyes looked through you or past you—it was hard to tell. What was easy to tell was that they made no eye contact at all. Well, I thought, OK, these are the contingent from Mars. If their religion called for them to be inhuman, so be it.

I sat down at a table in the conference room with Christina, the ever-ready Jeremiah, a nice-looking young woman lawyer from the

ACLU, a black judge from the Federal district court, a Latin American diplomat, and a few silent, sleepy, humble Moonies. Jeremiah was bug-eyed from sleeplessness, but he was intent on making an exuberant show. He told jokes to the diplomat. (The diplomat was later to speak at the podium on the evils of Communism in his country, praising the Unification Church's CAUSA, which had given his government material aid in combating the red menace . . .)

To start things off, a leader from each table stood and identified himself and his organization. A Scientologist from across the room stood and delivered a short, unfriendly, stilted introduction. (But even these superior beings betrayed a slight nervousness at finding themselves in the company of alien, "uncleared" humans.) Christina stood up and told the assembly that she was the Public Relations director of the Unification Church. The minister across from us said he represented a local Protestant church. To my eyes, he and the people at his table looked refreshingly American and normal, the men in blue or dark grey suits, their wives arrayed with suburban bouffant hair styles. They had been looking around with increasing anxiety at the Scientologists in the back and the Moonies across the way. I was suddenly embarrassed to be at the Moonie table. The minister glanced around, looking as if he were having second thoughts about bringing himself and his flock into such strange company.

The Scientologists exuded an adamantine superiority, but something was not quite right about the pose. It was as if there was nothing alive behind the mask. The Moonies gushed and smiled and tried to love one and all, but most were dead on their feet, and it showed. After lunch a panel discussion took place in a side room. As I walked in among little groups of chattering people, David Bromley (or was it Anson Shupe?) collared me and said excitedly, "Are these groups normative?! The question is, are they normative?!"

I asked him what he meant by "normative," and he stared at me for a moment, then rushed on. (David Bromley and Anson Shupe had collaborated on a series of sociological studies of the Moonies. They took a neutral stance, and became—naturally—subjects for Moonie manipulation and love-bombing. The sociologists gained careers that broke new ground for their science, and the Moonies had a pair of academic defenders in the legal realm. After the conference they published a book called *The New Vigilantes: Deprogrammers, Anti-Cultists, and the New Religions*.)

People took their seats. Up front was a long table with three people sitting behind it, facing us. One was William Ball, a constitutional lawyer famous for arguing religious liberty cases before the Supreme Court. He talked about the status of the Bob Jones University court case. The Christian college was segregated; the government wanted to force it to desegregate.

I don't remember who the second speaker was, but the third person at the table grabbed my attention. He didn't give a speech, but answered questions as a (normative?) representative of the Unification Church. He was thin, willowy, pasty-faced, and about twenty-five. (But you could never tell about Moonies. They tended to look a lot younger than their real ages). He seemed to be adrift in his own world. When someone asked him a question, he mumbled and stumbled and said nothing clearly. But it was his tone and accent that got to me. It was high and feminine and half-musical and Asian. It might have been Onni speaking. I was ashamed.

I was ashamed for the young man, for myself, and for the Family.

First: what possessed the Moonie higher-ups to put this poor specimen on display? He advertised nothing but the psychological dregs of the cult.

Second: It chilled me. The young man's personality was enfeebled. He had all but disappeared under the Moonie juggernaut. He had been replaced by the voice and the very mannerisms of his local guru. I imagined all the training sessions, the late night family meetings, the care and coddling, the constant carping demands, Boonville and Camp K, the perpetual blare of Onni in his brain—I didn't know what had happened. But I knew this man-child was archetypically brainwashed. Finally that word was real, and meant a real thing.

And Christina didn't realize it! Nor any of the others. It was as if no one had eyes and no one had ears. The Scientologists were concerned with sustaining their own mental light-opera. The Moonies were dead tired, and in any case, to hear this heavenly child speak in the voice of Our True Parent would be familiar to them, unquestioned, something normal—if it registered at all, which I doubt.

Any regular folks (I was about to say: real people) in the audience were probably too polite and simply dismissed the chirruping

Moonie-monster from their minds. Moreover, they couldn't know, as I knew, what Onni sounded like, and how this man sounded just like her.

It was the end of the show for me. I walked out of the Sir Francis Drake Hotel without even a good-bye to my once-beloved Christina. That was my last contact with the Unification Church.

In the Fall of 1981 I signed on with San Francisco State University, majored in philosophy, and received my B.A. in the spring of 1983. That was my real life track, but the religious question was always there—that was also my real life track. One summer day in 1981, I made another stab at Catholicism. Some friends had recommended a priest connected with the University of California Medical Center in San Francisco. The parish was exciting, I was told—filled with young professionals and academics, and the priest was young and smart and involved. I called for an appointment and visited him in his flat out on Tenth Avenue. He was indeed friendly—a refreshing contrast to my previous chilly contacts in Boulder. I asked him about the eternity of hell, a doctrine that had always disturbed me. By this time, though, I knew that the theological questions I asked had no easy answers, nor in some cases any rational answers at all. The mystery of iniquity remains a mystery, even to the brightest minds in the Church. Since that time I have read St. Augustine and Fr. Daniélou on the subject, and still there is no answer. Genuine religion is higher than the highest human minds. It's people like Sun Myung Moon who try to rationalize it all and always fall short.

The priest told me that though the Church believed in hell, it left the question open as to whether anyone was in it. Technically, he may be correct, but at the time I thought it was a cop-out answer. Then he talked about a group of people who would come over and meditate a couple times a week. He showed me the meditation room.

The room was lined with the same red and yellow pillows (called zafus) we had used for meditation high in the Rocky Mountains, in another country, in another age, under the auspices of a Crazy Wisdom lama from the wild steppes of eastern Tibet. I almost laughed. I almost launched into a lecture on the different sects of Tibetan Buddhism, and how you were not supposed to use the red and yellow zafus, since they were special to the Karma Kagyu Buddhist sect. They were not for public sale or public use.

I realized in a flash that I could entertain this priest for hours about my Buddhist adventures (a story with the real thing, a real Tibetan lama), and he would be attentive and excited. I despaired. Was the Church so vacated of spiritual substance that the best and the brightest had to go elsewhere? I was trying to step up to the higher mysticism of the Church while this priest and his clientele were co-opting a religious expression I had left behind in Boulder. I felt like I was light-years ahead of the priest in experience. I was polite; I said nothing about my Buddhist past.

Back in the living room, we sat and talked again (my heart wasn't in it), and then he gave me a book to take home and read. The book was called *The Sacraments Today*, by Juan Luis Segundo, S.J. It was liberation theology, though at that time I didn't know the name of the beast. Throughout the book the author criticized what he called the magical, supernatural view of the sacraments. He transformed Catholic words from their traditional meanings and applied them to new realities, always communitarian, political, and Marxist, and never personal or mystical. Sin was the sin of the ruling classes (who had co-opted most of the Church hierarchy).

Religious deliverance was the overthrow of political and economic tyranny. All the sacraments were gutted of their original supernatural meanings and reduced to temporal and communitarian ends. The whole Faith was in effect transformed into a propaganda brief for proletarian revolution.

Marxism and Buddhist meditation: the new Catholicism. At least for this particular San Francisco priest, and probably for most of his bright Catholic friends, that was the emphasis. That is what the priest thought would appeal to me as a potential convert, and that was presumably what he believed in. The interview and the book kept me out of the Church for another two years.

The non-Catholic—or even the Catholic—reader may wonder why, after these inauspicious contacts with the Church, I didn't move to one of the Protestant denominations that present forthrightly the doctrines of original sin and redemption and Our Savior. I have already spoken to the issue. I didn't care for the Jesus people who sent everyone to hell who didn't believe the way they believed, I did not believe in justification by faith alone, and I had a hard-won antipathy for sectarian religion of any sort. Jesus Christ founded the Catholic Church and promised He would never abandon it. Entering the Church was proving to be difficult, but in the outcome, that was all to the good. It made me look past persons and into the heart of the matter. It made me realize there would be troubles ahead, and it prepared me, just a little, for those troubles. What did Our Lord say about a pearl of great price? I was more than ever on the lookout for the right entry, some occasion where the aura of welcome would work both ways.

After graduating from San Francisco State, I was accepted for a Masters program at the Graduate Theological Union in Berkeley. This is a consortium of nine schools, six Protestant and three Catholic (Dominicans, Franciscans, and Jesuits), just up the hill from the University of California. In the summer of 1983 I visited the Dominican School at G.T.U. several times and talked about the Faith with my good friend Fr. Antoninus Wall, O.P.

Here (finally) we come to the end of this black comedy conversion story that started with a spontaneous prayer on a hill in Point Arena, California in 1973 and ended a decade later in the Dominican chapel in Oakland.

A fellow student from my years at San Francisco State had also come to G.T.U. He told me about a Byzantine Rite liturgy that was celebrated Sundays at the Dominican chapel by a biritual Roman priest. I went with my friend to this Mass, listened and tried to sing along with the exquisite Greek music, and decided that here and now I would try again. After the Mass, I approached the priest, Fr. Owen Carrol and (with little hope) mumbled something about wanting, possibly, to become a Catholic. He looked at me rather sternly, and said that I should not be overly enamored with the Eastern rite. It was beautiful, of course, but a beautiful service was not the reason to convert. (He probably thought I was one of those people who define their whole religion by a particular form of worship.) Then he said, "The communion with Rome is essential. The gates of hell shall not prevail against the Church."

I was intensely gratified. A real Catholic priest saying a real Catholic thing! I wanted to throw my arms around him. I wanted to fall to my knees and praise God. My heart started beating faster—with hope.

Fr. Carrol asked me about my intellectual background. What had I read that had brought me to the point of conversion? I said

G.K. Chesterton and Mircea Eliade (the anthropologist of religion) and Graham Greene and Thomas Aquinas (I had taken a course in Aquinas at S.F. State) . . . I must have named the right names, because Fr. Carrol's eyes lit up.

I received instruction from Fr. Carrol for a couple of weeks, and then in a (thank God) decisive moment, I said yes. The next day was cool and sunny. I spoke my General Confession on a park bench near the Eucalyptus Grove on the U.C. Berkeley campus. The spiritual relief I received when all the sins of my past life were forgiven was subtle—but oh so light! Fr. Carrol's hand hovered an inch over my head as he spoke the words of absolution, and I, I felt the old guilts and anxieties lift off me—it kept me on air the whole rest of the day. A week later, on October 16, 1983, I was Chrismated according to the Byzantine rite, with oil touched to my ankles, my hands, my face and my forehead, sealing the Holy Spirit. After ten years of refusing to accept what I already knew.

Another decade has passed. Much to my dismay, my conversion did not park me on the front porch of paradise, marking time in blissful serenity, waiting for death and immediate entry into the Court of Heaven. Sin did not stop in its tracks, but popped up more rudely, and in all the places I thought to have conquered. Temptations grew more insistent as they grew more recognizable. A friend told me that new Catholics often experienced it: come into the Church and all hell breaks lose.

But because I had come in so late in life, after such a journey, I was prepared for disappointments, if not in myself, then in the Church. The first disappointment was Catholic academics.

On the M.A. level I could pick and choose and steer clear of shallow modernist theologies. I stayed mostly with the Dominicans, who had by-and-large retained the Faith because of their knowledge of St. Thomas Aquinas. (Realist philosophy is the only underpinning to the Faith and the world; without it there is no defense against descending to a swamp of subjectivism where each person creates his own reality.)

But on the doctoral level I could not avoid the reigning theologies at the other schools in the G.T.U. "Process theology" was championed by some of the Franciscans and Jesuits. It depended on the philosophy of Alfred North Whitehead, with a pat on the back from Teilhard de Chardin. The idea is that God is within the track of time, and He and we and the world all evolve towards perfection together. Feminists, in particular, climb on that bandwagon, since social change (in their direction) is easily thrown into the "process." God and we and the world might then reach the perfection that is female, or rather, male in a female body. That freakish ikon seems to be the logical end of feminist theology.

My critique was just as easy: God is by definition Truth, and Truth is Immutable. A world trapped inside time is a world that can move only towards solipsism. The religious instinct is nothing if it is not an attempt to reach out to that Unchanging Divinity which is our source and our end and which provides the standard by which the world and ourselves can be judged. To place God underneath Time is to reenact the ancient Greek legend of Cronus (Time) devouring Uranus (heaven)—which, in effect, is what the modern world is doing as it gobbles up the Absolute and turns Him into a malleable instrument of human wills. I remember a twenty minute phone call with the Jesuit feminist theologian Sandra Schneiders, she shouting "Change, change, change!" and me shouting "Eternity, eternity, eternity!"

Because I could not avoid the professors who held a philosophy contrary to mine and who held a veto power over every step of my doctoral program, I had to kick back and finish my M.A. and embark on a career in Catholic journalism. It has something at least to do with my first love, which is writing.

The second disappointment was to see so many Catholics lusting for an emotional experience of the Holy Spirit and falling into delusion.

A friend nagged me into attending a charismatic Mass in the Oakland hills. We arrived just after the Mass had started. There was a large hall, with the sanctuary at one end, bare of altar rail, bare of everything except a table and a twisted crucifix on the wall done in Swedish Modern. People were crowded into rows of collapsible chairs on each side of the room. The spirit was lively. A man on the other side of the room was mouthing a string of syllables that sounded like "Mala, mala, mala"—others picked it up, and "mala mala mala" chorused around the hall. A woman on my side stood and "prophesied"—I can't remember what she said. (You can be sure there was nothing in the prophecy about conforming to the rubrics of the Mass.) An elderly priest walked into the hall and up near the sanctuary, where he talked of his illness, how he was getting better, but he needed more prayers from the people. Twenty people gathered around him, those nearest putting their hands on his head and shoulders, speaking in tongues. (The significant sound still consisted of a lot of "mala mala's.") The old priest was gratified, gushing his joy like a ten-year-old girl.

That was the Liturgy of the Word. The Liturgy of the Eucharist had us all marching up to the sanctuary in a crowd around the altar table. The big event was the kiss of peace. Circles of people moved around the altar, clockwise and counter-clockwise, me insisting on shaking hands with (not hugging) the men, but being gripped in full fierce hugs by buxom women over forty. The Eucharist was communal, each in turn giving the Body and Blood to the one next to him or her.

After Mass I talked to a woman in the kitchen where we had all gone for coffee and cookies. Of course I had the Way Ministry zinging in my head, and I privately thought that all these Catholics were kidding themselves. (They couldn't even vary the simple mellifluous syllables with a few "gloptiggles" and "riptans." Apparently the spirit who visited the Oakland Mass was not overly articulate.) I was interested in the feelings these people experienced when they gave forth with the utterances of the angels. To my mind, authenticity in this area depended on a fully sundering sort of experience. I said, as cautiously and as politely as I could, "I'm just a little skeptical. It seems to me if a person is really overwhelmed by the Holy Spirit, he must feel something huge and strange happening within himself. Do you see what I mean? I mean, this is God taking you over..."

"No," she said. "It's nothing like that. I just let go and let the Spirit talk."

"Oh," I said.

In this case I suggest we have a cult mentality in people who are desperate to believe the unbelievable. But they do it to themselves. No cult-master sets the tone and demands obedience to his every whim. Manipulation is inter-mutual, if it is present at all. It consists of each person implicitly convincing another, and in that act, convincing himself. The elderly priest loved to be loved, as we all do. To my eyes his gushing was pathetic, but I am one who wants to see dignity in the elderly. He bought into it because it felt good, with the excuse that it seemingly had some scriptural warrant. Communal prayer can sometimes effect healing. In that sense there was nothing counter-Christian about the event.

But the Mass was badly corrupted, the group of people lost my respect as they gabbled and garbled and hugged each other to death, and the sense of it was not people worshipping God, but people trying to feel good about themselves. You are somebody special when the Holy Spirit speaks through you, and all the better if it's happening all around you. That makes it real. So we are all special people—not pathetic, lonely, frustrated individuals without a tribal culture to make us one body, one soul.

In a later chapter we shall see classic cult aspects taking over a charismatic community. In that scenario we will find a willful and self-assured leader, a shepherd of souls, with all the totalitarian consequences that kind of intimate government brings.

But most Catholic charismatic events are no different from Pentecostal services anywhere.

Not too long ago I attended one at the University of Portland. Fr. Ralph DiOrio, the famous Catholic healer, was in town. The huge athletic auditorium was packed to the rafters with at least two thousand people. The first thing I didn't care for was Fr. Ralph making cute jokes at the expense of the bishop (an assistant bishop of the Portland Archdiocese) sitting behind him on the stage, Fr. Ralph humorously implying that the Church hierarchy were a bunch of buffoons. The second thing was Fr. Ralph's saying that it made no difference if you were Catholic or Baptist or Lutheran. "If you're Baptist, don't change your faith. Be a better Baptist." (This statement received a big round of applause.) The third thing was Fr. Ralph's assuring us that it was not he who accomplished the healings, but Jesus working through him—and then immediately launching into an anecdote about how he had healed so and so right in the rectory: each of these many stories followed by another round of applause from the adoring congregation. The humble Fr. Ralph was in his glory.

Later, to get the healing mood right, Fr. Ralph divided the whole crowd into three sections with a sweep of his hand, and had each section start a particular chant, all in unison. (I was high above the stage area, in the third tier, towards the rear, sitting with my friend and a couple of his friends.) Our section chanted "Abba, abba, abba," slowly, sonorously. It reminded me of Hindu "Om circles" I had taken part in once or twice in Boulder. "Abba . . . Abba . . . Abba . . ." was a lot like "Om . . . Om . . . Om . . ."—in fact I turned to my friend and sang "Om . . . Om . . . Om . . ." in his ear.

But then, just to my right, a lady started gobbling with the talk of the Holy Spirit, and I thought, uh oh, here we go again.

A few minutes later I left. (We were already an hour and a half into the show.) My friend later told me Fr. Ralph had kept the event going for six hours. The friend was too polite to get up and leave, but he agreed with my comment that it was a stage-managed event. You can get the same thing from TV Holy Spirit shows.

Maybe there were some healings, I don't know. I wouldn't have known even if I had stayed for the climax of the program, since, like Protestant versions of the same thing, you never know who's kidding whom or what's real and what's not. At the time I thought, maybe I can get healed (I had a bad back), but only if I lose myself in the chants, the gobbles, Fr. Ralph's charisma, the rising momentum of a communal spirit—and I said NO!—I've already been a Moonie.

Was I overly skeptical because of my Moonie past?—so that I imposed a former experience unfairly on a present event that was only superficially similar? Perhaps. But Moonie past or no Moonie past, I can sense when I am being subjected to manipulation; when a crowd is being warmed up to a high pitch of enthusiasm; when I am being called upon to throw away my self and become one with a mob spirit. If the Lord God wants to heal some illness in me, I don't think He requires that I temporarily jettison my critical reason—my gimlet-eyed testing of the spirits—in order to receive that healing.

The third sort of disappointment, more of a shock than a disappointment, was to realize that being Catholic is no defense against losing yourself in a cult. When I began a journalistic investigation of sectarian Catholic movements in 1988, I had no idea they would exhibit the same soul-shrinking characteristics as the Moonies, the Scientologists, or the Way Ministry. Of course every sect has its own special flavor and its own degree of control, as we shall see.

A sect or communal movement of any kind can look good and even be good to begin with. And many can remain good and never take on the characteristics of cults. Individuals and families looking for a more profound religious life often gather together and organize and build communities that involve everyone concerned in a more fulfilling style of worship. There is really no telling how or when such groupings may develop characteristics destructive to souls. The only warning I can give is to be on the lookout for anyone who tells you to give over your innate responsibility of conscientious judgment to him, your inner "yeses" and "nos."

Catholic religious orders ordinarily require a vow of obedience. That is a perfectly legitimate requirement. It is conducive to humility and the end of that self-adoration that separates you from God. Obedience to religious superiors is active and outward, and it is inward as well since it involves an inward assent. That assent, however, still requires a judgment of the mind. It is when the inner self begins to get confused and dulled in thinking, when the self seems to fade into the atmosphere and can no longer judge right and wrong, that something destructive is taking place. A lot depends on the character of religious superiors and on the grace of God.

There are a couple of danger signals: when a movement results from a rejection of higher church authority and when a movement carves out a kingdom within the Church, effectively if not openly removed from higher church authority. In both cases, I think, the corrective grace of the Holy Spirit can be lost along with the corrective guidance of outside churchmen. Even when everything is legitimate, in certain groupings evil persons can assume leadership, and then followers under the vow of obedience can be in trouble. (In this age, when many religious superiors spit in the face of higher authority, I think more cults will develop within the Church.) Again, it comes down to the point where you are losing touch with your practical and moral judgments. That is when you must wrench yourself out of the scene in order to save your soul's integrity.

But that is easier to say than to do, when processes of mental control are so subtle and often seem to grow up automatically in a tightly bonded group setting. By the time an evolving community becomes a cult, it is often too late for its members to realize that fact. I went through the Moonies, and so have the experience of a veteran, but I cannot claim that I have a permanent and solid defense against cultic involvement, even knowing what I know. Just as there is very little defense against a love that turns into a betrayal, there is very little defense against a loving community that turns ugly.

During my student years at the Graduate Theological Union in Berkeley, I lived in an apartment owned by the Dominicans. A few blocks east, on another part of what we affectionately called Holy Hill, is a Jesuit residence house where I spent many hours talking of truth and Christ and the Church with a good friend who has gone on to become a good priest. A block west of the Jesuit house is a Tibetan Buddhist temple painted bright yellow, with prayer flags blowing in the wind and prayer wheels spinning on the cornices, and across the street from the Buddhist temple, on the near side, is the big white Georgian house fronting Hearst Street where eighteen years ago I sat on the floor with a hundred other woebegone workers for the Kingdom of Heaven while Onni lacerated us for our laziness and infidelity. The sidewalk on the west side of the house is above the level of the window, but if I knelt down I could see into the kitchen, where a bowl of white flowers rested on a table and, leaning against it, a small color photograph of Sun Myung Moon.

Somewhere in the same neighborhood is the hidden mansion where Onni and Dr. Durst sat on thrones like Byzantine hierarchs while we bowed and scraped and scraped and bowed and sold the best years of our lives for a mess of pottage.

The Catholics you will meet in the second part of this book have, I am afraid, done pretty much the same thing.

Part II:

Catholic Cultists

Chapter Eight

A Mighty Fortress Is Our Sect

The Fatima Crusaders, aka the Tridentine Latin Rite Church, aka the Congregation of Mary Immaculate Queen of the Universe, is a small sect of several thousand members who claim to be the last Catholics on the earth. Those others, that 900 million having Pope John Paul II at their head, are all apostate and in a state of manifest heresy and have been since the death of Pope Pius XII.

The claim is laughable on the face of it, but since it is only an exaggeration of the position held by many ultra-traditionalist Catholics, it bears further inquiry. The stumbling block for these people is the Vatican II Council and the revised style of the Mass. In particular, the claim is that the changed form of the consecration of the wine in the New Mass has invalidated that Mass, and the supposed encouragement of religious syncretism in *Dignitatis Humanae* represents a suicide of the Church. In a more general sense, the Vatican II documents as a whole are castigated as promoting that modernism so severely condemned by Pope St. Pius X in *Pascendi Gregis* and in other papal documents since that time. The effectively existentialist and subjectivist theology of Karl Rahner and the fantastical evolutionism of Teilhard de Chardin are said to have had an influence on the Council proceedings to the point of destroying the traditional Faith along with its philosophical underpinnings.

These issues have been argued over ad infinitum in the past two decades. Devout and intelligent Catholics have worried over the proper interpretation of the Council's *Dignitatis Humanae* and *Gaudium et Spes*; the claim of modernistic infection has merit for many; and certainly some passages in the Conciliar documents are so ambiguous that contradictory interpretations can be entertained. To be sure the so-called "Spirit of Vatican II," that cloudy complex of interpretations promoting a this-worldly, anti-supernatural viewpoint, abrogating to mankind the prerogatives of God, has been a continuing disaster to the quality of worship in the post-Vatican II Church. Liberals read the Conciliar documents one way, conservatives another—but the matter should have been put to rest (at least in terms of magisterial guidance) by Pope John Paul II's statement of November 6, 1978—"That the Council must be understood in the light of all Holy Tradition and on the basis of the constant Magisterium of the Church." If local hierarchies and laity would but follow the light emanating from the See of Peter, all would be well.

That's not good enough for the Fatima Crusaders (or for the Lefebvrites or for any number of schismatic Catholic communities dotted around the world). Here is a summary of the Crusaders' position, quoted from their literature:

> We declare that the New "Mass" is invalid . . . . We declare that the introduction of this New "Mass" also signals the promulgation of a new humanistic religion in which Almighty God is no longer worshipped as He desires to be worshipped . . . . Those who have accepted this New "Mass" have, in reality and without taking notice of it, apostatized from the true Faith; they have separated themselves from the true Church and are in danger of losing their souls because outside the Church founded by Jesus Christ no one can be saved. For this reason, we invite the faithful to return to their Faith from which they have strayed.
>
> We reject the heretical Decree on Religious Freedom which places the divinely revealed religion on an equality with false religions. This decree is a clear and evident sign of the denial of our holy traditions by the apostate and schismatic hierarchy.[1]

What makes the New Mass invalid? There are several points of contention, but the most significant is the change in the words of the consecration of the wine—the old form was "which shall be shed for you and for many unto the remission of sins." The New Mass replaces "for many" with "for all."[2] The argument is made that "for all" suggests universal salvation, or in any case makes a mockery of the magisterial teaching that there is no salvation outside the Church. The response is first that the magisterial teaching admits salvation outside the Church in the literal sense by means of the "baptism by desire," whereby good men, ignorant of the claims of the Church, nevertheless, conform themselves to the will of God and can be saved by Christ even if they do not know Christ.

How have the Fatima Crusaders justified rejecting the papacy and going into schism (while claiming that it is not they, but the "Conciliar Church," that is in schism from the Faith)? The logic is as follows: the Pope, being infallible in matters of faith and morals, cannot err in these matters. But all the popes since Pius XII have in fact erred by continuing to approve the Vatican II Council. Therefore, they cannot be true popes, and the See of Peter is vacant.[3] This position is known as *sedevacantist*, and it is held in extreme or mitigated forms by more than a few traditionalist would-be Catholics.

The immediate problem that arises is that of ecclesiastical authority. Traditionalist sects like the Fatima Crusaders must forever attempt to legitimatize themselves through episcopal consecration. Thus Francis Schuckardt, the founder of the Crusaders, got himself ordained by a bishop of the Old Catholics, a sect which broke away from the Church after the First Vatican Council, but which supposedly retains a valid, if illicit, apostolic succession of bishops. After Schuckardt left under a cloud of scandal in 1984, the Crusaders placed themselves under the authority of first one, then another, bishop in the "lineage" of the Vietnamese schismatic, Archbishop Ngo-Dinh-Thuc.

Rome's policy towards schismatic movements seems, at least in recent years, to be one of caution and compassion. Every attempt was made to get traditionalist Archbishop Lefebvre and his Society of St. Pius X back into the fold. The end of tolerance seems to come at the point when the schism is "formalized" by the schismatic bishop's consecrating other bishops, and thus perpetuating the schism. (Bishops can consecrate priests and other bishops generation after generation.)

To forestall these validating maneuvers, excommunication follows *ipso facto* when a schismatic bishop consecrates another bishop without papal approval. Archbishop Lefebvre and the bishops he consecrated on June 30, 1988, were all made excommunicate by that very act. Similarly, Archbishop Ngo-Dinh-Thuc was formally excommunicated along with those he consecrated as bishops in 1983.[4] The Fatima Crusaders, then, and the bishops who provide their "validation" are all in a state of excommunication from the Catholic Church.

The name "Fatima Crusader" conjures up an image of an "army" fiercely loyal to the message of Fatima and dedicated heart and soul to Our Lady. It seems to be a movement akin to the Blue Army and other strongly-Marian advocacy groups. It is rather another case, like the phoney apparitions at Bayside, of Our Lady being ill-used by her ostensible friends. (Incidentally, it should be made clear that the Marian journal *Fatima Crusader* published by Fr. Gruner in Canada has nothing to do with this sect.)

There is indeed a historical connection between the Fatima Crusaders and the Blue Army, but one which shows the Blue Army in a good light.[5] Francis Schuckardt himself was in the higher echelons of the Blue Army and an international spokesman for the group before they kicked him out in 1967 for condemning Vatican II and Pope Paul VI. The next year he started his own "apostolate," called the Fatima Crusade, in Coeur d'Alene, Idaho. By the early 1970s the official name had become the Tridentine Latin Rite Church. In 1977 the sect purchased the formerly-Jesuit Mount St. Michael seminary in Spokane, Washington. This complex of buildings remains the headquarters of the group. There is also a convent and several schools in the TLRC's "City of Mary" in Rathdrum, Idaho, in Coeur d'Alene, and at Mount St. Michael's in Spokane.

At its high point in 1984, the sect had perhaps 800 members in the Spokane-Coeur d'Alene area, and perhaps as many more in various "missions" around the country. (Membership numbers in the "mission churches" have most likely been wildly inflated.) In 1983 it seems that a move was contemplated to New Zealand, but advance negative publicity scotched that effort.

Schuckardt seems to have reached an advanced state of megalomania in 1978 when he purportedly had a vision of the Blessed Virgin, the contents of which he did not reveal. But since that time on various occasions, he was seen wearing white papal vestments.

We can only suppose by these external signs what sort of revelations were occurring in the inner sanctum of the sect.

What else was occurring in the inner sanctum was revealed by ex-members, who in 1984 charged that Schuckardt had called them into his quarters late at night ostensibly to massage him, but who were required to take off their clothes and lay across his body.[6]

Charged with repeated acts of homosexuality by his next-in-command, Fr. Denis (Robert Chicoine), he absconded with some $250,000 and about twenty followers and later was convicted in California of trafficking in cocaine.[7]

Fr. Denis remained in charge of a much reduced One True Church. More than half had left when Schuckardt revealed some weaknesses of the flesh. The search was on for another "validating" bishop, and by 1985 one was found in the person of the excommunicated George Musey, who reordained the Mount St. Michael priests from the Old Catholic lineage into the more recent schismatic lineage originated by Archbishop Ngo-Dinh-Thuc. A little more than a year later, in a contentious meeting on September 10, 1986, Musey was ousted. He had angered many of the locals (meaning Robert Chicoine) by assuming too close a control over the group. Robert McKenna stepped in to take his place.

Bishop McKenna had been consecrated by Thuc-line Bishop Guerard des Lauriers three weeks earlier. In fact, the timing of Musey's ouster and McKenna's consecration suggests a planned action by Des Lauriers, McKenna, and Chicoine, with the provision that McKenna would leave the cult well enough alone. Unlike others of the Thuc lineage (including its originator), Des Lauriers and McKenna were not strict sedevacantists. Des Lauriers, once a Dominican, had developed a theory of the heretical papacy which kept the Vatican II popes as real popes—maybe. The formula used was that the present pope, in adhering to the Vatican Council, was ignorant, but not culpable; able to abjure his errors; so "materially" but not "formally" remained the true pope. This compromise caused no end of trouble in the Mount St. Michael faithful, and especially in their offshoot centers in California and elsewhere.

Since the Schuckardt scandal, the sect has slowly recovered in membership. By 1988 there were reportedly about 500 families in the Spokane area, along with a number of priest-missionaries with small flocks in Los Angeles, Phoenix, Akron (Ohio), and New Zealand. Supposedly there are also Fatima Crusader cells in Australia, England, Mexico, and in several European countries. It is impossible to get hard numbers for these "mission churches"—Fr. Kent Burtner, an expert on cults who investigated the TLRC in 1983, says that claims of a hundred members at a particular location would, on investigation, shrink to ten or fifteen. In the Spokane area itself as of

1988 there were about 80 nuns in three convents, twenty or so male religious, and six priests.

In 1991 a local Fatima Crusader priest, Mark Pivarunas, ordained first in the Old Catholic line, then in the Thuc line by George Musey, was consecrated as bishop by the Mexican Moises Carmona, who was one of first of the Thuc bishops. With the elevation of Pivarunas the Fatima Crusaders now have their own bishop-in-residence. Fr. Robert Chicoine, the power behind the throne under Schuckardt, engineer of Schuckardt's ouster, and local leader afterwards, now heads up a CMRI center in New Zealand.

According to a source intimately familiar with the ins and outs of Mount St. Michael, a further power play had occurred. Fr. Pivarunas led a rebellion against Chicoine two years ago, and Chicoine was given a vote of "no confidence" as Superior General of the TLRC. Pivarunas took over as Superior General and established a local dictatorship as controlling as anything Schuckardt or Chicoine had established in the past. In 1991 Pivarunas picked a fight with McKenna, the then titular bishop of Mount St. Michael, leaving Pivarunas in full local control.

While the 34-year-old Pivarunas engineered a bishopric for himself, he kept his community under strict obedience not to give away the secret. So it was only on the eve of the consecration that the other Thuc line bishops got wind of the action. Six of these bishops (McKenna, Musey, Oliver Oravec, J. Vidar Elmer, John Hesson, and the South African Richard Bedingfeld) signed a statement aimed at making the TLRC more open to higher-level (Thuc-line) ecclesial control. Meanwhile Carmona was in his dotage, being gently handled by some nuns who conceived it their duty to censor his incoming mail. So he never learned of the dispute over control of the Crusaders. Pivarunas was able to perform an end-round and show up in late September 1991 as a newly consecrated bishop. Now any submission to the larger fold of Thuc line bishops is gone—not that such a connection would make much difference, since the whole schismatic hierarchy is nothing more than an unsanctioned imitation of the Catholic reality.

What does the TLRC believe, aside from its dissent from Vatican II and the *Novus Ordo Missae*?[8] It believes it has in hand the infamous Third Secret of Fatima, which is purported to assert that the world is due for a grievous judgment, when the great majority of people will be killed, and those that remain wish they had been among the deceased.

It believes that Vatican II's "apostasy" is explainable by the fact that Freemasons have taken over the Church. Pius XII is alleged to have been poisoned. Paul VI was supposedly a Grand Luciferian Master of the Freemasons. The United States government was formed by Freemasons, and nearly all Catholic bishops in this country have succumbed to their line of thought. What the Freemasons supposedly desire is an end of the Catholic Faith, one world government, and one world humanistic "religion." In much of this they have already succeeded, as the state of the Church and the state of the world attest. The fact that all but a few Catholics acquiesced with hardly a murmur to the "new Church" and the New Mass is taken to be none other than that mass apostasy predicted in the end times by Scripture. The TLRC is thus a Remnant Church, with a huge apocalyptic burden and a huge responsibility. Needless to say, an overwhelming burden is thus placed on individual Fatima Crusaders. Their strict obedience and prayers are the only thing standing in the way of the Anti-Christ.

And what about the Jews? Firstly, the Jews today are not the real Jews, who were all wiped out by the Romans in the Jewish rebellion in Palestine in A.D. 66. Present day Jews are actually descendants of an alien race that took over the Talmud and spent the next two millennia in vicious enmity to the Christian Faith. They were responsible for the Bolshevik revolution in 1917, and they started World War II as a part of their master plan to take over the world. They are Christ-killers (despite the contradictory notion that they are not descendants of the Jews responsible for the Crucifixion).

(Anti-Semitism was roundly denounced by at least three popes who have the approval of the TLRC: Pope Benedict (1914-22), Pope Pius XI (1922-39), and Pope Pius XII (1939-58). Pius XI wrote: "Anti-semitism is a movement in which we Christians can have no part whatsoever.... Spiritually, we are all Semites." It might be pointed out that if Jesus Christ had been Chinese, the Chinese would be called Christ-killers. If He had been an American, Americans would be called Christ-killers. In regards to Bolshevism, it might be noted that Lenin was not a Jew. The Jews who did take part in the Russian Revolution were later purged by Stalin. In regards to World War II, it was Hitler's bizarre notion that international Jewry forced his hand. Does the TLRC take its history directly from Nazi propaganda?)

We are perhaps gaining some idea as to what happens in a schism that becomes a sect that becomes a cult. There is, some would argue, a legitimate fear of massive divine judgment, and this may legitimately result in a very worried apocalyptic stance. But there is no legitimate reason to falsify history or to exaggerate conspiracies or to descend into a virulent hatred of imagined enemies. In fact, the proper response to an apocalyptic fear is to prepare for eternal life by actively loving God and neighbor.

But fear and hatred of outsiders is a chief mark of cults. It is a matter of psychological tightening combined with elitist arrogance, of demolishing the beast in one's own heart by exaggerating the beast in another's. It is to manufacture a culpable rather than an innocent or ignorant enemy. There is no doubt that Freemasons, especially in Italy, continue to conspire against the Church. There is no doubt that a good many Jews were Communists in the early decades of this century. But so were a good many non-Jews. There is no doubt that 350 years of rationalistic and subjectivist philosophy in the West have undermined the morals, manners, and faith of many. But the mark of paranoid thinking, and thus of cultish thinking, is to turn ignorant error into intentional conspiracy, legitimate opposition into deviltry, and, especially on the Jewish question, it is to lose one's reason.

In fact, to lose one's reason in favor of the reasoning of a leader is comforting for the uncertain mind, but it is a dehumanizing thing. It is one of the things demanded by the leadership of the Fatima Crusaders. The following is a quote from the *Inland Register* (the diocesan newspaper of Spokane): "Accepting Bishop Schuckardt as their religious superior, TLRC members continually subject their reasoning powers to Bishop Schuckardt, all ex-members said."[9] In 1975 all books of members were confiscated, and only those sanctioned by Schuckardt were thenceforward allowed. Two years earlier Schuckardt had placed the whole community, then located in Coeur d'Alene, under interdict until everyone had signed a loyalty oath to him.[10]

As the "last remnant of true Catholicism," the cult is of course oppressed by the fiercest machinations of the devil. All outsiders are possessed by Satan. Virtually everyone outside the group is going to hell, including all Catholics in allegiance to Pope John Paul II—that is, all "Conciliar Catholics." Any member who leaves the TLRC is *ipso facto* possessed by Satan. Within the group, the devil is constantly at war with the souls of the remnant faithful. Everyone must therefore be constantly on guard.

The following is quoted from the *Tridentine Latin Rite Church*, an investigative report published by the Spokane diocese's *Inland Register*:

> "This is one of the very few Catholic communities left on the face of the earth, so all the legions of hell are naturally going to concentrate on destroying this community," Bishop Schuckardt states.
>
> "And we must be careful that the devil never catches us in a moment of weakness, a moment of doubt, a moment of contradiction or sorrow, or that we are feeling sorry for ourselves."[11]
>
> [Ex-members say] TLRC leaders stress that the devil has declared an all-out war on your souls and the community, causing members to suffer from severe mental strain . . . . We were told that our weapons to combat Satan were work, prayer, penance, and sacrifice, but soon it became evident that no matter what you did or how much you accomplished for the church, you always fell short of what God expected.[12]

In such a terrible and subtle spiritual war, the cult will not countenance a competitive loyalty—that of mother for child or wife for husband. This is the language Fatima Crusaders use: "People are only too willing to look at the natural and forget the supernatural. Our stand is attacked so often because we place the supernatural (our union with Christ) first over a natural union (a family unit)."[13]

And how! The Sawyer family were with Schuckardt and the Crusaders from 1966 to 1981. They are only one of many families who had thrown one or more of their children out of the home to fend for themselves—because those children had rebelled against the harsh discipline of the cult and therefore had caused the parents to be "enemies of the church."[14]

What is that discipline like? The wooden paddle is used liberally in school. On one memorable occasion—memorable because it became public knowledge—forty whacks were administered to each of some thirty-five boys for failing their classroom assignments. In

1976 a Brother Welsh served five days in jail and was given two years probation for "excessive spanking" of a ten-year-old. The child was hospitalized due to the severity of his wounds.[15]

Marriages are often broken when a spouse refuses to accept the TLRC as the One True Church. The loyal member is told to choose between the church and marriage to an "infidel." One former member says: "I know of several spouses in the TLRC who are going through the motions of being a faithful member because they know that their wives will leave them and take the kids with her, if he ever calls for a showdown on 'either me or this church.'"[16]

Let us follow the plight of one family in some detail, just to get the flavor of this "superiority of the supernatural over the natural." This family was in the cult for some thirteen years, from 1969 to 1982. First the mother's statement:

> Probably the worst single thing was when we were told by Father Denis (Robert Chicoine) to put our three sons, ages 14, 17, and 18, out of our home and literally out on the streets because they refused to attend the school at St. Michael's. If we refused, we (my husband and I) would not be allowed to receive the sacraments. We were not to have anything to do with them at all. At this time (1979), Fr. Denis told me I was "too attached to my husband and children." We sent our boys out.[17]

Next, the statement of one of her daughters. She is 18 years old. It is 1982, three years after her brothers have been kicked out of the family. Before and after every school year, retreats are held for the school children. During these retreats the regimen is prayer, lectures far into the night, more prayer, and absolutely no talking. Watches are taken away, so the passing time becomes a blur ordered only by the retreat masters. The daughter has just finished her senior year:

> By this time, most of my family had left the Crusade. On the last day of the retreat, Father Denis called juniors and seniors into an office one by one. He talked to me last.
>
> He started by asking me what my vocation was. I answered that it would be a single life. He said, "Why not be a religious? [a nun]. I told him I just couldn't do it because I have a back deformity and ulcers. He said, "Those ulcers could clear up. They're from living at home,

and the turmoil between the boys that have left and those that are trying to do right." He told me that I was of age and could make my own decisions. I felt he was pressuring me.

I said, "I know, Father, but really there is no decision to make, because this is the only truth. If I leave here, I'm damned. He said, "that's right," and advised me to leave home, and don't even go back after the retreat.

I couldn't bear the thought of leaving my family! The last few hours of my retreat I cried and cried because I didn't want to leave them, but I knew I'd be damned if I didn't.

Let us recall that this young lady had spent her whole life being educated to the belief that outside the gates of the TLRC was only Satan and death and hell.

Lastly, another daughter remembers her school days in the TLRC:

Between the first and fifth grade it was the same thing each year. Getting whacked with different sized paddles for everything I did wrong, like not having homework done, or for what they called poor excuses for being absent from school.

When I was 12 and in the sixth grade, I got in trouble for telling a bad joke, but I didn't do it. This was something that had happened a long time back, but Sister Clarita [who had been a real nun in the Order of Notre Dame de Namurs before joining the Crusade] had just found out about it.

She told my dad that he had the choice of cutting my hair as punishment himself or letting her cut it. My dad knew how the nuns cut hair (like a boy's army haircut) so he cut it himself, not as short. I was also to stay with Sister Lucia (Mary LeStage) at the City of Mary (in Rathdrum, Idaho) for a week. This all happened on Ash Wednesday in late February of 1978. The week was full of punishment and public penances. They thought my attitude to them was very bad, so on the following Monday I went to Mount St. Michael in Spokane to talk with Father Raphael (John Ellis). He told me I would have to spend another week with the nuns, or how ever long it would take for my attitude to change.

On Wednesday, after one week there, I ran away from the City of Mary, but my dad found me after about six hours and took me back up there. If he did not, he and mom would be refused the Sacraments, etc.

On Thursday, the day after I came back, I was sorting a box of carrots, putting the rotten ones in the trash. I put two carrots that I thought were rotten in the trash. Sister Lucia and Sister Clarita saw this and came over and said that they were still good and that I was going to eat them for lunch.

When lunch came, they put these two carrots in front of me with a knife and told me to cut the rotten green and black stuff off. There wasn't even 1/8 of the carrots left that was good. I was to eat that and the rest of the rotten stuff that I took off.

I started eating the carrots and I threw them up. They made me eat them again and I threw them up again. I just couldn't keep it down.

Sister Lucia got the razor strap out and said she'd count to five, and if I didn't eat a spoon full of my vomit, then she would give me five whacks on my rear end. I got five spoon fulls down before I threw up again. After this, the other nuns there told Sister Lucia to move me to another room because they were getting sick watching me.

I went into another room and threw up all over a chair. I was made to kneel by the chair to lick the throw-up, but I didn't want to. Sister Clarita told me to say either "Jesus, I love you" and lick the vomit clean or say "Jesus, I hate you." I had all I could take, so I said, "Jesus, I hate you." Sister Clarita got on top of me and started punching me in the face for saying what I did.

Finally, because I didn't want to get any more beating (I already had a black eye and a very sore bottom), so I ate all the rest of the vomit up.

What had happened to the sanity and good sense of this girl's parents (not to speak of the sadistic Sr. Clarita)? It seems that they sympathized with her plight, but made their daughter go back to the hell she had tried to escape because they feared for their own souls. (They would be refused the Sacraments.) Outside the cult they would be damned. Inside they were condemned to obey the arbitrary dictates of the leaders—or be damned.

The solid wall erected around the group, isolating it as an island of the blessed in a sea of irredeemable evil while, within, the individual soul is given over to the tender care of the cult leader—all this is shockingly similar from one cult to another.

The irony for me is that I came to the Church after a long journey in the land of do-it-yourself religion. Rome, and only Rome, is the touchstone of reality, the very opposite of a cult. The Catholic Church is huge and venerable and wise with the wisdom of the ages. Its authority is not something crushing your face every nanosecond of the day and night, consuming you, and killing your soul, but is spread out from your parish to your diocese to the Vicar of Christ, encompassing the whole world. Its many-tiered structures allow personalities to exist, for good and for evil. (The wheat and the tares will be sorted out at the Judgment.) Its meaning and its life are spread from here and now through twenty centuries of violent and exalted history. Its spirit underpins the universe. It has coped with every rebellion and schism and false faith imaginable.

Surely no Catholic (I thought) could fall into the trap of the cults. But many have, usually in the search for a stronger faith, a more involved Catholicism. It seems that just as the world breeds cults to provide a coherence missing in the world, Catholics go cult-ward to find a coherence missing in the Church. In this time of troubles, they seek the old certainties.

NOTES

1. Statement of Archbishop Ngo-Dinh-Thuc, May 26,1983; quoted in *From the Bounties of the Sacred Heart*, a publication of the Fatima Crusaders.
2. See *Reign of Mary* (the Fatima Crusaders' magazine), Spring 1987, p. 4.
3. "A Man from God Called John?" in *Reign of Mary*, Summer 1986.
4. Bob Cubbage, *Tridentine Latin Rite Church*, 1986 ed., an exposé published by *The Inland Register*, newspaper of the Spokane Diocese.
5. Historical information on the Fatima Crusaders is taken primarily from *Tridentine Latin Rite Church*, 1986 ed.
6. *TLRC*, 1986, p. 35.
7. Information provided by the Cult Awareness Center, Portland, Oregon.

8. See *TLRC*, 1986, Chapter III, "Political Beliefs."
9. *Ibid.*, 25-6.
10. *Ibid.*, 26.
11. *Ibid.*, 23.
12. *Ibid.*, 27-8.
13. *Ibid.*, 22.
14. Letter on file at the Cult Awareness Center, Portland, Oregon.
15. *TLRC*, 1986, p. 9; also, document from the Cult Awareness Center, Portland, Oregon, by Fran Bahr.
16. *TLRC*, 1986, p. 25.
17. This and the following two quotes are condensed from affidavits sworn before a notary public on May 15, 1983.

Chapter Nine

Dona Lucilia of the Flashes

You may have seen them marching down Broadway in New York City, protesting *The Last Temptation of Christ*, or a few years ago, demonstrating against the blasphemous French film, *Hail Mary*. A disciplined army of well-dressed young men, aggressively Catholic, wearing red caps, holding aloft brilliantly-colored pennants picturing a gold lion rampant on a crimson field. Depending on your point of view, the sight may have been stirring or ludicrous, or both at once. Who are they, these specters from the fourteenth century, these paladins of a past or future medieval dream?

Their official name is the Society for the Defense of Tradition, Family, and Property, better known as the TFP. Headquartered in Brazil, the organization has centers in at least twelve countries. In some of these countries the name is different, perhaps to give the impression of local autonomy, perhaps to confuse the process of identification. In Spain, for example, the TFP is known as the Covadonga Cultural Society. In Bolivia the title is Young Bolivians for a Christian Civilization; in Canada it is variously TFP or Young Canadians for a Christian Civilization. An alternative name in the United States is Foundation for a Christian Civilization. In addition to these, there are TFP branches throughout most of Latin America, in France, and in Rome. According to Mario Navarro de Costa, the TFP "nuncio" in Washington, the organization has recently moved into Australia, New Zealand, the Philippines, and India. The world center in Brazil has some 1500 to 2000 fully-dedicated, full-time members, and the various national branches have anywhere from ten or so in the last-named countries, to more than 100 in Spain. The American TFP, headquartered in Bedford (Westchester County), New York, has some 100-200. Part-time members, friends, and collaborators bring the number to many thousands in Brazil, in every major city. TFP associates in the United States are said by Director of

Communications Stephan Schneider to number some 22,000, with TFP publications like the American TFP Newsletter going to some 45,000 Americans.

The founder, director, and spiritual leader of this intercontinental network is the 85-year-old Plinio Corrêa de Oliveira, son of a coffee plantation-owning family, born in São Paulo in 1908. Active as a youth in the Marian Congregations forming in Brazil in the 1920s, he was instrumental in founding University Catholic Action at Largo de S. Francisco Law School in São Paulo. He graduated from this institution in 1930.

In that same year, a military coup had brought into power a "provisional government" headed by Getúlio Vargas. For a couple of years Vargas staved off pressure to hold a Constitutional Assembly, but in 1932 a "legalistic," or "constitutional," revolt in São Paulo forced his hand. In preparation for the Assembly, Plinio helped organize a Catholic Electoral League under the auspices of São Paulo Archbishop Leopardo de Silva. As the League's candidate, Plinio, at the age of twenty-four, was elected to the constitutional convention in 1933. Due to the Catholic party's efforts, the new Brazilian constitution was to contain provisions for anti-divorce legislation, religious instruction in public schools, and voting rights for religious.

Plinio was defeated in a return bid for a seat in the legislature—apparently he had angered a powerful Catholic prelate—and the next year we find him teaching history at a branch college of the University of São Paulo. Later he was to teach at two other São Paulo institutions, which subsequently became part of the new Pontifical Catholic University in São Paulo.[1]

So far we can recognize a young man of profound Catholic devotion, intellectual capability, and organizing skill. In August 1933, he was made director of *Legionário*, the journal of the Marian Congregation of Santa Cecilia, and it was here that the nucleus of the TFP was formed. Writing for this magazine were Msgr. Antonio de Castro Mayer and Fr. Geraldo de Proenca Sigaud, two ecclesiastics who were to remain colleagues of Plinio and collaborators of the TFP for several decades. Both were finally to have a falling out with Plinio. These desertions, especially De Castro Mayer's, are significant in revealing the movement of the sect away from Catholicism and towards a demagogic anti-Church. This development will be discussed later in its proper place.

The *Legionário* soon became the semi-official organ of the Archdiocese of São Paulo. From the very beginning, its program was an unrelenting attack on Communism, on "revolutionary tendencies in centrist movements,"[2] and on the extreme Right. (It should be recalled that in the 1930s, essentially secular totalitarian movements of both the extreme Left and the extreme Right contended for power not only in Europe, but also in the Americas, and especially in Latin America.) But it is the phrase "revolutionary tendencies" that is the key to understanding the TFP. If the attack is, broadly speaking, against Right, Left, and Center, there is little room for concord with any force in the political spectrum: the effect is to isolate. Further, the determination of "tendencies" is a highly speculative undertaking and in practice will amount to a forceful personality deciding what he likes and what he dislikes and placing everything he dislikes into the camp of the enemy.

In the late 1930s Catholic Action made its appearance in Brazil. What was now known as the *Legionário* group opposed what it considered progressivist, egalitarian, and liberal tendencies in Catholic Action and in the early lobbyings for liturgical reform.

It attacked Jacques Maritain's alleged philosophical accommodation of leftist workers' movements in France (which had offshoots in Latin America). It attacked the whole "modernizing" program—a program that included eliminating Marian devotions, diminishing the distance between priest and laity, and downgrading the practices of private prayer and Communion outside of Mass. Behind the liturgical movement, the *Legionário* group (and many other Catholics, of course) discerned a denial of true Catholic spirituality, especially in the areas of "fleeing occasions of sin [and] fighting against one's disorderly passions."[3]

The opposition to leftist influence in Catholic Action, culminating in the publication of Plinio's *In Defense of Catholic Action* in 1943, caused a storm of protest. Plinio and the rest of the *Legionário* group were ostracized by most of the Brazilian Catholic world. (The subjugation of large masses of Catholics to political Left or Right is nothing new.) In 1945 Msgr. Castro Mayer was moved to a parish in Belém, a city near the mouth of the Amazon far to the north. In 1946 Fr. Sigaud was transferred to Spain. In 1947 what remained of the *Legionário* group, having lost its ecclesiastical support, withdrew from the newspaper and went, as it were, into exile. There were nine left in the group, and these nine went underground, praying together, studying together, and absorbing the ideas of their leader Prof. Plinio. It was in this three year period of exile that an ever-tightening bond of mind and soul was formed that eventually became the driving power behind the TFP. Here the group concentrated itself into a fervent devotion to Our Lady according to the prescriptions of St. Louis de Montfort, developed its rigid polemic against Communism, socialism, liberalism, and democracy, and attached itself to the messages of Fatima.[4]

Possibly also, in those dark days of abandonment and perceived persecution, the TFP developed a "Strategy of the Two Truths" : the truth as told to the irredeemable outside world (including the world of priests) and the truth as known only to initiates.

The way out of the darkness began with the "rehabilitation" of the two friendly ecclesiastics. In 1947 Pope Pius XII appointed Fr. Sigaud to the bishopric of Jacarzinho (a town some 200 miles west of São Paulo), and in 1948 Castro Mayer was made bishop of Campos, a city near Rio de Janeiro. The two priests, now bishops, were, so to speak, back in the neighborhood. In 1951 Castro Mayer established the magazine *Catolicismo* and virtually turned it over to the direction of Plinio and his group. According to TFP literature, the program of *Catolicismo* was "to alert the public and encourage them in the struggle against the factors of religious, moral, and cultural deterioration stemming from contemporary neopaganism. Above all, it promoted reaction against progressivism and 'Catholic leftism.'"[5] The old *Legionário* group was now the *Catolicismo* group, and it is in this organ that Plinio was to publish his ideas and critiques for many years. During the 1950s, *Catolicismo* grew in circulation and influence in the population corridor between São Paulo and Rio de Janeiro. Congresses and seminars were held, advancing the *Catolicismo* viewpoint. Eventually seminars were held on a regional basis, becoming the germ of today's TFP "SEFACS," or Specialized Education and Formation in Anti-Communism Seminars.

In 1960 Plinio instituted the Brazilian Society for the Defense of Tradition, Family, and Property. From the very first, a major focus of the TFP had been to oppose any and all land reform programs in Brazil. Its first action as an organized entity was to promulgate a pamphlet co-authored by Plinio, the economist Luiz Mendonca de Freitas, and Bishops Castro Mayer and Sigaud. The pamphlet was called *Agrarian Reform—A Question of Conscience*. It argued for the sacredness of the right of property as a law of God.[6] It was written in response to the Agrarian Revision Bill being considered by the state legislature of São Paulo in 1960—a precursor to a national land reform bill introduced in the next year by newly installed president João Goulart.

During the Second Vatican Council, Plinio circulated an essay entitled "The Freedom of the Church in a Communist State" among the fathers of the Council. In December 1963, the TFP collaborator Bishop Castro Mayer presented to the Vatican Secretary of State a petition signed by 213 of the Council Fathers condemning "Marxism, Socialism, and Communism in their philosophical, sociological, and economic aspects." In February 1964, Archbishop Sigaud—the other close ecclesiastical friend of the TFP—presented a petition to Pope Paul VI asking for the consecration of Russia and the world to the Immaculate Heart of Mary in accord with the instructions of Our Lady of Fatima. The pope heeded neither petition.

After the Council, Plinio's essay was enlarged and distributed throughout Brazil. It was during this campaign that TFP members first appeared on the streets with red banners emblazoned with a gold lion and the words "Tradition, Family, Property." The date was March 30, 1965. The characteristic red capes were added to the repertoire during a 1969 campaign denouncing charismatic groups.[7]

The "bible" of the TFP—read reverently and even memorized by initiates—is a book written by Plinio in 1959 called *Revolution and Counter-Revolution*. It sets out a thesis which, in a feeble way, has been followed out in public action by members of the organization. The thesis of the book is that the present state of rampant atheism, materialism, libertine behavior, and disrespect for the Church in its pure and traditional form has as its basic cause not only the theories of Marx and the devious practices of Communism, though Communism is and remains the prime example of the underlying evil. The real enemy, behind Communism, socialism, liberalism, and democracy, as well as behind the atheism and libertine perversity of Western culture, is the "Revolution."

The "Revolution" is that which "desires to destroy a whole legitimate order of things and to replace it with an illegitimate situation." It is thus a broader and deeper assault than any one or more of its symptoms. And what is the "order of things" that is being destroyed? It is Medieval Christendom.

"Now," Plinio explains, "that Christendom was not just any order, possible as many other orders would be possible. It was the realization, in the circumstances inherent to the times and the places, of the only true order among men, namely, Christian Civilization."[8]

The Revolution began with a loosening of morals, manners, and transcendental motivation and belief in Fifteenth Century Europe. This disintegration of Christian spirit in favor of self-regarding humanism was followed by the first external event of the Revolution, the Protestant Reformation (or, as Plinio calls it, the Pseudo-Reformation). Pride and sensuality were the two underlying ingredients of the Reformation. Pride took the form of a demand for individual or private interpretation of the scriptures and a rebellion against ecclesiastical authority. Sensuality took the form of the introduction of divorce in the lay community and a married clergy.

The second outstanding event of the deeper Revolution was known as the French Revolution, which, besides exhibiting a murderous anti-clericalism, added to the rebellion against the civil order. It was a revolt against monarchy and aristocracy, and in their place, an affirmation of egalitarian popular sovereignty. The third stage of the Revolution, Communism, grew out of the other two. And according to Plinio, behind all these historical events is a conspiracy.

> To produce a process that is so consistent and so continuous as that of the Revolution across such a huge and uncertain time span seems to us to be an impossibility without the action of successive generations of conspirators of an extraordinary intelligence and power.... The master sect, around which all the others are organized as simple auxiliary forces (sometimes consciously, and sometimes not), is Masonry.[9]

Later on in the TFP "bible," Plinio argues that many may be infected with the Revolution (now considered as a quasi-mystical force) without knowing it; that some may be partially Revolutionary and partially Counter-Revolutionary; that "semi-Counter-Revolutionaries" are actually fully in the Revolutionary camp. "Thus, as a consequence of the unity of the Revolution, the authentic counter-revolutionary can only be one who is totally such."[10]

At this point we encounter the profound error in the TFP thesis. Given all the philosophies, all the morals and mores of people, all the political and social and economic systems, all the "tendencies" and "veiled" aspects of life—in short, the whole landscape of humanity—who can possibly determine in all cases what is Revolutionary and what is Counter-Revolutionary?—especially when the Revolution itself is such a billowy, shadowland entity? The consequence of such a rigid, yet all-consuming, division of reality is to make anyone who disagrees with its author in any way, a member of the army of evil. In practice it results in an utter dependence on the authoritative discernment, and therefore the dictatorship over souls, of Plinio Corrêa de Oliveira, and no one else.

The manual goes on to define the characteristics of a good Counter-Revolutionary. He knows the Revolution and the Counter-Revolution thoroughly; he loves the Counter-Revolution and hates the Revolution; he "makes of this love and this hatred the axis around which all of his ideas, preferences, and activities revolve."[11] The TFP adept must not only know both sides of this great divide (presumably by consulting Prof. Plinio on every occasion), but he must love the one and hate the other with a passion that is all-consuming, to the extent of engendering all of his ideas in terms of this implacable enmity.

One can easily predict hatred swallowing up love in the TFP foot-soldier, for what he is to love has disappeared from the earth and remains a specter of Medieval glory. What is hated is the whole of the modern world. The objects of hatred are concrete, near-at-hand, and highly visible, while the objects of love are the province of a dream, realized, if at all, only in the little remnant army of truth making up the TFP. All the cults end up doing this. They divide the universe into themselves as the lodestar of all truth and the whole world outside the boundaries of the cult as the fundament of evil.

I think Jesus Christ had these things in mind when he encouraged us to love our enemies. God alone knows the depths of the human soul, and He knows how damaging to our souls is the thought, all too human, that there can be nothing good in what seems to compete with our viewpoints, our loyalties, or our tight little bonding arrangements.

Up to this point we can discern a Catholic lay organization of a strikingly nostalgic political persuasion, anti-democratic, and fiercely opposed to anything having "affinities" to Communism, within the Church or without. In particular it has poured out its wrath on Vatican II and the *Ostpolitik* of post-Vatican II foreign policy (seen wrongly as allowing the infection of Communism into the highest reaches of the Church). In Brazil it launched a major attack on the Christian Democratic Party and the Brazilian bishops who during the worst of the repressions under a succession of military dictators called for an amelioration of those repressions. Behind all the rational argument, the steady stream of declarations and pamphlets, the enmities and street demonstrations, the purportedly super-devotional Catholicism, some have found a single motivating force—that being the defense of privilege and the great plantations. Remember that Plinio comes from the aristocratic class of plantation owners. But it would be vastly inaccurate to reduce the whole movement to an economic motive. There is as well an overriding politico-mystical dimension, wrapped up in a fantasia of the "golden age" of medieval Christendom. (I wonder if, when God asked St. Francis to rebuild the Church, He considered the Church of the Thirteenth Century to be enjoying a golden age.) Is there something more here than the old-time religion and the old-time politics? Is there something (besides the TFP "bible") that would make us describe this organization as a dangerous religious cult hiding under the public veneer of traditional Catholicism?

The suspicion first comes to the fore when one notes that in 1970 Plinio began sending out caravans of young TFP personnel around Brazil, distributing his writings and other TFP materials. These soon became "permanent caravans." Now, "permanent caravans" means life on the road, always on the go, with no home besides a Volkswagen bus. These must have been superbly dedicated young men, especially when we learn from TFP literature itself that the "caravans" were funded not by the TFP, but depended on the charity of strangers in the countryside—"for room and board and other necessities."[12] There is a striking similarity between these caravans and the Mobile Fund-raising Teams of the Unification Church, who likewise have to fend for themselves and sleep catch as catch can on the jolting floor of a Dodge van. In the Moonie case the object is to sell flowers and raise money with as little overhead as possible by using an army of willing slaves; in the TFP case it was (in the 1970s at least) to sell books promoting the sacred right of private property and the Fatima "anti-Communist" message. Without pressing the comparison too far, we can say that in both cases day-to-day life was extraordinarily uncomfortable and endured only because of the uncommonly heroic devotion of these young people to their respective leaders. One informant tells me that he came across a TFP van in upstate New York; the young men inside had been sent on a book-selling tour without funds of their own for gas or food or lodging, and there they were, parked on the side of the road in the middle of the night, hungry and demoralized. He bought them dinner and gave them enough gas money to get back to the TFP "seat" in New Rochelle.

Perhaps the "SEFACS" are the TFP's version of Moonie training sessions. Fr. Kenneth Baker, S.J. (publisher of the *Homiletic and Pastoral Review*) gave me that impression when he talked about his run-in with the TFP several years ago. He talked of the TFP convincing parents to send their sons up to the Mt. Kisco, New York center, where they stayed up all night, drowning in a barrage of information. It sounds like something tougher and more sudden and more military than Boonville. A New Jersey parent who was involved with the TFP for a time told me about the changed personality, the changed accents, and the rote vocabulary of TFP initiates. The same thing happens to a Moonie when his personality fades away, and he turns into a cardboard ape of the god of the cult.

And then there were the defections and attacks. One of the two ever-faithful ecclesiastical friends of the TFP, Archbishop Sigaud, parted ways with Plinio in 1970, declaring that TFP members "have already done much for Brazil but now they are becoming harmful."[13] The other great friend, Bishop Castro Mayer, broke with the TFP in 1983 or 1984. This is the more serious desertion, since Castro Mayer had been a mentor to Plinio and a public promoter of the TFP cause from the early days of the *Legionário* group until just recently, a period of some fifty-five years. Imagine a prelate spending his whole ecclesiastical career befriending, defending, and promoting a movement and, after a lifetime's investment of intellect, heart, and soul, finally realizing he had been had.

The attacks came from within the Catholic Church and without. In 1970 the Cardinal Archbishop of Salvador, Eugenîo Sales, issued a public statement condemning the TFP and praising the TFP-maligned "red Archbishop" Helder Câmara.[14] (Câmara's great crime in TFP eyes was his friendliness towards land reform. Even the military dictatorship of the time decreed an "Instrumental Act" providing for the expropriation of large estates.)

One reason for Archbishop Sigaud's defection was his agreement with the "Instrumental Act"; another was his obedience to the *Novus Ordo Missae* promulgated by Rome in 1969. At the time of his formal disassociation from the TFP, he is quoted as saying, "because of a problem of conscience [I] could not fail to support the government, nor be against the Pope."[15] One must assume, then, that the TFP had gone on record as opposing the liturgical reform, as well as opposing the governmental decree.

In 1975 what the TFP calls a "media uproar" resulted in hundreds of articles accusing the TFP of "having Nazi-Fascist tendencies, of carrying on subversive monarchist activities, and luring and training youths for the practice of violence." A parliamentary Commission of Inquiry in the State of Rio Grande do Sul investigated the organization. The Commission's brief was to examine the "activities, purposes, financial support, [and] methods employed to recruit its active members and to perform its work." The charges against the TFP included "paramilitary regimentation of militant members, possession of arms and munitions, profession of neofascist ideology or methods, as well as disturbing the peace or the public order [and] transgressing the National Security Law." The Commission was unable or unwilling to substantiate the charges, and the inquiry was eventually dropped.[16]

Another case in the same year involved the TFP in "inducement to flight, reckless transfer, and concealment of minors." A police inquiry established that the minor in question had been given over to the TFP through a legal guardianship contract signed by his parents. This satisfied the authorities that no law had been violated. The boy meanwhile resided at the local TFP center, where he received "moral and intellectual formation."[17]

The attacks on the TFP came not only from the press or from socialists and Communists, but from the State itself, and this at a time when the TFP was slavishly promoting the licitness of the military regime. Acting on the logic of *Revolution and Counter-Revolution*, the TFP had managed to make enemies of nearly everyone.

In the case of the guardianship of the minor, we have certain evidence of at least one form of TFP recruitment. The TFP is interested in recruiting young men, preferably minors, so that they can be formed into "warrior monks" fervently loyal to the cause. And one way they do this is by securing guardianships of the minor sons of parents favorable to the TFP viewpoint.

It was in connection with another recruiting device, that of establishing schools for boys in order to initiate them into TFP doctrine, that the first major exposé of TFP inner workings came to light. L'ecole St. Benoit was established near Tours by the French branch of the TFP in 1977. Parents soon became upset at the changed attitudes of their sons. They found a secretiveness and glib dissimulation far beyond what could be considered normal. A prevailing pattern was the boys' increasing dislike and enmity towards parents. A meeting between concerned parents and school officials was finally held on March 24, 1979, where the parents first learned that their own children's odd behavior weren't special cases, but part of a general pattern existing throughout the school.

Sometime afterwards, a comprehensive document titled "Beware of False Prophets" was issued by an anonymous coalition of former TFP activists and associated priests. The exposé circulated among traditional Catholics in France and was distributed in Paris to embassies of countries having TFP chapters. But it made a special splash in Brazilian newspapers. In response, Plinio wrote a letter printed in *O Estado de S. Paulo* (August 22, 1979) protesting "the involvement of the venerable name of his dear mother in a media uproar against the TFP."

The French report notes that Dona Lucilia (Plinio's deceased mother) was so highly venerated within the cult that not only was her picture carried in processions, kissed, and her gravesite made into holy ground (people would touch rosaries and rose petals to her tombstone), but further, that TFP members were in the habit of improving on the Hail Mary in the following manner:

> Hail Dona Lucilia, full of grace, the Lord is with thee.
>
> Blessed art thou among women, and blessed is the fruit of thy womb, Plinio.
>
> Holy Dona Lucilia, mother of Plinio, Pray for us sinners now and at the hour of our death.

The blasphemous prayer suggests a rather exalted status for this Mother of this Son. I am Catholic, and as I read this mockery of a nearest and dearest petition to the Virgin Mary, I am ashamed for these cult-Catholics who think this is not the foulest sort of poison to throw into the face of God.

Earlier we spoke of a "strategy of the two truths." To understand the TFP, we need to see it as having a well-engineered, but deceptive, public persona and a secret "higher truth" operating within. The public persona is politically and economically conservative, which allows it to infiltrate New Right lobbies like the Free Congress Foundation in Washington, D.C., and ally itself with traditional European right-wing movements like the French *Lecture et Tradition* and the Italian *Alleanza Cattolica*.[18] The TFP naturally keeps its inner face hidden from such superficially likeminded groups. As to religion, the persona is fervently Catholic, loyal to pope and magisterium, but understandably dismayed at the theological modernism, leftist politics, and liturgical desacralization that have played havoc with large parts of the post-Conciliar Church.

The secret inner doctrine, as revealed by the French exposé and corroborating sources, is another story altogether. The initiate is led step-by-step, ever so subtly, into the esoteric truth. Recruits are preferably teenage or pre-teen boys. (Women need not apply.) The younger the better, for the young can be educated more easily into something romantic and self-exalting. The training in many TFP centers includes karate, judo, and other Asiatic commando skills. Soon they learn that the whole adult world, with few exceptions, is corrupted by the Revolution. They learn that their own mothers and fathers are "FMRs," or "Fountains of My Revolution." The boys themselves are thus infected with the Revolution to some greater or lesser extent, a corruption infused by their parents. But Dr. Plinio will save them. Dr. Plinio can discern, with merely a glance, or by looking at a photograph, if a person has "TAU," and thus is fit material for the Counter-Revolution. Learning he has the quality of TAU exalts a boy in his own mind and at the same time drives a wedge between him and his parents and between him and the whole outside world. He has a new family now, and a new "father," and in this family he has a very serious part to play. His apostolate is greater than that of a priest (the time for priests is over), for he will help bring in the Reign of Mary, and in that Kingdom he will be a prince. But none of this may be learned by anyone on the outside. He is sworn to secrecy, and he must learn to dissemble—thus the dissimulation, the lying, the secretiveness and the increasing dislike and belittling of parents noted with such pain by fathers and mothers in France and in the United States.

To be told by One Who Knows that you have the mark of salvation on your soul, that you will be mystically preserved in the chaos to come, and that in the Millennium you will be a knight-errant in the army of Mary the Mother of God—all this is pretty heady stuff!

The devotion surrounding Plinio has all the trappings of a personality cult. He is called Elias by his followers. A hat he left behind at the TFP "seat" in Mt. Kisco was placed on a bed and touched and venerated as if it were the relic of a saint. His every word is tape-recorded and sent daily to TFP centers around the world, there to be pondered by thousands of reverent disciples. Photographs of prospective members are sent to Plinio in Brazil for him to judge and discern what they reveal of the postulants' inner characters: this one is of no account; that one has homosexual tendencies; this one is infected with the Revolution; this other one has a superior vocation.

And this Chosen Hero shall lead the remnant through the massive chaos of the Bagarre (Armageddon) into the New Jerusalem.

This is the secret truth of the great prophet Plinio Corrêa de Oliveira. And the mother of the prophet is accorded the exalted veneration of *hyperdulia*. Here is a condensed form of her litany:

Dona Lucilia, pray for us.

Mother of Dr. Plinio, pray for us.

Mother of our Father, pray for us.

Mother of the Ineffable, pray for us.

Mother of all Eternity, pray for us.

Mother of the Axiological Principle, pray for us.

Mother of the Temperament of Synthesis, pray for us.

Mother of all purity, pray for us.

Mother of the Trans-Sphere, pray for us.

Mother of the Counter-Revolution, pray for us.

Fountain of Light, pray for us.

Consoler of Dr. Plinio, pray for us.

Mediatrix of the Great Turn-around, pray for us.

Mediatrix of all our graces, pray for us.

Dawn of the Reign of Mary, pray for us.

Dona Lucilia of the Smile, pray for us.

Dona Lucilia of the Flashes, pray for us.

Our help in the Bagarre, pray for us.

Cause of our preservation, pray for us.

Vessel of logic, pray for us.

Vessel of Metaphysics, pray for us.

Martyr of isolation, pray for us.

Queen of serene suffering, pray for us.

Dona Lucilia, our Lady and Mother, help us.

Pray for us, O Mother of the Doctor of the Church, that we may be made worthy of the promises of Dr. Plinio.

The document from which this litany was transcribed was sent to Bishop Antonio de Castro Mayer by a concerned Catholic on October 26, 1983. The inquiry included several questions:

(1) Are these prayers lawful or are they opposed to the true code of canon law?

(2) Are they in accord with the doctrine of the Church?

(3) Are these titles to be attributed exclusively to Our Lady or to any other person?

(4) Is this litany in accord with the practice and with the spirit of the Church?

Bishop Castro Mayer responds that "he never knew about [the litany's] existence. It attains to blasphemy." He continues, "Many of the different invocations involve great and grave errors against the faith, for example, calling Dona Lucilia the Fountain of Light (the Light which can only be Our Lord Jesus Christ), Mediatrix of all our graces, and others like it. The same can be said for the prerogatives attributed to the correlation of these invocations, like 'Ineffable' (only God is ineffable), Doctor of the Church (as if he were the 'only' Doctor of the Church, etc.)."

The bishop then answers the particular questions of the inquirer: (1) The litany is not licit, and is contrary to the correct code of canon law; (2) No; (3) No; (4) No.

The document ends with the signature "Antonio de Castro Mayer, Bishop" and the words "Campos, November 4, 1983, St. Charles Borromeo, Doctor of the Church." If the bishop had not before this time parted ways with Plinio, surely he did so after seeing the "litany" which he claims never to have seen before.

Let me add my outrage to that of the bishop. The crime in this sort of thing is that it closely echoes familiar Catholic litanies, except that Dr. Plinio and his mother are substituted for Jesus Christ and His mother. The message is driven all the more profoundly into the souls of devotees who chant it day after day and night after night, the copy-cat form recalling the prayers of their childhood on a subliminal level. "Pray for us, O Holy Mother of God, that we may be made worthy of the promises of Christ." This is right at the heart of orthodox Catholic devotion. To see it bowdlerized and junked up with eerie phrases from the books of Plinio is to recognize a substitute faith that mocks the Catholic Faith in its most intimate places. By ever-repeated innuendo, the prayer replaces Jesus Christ and the Virgin Mary with Dr. Plinio and his mother.

And what is the secret doctrine of this substitute church? The times are nearing the great Bagarre. The third secret of Fatima has been discerned: Satan has conquered the highest reaches of the Catholic Church. Church, priest, and pope are no longer relevant—"there will be no more guidance from a priest." Traditional Catholics and schismatic Lefebvrites[19] are mocked as mere "Trads." Priests are ridiculed behind their own backs. The Church has become a "Hollow Shell"—in fact, this is the TFP code name for the Catholic Church.

The Mass is no longer of any force or relevance—whether that Mass is *Novus Ordo*, Tridentine, or Byzantine. Confessions are faked—"tell the priest anything" was the instruction received by a former member. Only the sacrament of Communion remains valid, and so one notes the strange spectacle of TFPers standing outside a church for the bulk of the Mass, entering only to receive Communion, then leaving. (TFPers in Westchester County attended a Byzantine Rite Catholic church until the parish priest had had enough of their rude shenanigans and kicked them out of the congregation.)

This being the time of the Prophet, there is no priestly formation of TFP members. There is no catechism, except the catechism of Plinio. Priestly orders are not relevant; they are a fraud. In the time of the Bagarre, say TFP militants, they will assassinate "apostate" (i.e., non-TFP) priests and bishops. Since the TFP is the unique and only apostolate in the end times, its *modus operandi* is to infiltrate and destroy all other Catholic or secular right-wing movements because all so-called right-wing movements are, in fact, doing the left a service, in the same way that the Nazis brought about the advance of Communism by the reaction they provoked.[20]

(This is a wondrous logic. For it means that all opposition is counter-productive, and in particular this consequence can be applied to the TFP itself, in its fight against Communism. But the TFP, one must presume, is the exception to the rule.)

The Bagarre is just around the corner. The weather is watched closely for signs of the end. Portents are read into every political event. When the time comes, the soldiers of the TFP will lead the forces of good against the forces of evil. The good people of the world will fall in line behind the glorious red and gold banners of the TFP. When the chaos is ended, TFP cohorts will be the aristocrats of the new order, and Mary the Mother of God shall reign in person on this earth. The new order shall be a resurrected Medieval Christendom, with tournaments and feasts and a population of happy peasants full of mutton and ale. And the knights of the TFP shall be ever on the alert to strike down any remnant of evil.

Now let us return to reality. The TFP is a typical, if highly secretive, millennial movement. For all its mystical trappings—"Mother of the Trans-sphere"—it is essentially worldly in orientation. There is no "new heaven and new earth" in its view of the *eschaton*, and it is curiously lacking in any mention of Jesus Christ. The usual form for millennial doctrine to take is the familiar thousand-year reign of Christ on the earth. Who is to take the place of Christ? Will it be Plinio himself, or one who follows, with "Elias" his harbinger? A new "Marian pope" is predicted, and perhaps already found in the person of Gregory XVII (Dominguez Clemente), whose "Holy See" is a commune called Palmar de Troya near Seville in Spain.[21]

Where is the Second Coming of Christ in the TFP's apocalyptic vision? A social psychologist would find it quite understandable that there appears to be no male competition for Plinio in this scenario of the end times. The psychologist would see an inordinate love, even worship, of the mother and a corresponding hatred and belittlement of the father as being fertile ground for celibate and dictatorial egomania. He would expect a vivid persecution complex and a degree of paranoid self-exaltation. Plinio has no wife; he has "twice the spirit of Elias"; he is said to be a spiritual reincarnation of Charlemagne; his personal guardian angel is none other than St. Michael the Archangel.

It seems clear that the TFP apostle's engendered belittlement of his natural father—"Fountain of My Revolution"—is part and parcel of Plinio's demand for the destruction of any and all male competition and a corresponding demand that any and all authority needs be directed towards himself—likewise the ridicule and belittlement of priests, likewise the recruitment of pubescent boys to be molded and formed into subservient and celibate clones of the Prophet, likewise the alienation of adult men from their wives and the consequent destruction of families.

French children at L'ecole de St. Benoit were dissuaded from critical reflection. They were told that they had drunk Cartesian rationalism with their mothers' milk. They thought too much. Thinking, they were told, is demonic. Only a person irredeemably infested with the Revolution would dare question the brilliant and serene analyses of the Prophet.

A former friend of the TFP in New York State tells me that, though there is no Catholic catechetical teaching, there is a constant barrage of the tape-recorded words of Plinio, delivered on a daily basis from headquarters in São Paulo. And there is prayer—to Mary, in the form of the rosary. But the rosary is said so fast and with so little evident piety, he describes it as a "machine-gun rosary." This is also the TFP's own characterization—a barrage of Marian bullets aimed at the heart of the devil.

The demonization of reflective thinking and the practice of super-fast chanting are marks of the Moonies, the Summit Lighthouse, the Hare Krishnas, and the Fatima Crusaders. In the Way Ministry it is a constant stream of interior nonsense-talk construed as the language of the angels. In each case the reasoning power is clouded over by a light trance, resulting in subliminal and uncritical acceptance of the cult-master's words and a slow destruction of the independent will.

Plinio himself describes the process in, strangely enough, his indictment of the fourth stage of the Revolution. The fourth stage is found in the Structuralist theories of Claude Levi-Strauss:

> Structuralism sees in tribal life an illusory synthesis of the height of individual liberty and consented-to collectivism. In this situation, collectivism will end by devouring liberty. In a collectivism of this nature, the various "I's" or the individual persons, with their ways of thinking, their wills, and their ways of being, which are both characteristic and conflicting, intermingle and are dissolved—according to the structuralists—in the collective personality of the tribe. This tribal personality generates one thought, one will, and one style of being intensely common to all.
>
> Of course, the road to this state of things must pass through the extinction of the old criteria of individual reflection, volition, and sensibility. These will gradually be replaced by forms of sensibility, thought, and deliberation that are more and more collective.

Plinio applies this analysis to the modern charismatic movement, which the TFP abhors. But with more justice it can be applied to Plinio's own bizarre cult. There is more:

> In tribes, the cohesion among the members is assured mainly by a way of feeling common to all, from which flows common habits and a common will. Individual reason is limited in them to almost nothing. In other words, it is restricted to the first and most elementary movements that this atrophied state permits. This is a level of thinking that has been called "savage thought." This is thought that does not think, that is tuned only to what is concrete. Such is the price of collectivistic tribal fusion. It belongs to the witch doctor to maintain this collective psychic life. He does this by means of totemic cults that are charged with messages which are confused, but nevertheless rich, with phosphorescent fires or even with the flashes coming from the mysterious world of trans-psychology or parapsychology. The acquisition of these

"riches" will be the compensation that man will receive for the atrophy of reason.[22]

Phosphorescent fires? Flashes from the mysterious world of trans-psychology? These are the very phrases sprinkled through Plinio's descriptions of his own alleged mystical powers. Can he be so insightful about cults and the cult mentality and yet so blind to the fact that he is describing himself and his own totemic cult?

The mystagogue Plinio, wizard discerner of souls, son of the trans-sphere, is called by his followers "X-Ray." Listen to them now, fused into a common sensibility and a common will, atrophied in reason, chanting in the dark reaches of the night—

"DONA LUCILIA OF THE FLASHES, PRAY FOR US!"

NOTES

1. Short Biographies of Plinio Corrêa de Oliveira appear in *Tradition, Family, Property: Half a Century of Epic Anticommunism* (Mt. Kisco, New York: Foundation for a Christian Civilization, 1981.), 363 ff., and in Plinio's *Revolution and Counter-Revolution* (New Rochelle, New York: Foundation for a Christian Civilization, 1980.), 174 ff. The former book also contains a detailed history of the TFP, all, of course, from a self-glorifying TFP viewpoint.
2. *Tradition, Family, Property* (hereinafter designated *TFP*), 372.
3. *TFP*, 375.
4. *TFP*, 382-6.
5. *TFP*, 397.
6. *TFP*, 22.
7. *TFP*, 86 ff., 143.
8. *Revolution and Counter-Revolution*, 56.
9. *Revolution and Counter-Revolution*, 53-4.
10. *Revolution and Counter-Revolution*, 75.
11. *Revolution and Counter-Revolution*, 94.
12. *TFP*, 199.
13. *TFP*, 166.
14. *TFP*, 164.
15. *TFP*, 167.
16. *TFP*, 210 ff.
17. *TFP*, 214.
18. *TFP*, 307 and 325.
19. A chapter will be devoted to the followers of Archbishop Marcel Lefebvre.
20. From the French exposé "Beware of False Prophets."
21. Dominguez visited São Paolo, Brazil, and other Latin-American countries and entered into an alliance with certain "traditional Catholics." It has not been established that this means the TFP, though everything points in that direction.

Chapter Ten

The Seer of San Vittorino

Padre Pio, world-renowned stigmatist and mystic, died on September 23, 1968. Six months later, during Holy Week of 1969, another Italian religious reportedly received the stigmata. This was Br. Gino Burresi, a 37-year-old monk of the Oblates of the Virgin Mary. As Br. Gino's fame grew internationally, many devout Catholics assumed a kind of transfer of holiness had taken place. God had drawn Pio to His bosom, but had given us a replacement who would be a light and a symbol of sanctity, an exemplar to draw at least some of the world to holiness and keep the forces of darkness at bay. Who is this miracle-worker, this reputed spiritual beacon shining on the last decades of the 20th century?

Fr. Robert Fox's biography of Gino, *Call of Heaven*, reveals a childhood very early drawn to the religious life. Gino himself describes a day when he was struck by the supernatural. He was five years old. He had entered a small countryside chapel. "I began praying, but shortly after, I heard crying. I turned around, and there on the chair in the corner was a beautiful lady. She was crying and had a baby in her arms. The baby boy constantly looked at his mother and shared in her grief. 'Why are you crying? Has someone died?' I asked. She answered: 'Because men blaspheme me.' I asked, 'What must I do?' She responded: 'Give me your heart, sacrifices, and prayers.' Our Lady instructed me in the message of Fatima from my earliest years."

At age 14, the young mystic became an aspirant in the Oblates of the Virgin Mary at Pisa. The year was 1946. Troubles concerning vocation followed and bedeviled the young man for years. By turns he was attracted to the Franciscans, the Capuchins, and other orders. Trouble also came in the form of a girl from his village who wanted to marry him. Indecisions and temptations finally resolved, in 1956 Gino became a fully professed monk of the Oblate order. Humble, pious, submissive, he filled his days as a catechist and janitor, mother hen to seminarians, and helper of the poor. A reputation for holiness followed him to St. Helena's Church in Rome. The pious and the curious visited in increasing numbers. They would see the young brother (so self-effacing that he had rejected the priesthood) kneeling before a statue of Our Lady of Fatima, deep in prayer. Imbued with the message of Fatima, Br. Gino received permission to form an offshoot of the Oblates called the "Pious Congregation of Our Lady of Fatima." The Congregation spread Marian devotion and the Fatima message throughout Italy, France, Belgium, and Germany. In 1964 the Congregation moved its headquarters to San Vittorino, a few miles north of Rome.

Br. Gino seemed like a godsend to the Oblates of the Virgin Mary. The Institution had been founded by the venerable Fr. Pio Bruno Lanteri in 1816. From its beginnings the Oblates attacked the heresies and errors of the day, defended the Holy See against its enemies, and devoted itself to the honor of the Blessed Virgin Mary. By the late 1960s it had fallen on hard times. As large parts of the Church entered a period of experiment with liturgy and theology after the Second Vatican Council, aspirants to a traditional, devotional, "outdated" religious order were few and far between—until a reputed miracle-worker came along and drew the spiritually thirsty like a magnet. By the early 1980s, Gino had in a sense taken over the whole order, as a hero of holiness, as a fountain of spiritual authority, as a renowned stigmatist and mystic.

The beginnings of San Vittorino were rocky. Gino built a little shrine there in 1961, then a "crypt chapel" in 1964. A college seminary was built in the 1960s, but it remained empty until eight English speaking students arrived in 1971. Plans had been approved for a Sanctuary of Our Lady of Fatima in 1970, but the church took some time in the building, and it was not consecrated until 1979. In 1972 fifty-two postulants for the seminary arrived from the United States, Canada, Ireland, and England. In 1973 fourteen more came, all foreigners.

Apparently Gino's reputation grew internationally, but less so in Italy, during those early years. There was a large turnover of seminarians, for unknown reasons. Many left after a short stay, and many more came to fill their places. The first Italians joined in 1974. In 1976 there were eight Italians among twenty-six postulants. In 1978 thirty-one came from the United States and thirteen from Italy. A Fr.

Joseph Breault (O.V.M.) spent a good deal of time in the United States, recruiting, and back at San Vittorino, smoothing out the troubles of the American students.

On May 13, 1978, Gino established a convent at San Vittorino, named the Oblate Sisters of the Virgin Mary of Fatima. The sisters' program was to include a pious devotion to the Blessed Mother, aid to the poor, an apostolate of "good" publications, and furtherance of the work of the priests.

The biography of Gino abounds with the supernatural. Pilgrims to San Vittorino often smelled the odor of sanctity in the presence of the mystic. The odor would come and go and return to the pilgrim sometimes after he departed from the august presence. Gino painted pictures supernaturally, or at least very swiftly. He would disappear overnight and return with a completed, oil-painted holy picture, often portraying the Virgin or the Virgin and Child. Gino blessed the sick, and they were healed. Like Padre Pio before him, Gino bilocates, appearing at the bedsides of the dying, bestowing spiritual comfort. He is six feet tall, an imposing presence among his fellow Italians. His dark eyes pierce the soul. He peers into the minds of penitents; he knows their secret sins.

Every December 8 and May 13 he is visited by the Blessed Virgin Mary. On these occasions the Virgin blesses holy objects that have been left with Gino and showers them with the odor of sanctity.

Every year during Holy Week, the mystic endures a death and resurrection. His sufferings intensify on Holy Thursday. He groans and rolls around in agony. His undershirt must be changed many times as it becomes soaked with sweat. But the sweat does not smell like sweat; it exudes the odor of sanctity. On Good Friday, the wounds of the stigmata become unbearable. Gino gasps for air. Doctors are always present during these last few hours of the crisis, ready with an injection to revive the heart. For the heart of Gino stops beating. And then it begins to beat again. Gino slowly revives, but he is profoundly shaken. He is too weak to stand or walk until many hours have passed.

Stories are circulated of stranger events, if not so profound. Vinegar has turned to wine under the ministrations of Gino. Doves alight on his shoulders. Fish in ponds allow themselves to be petted. Rosaries multiply. Gas for cars appears like magic. In 1983 Brother Gino became Padre Gino. Perhaps by now he had overcome his doubts about his worthiness for the priesthood. Perhaps it seemed silly for a miracle-worker with a swelling international reputation, an oblate religious with the mantle (perhaps) of Padre Pio, to go on refusing the charism to say Masses and hear confessions, especially since he was widely acclaimed to be graced with the knowledge of the hidden thoughts and sins of those who came into his presence.

The Oblate Sisters drew many postulants, a large percentage from the United States. Gino's fame grew apace; millions of dollars poured into San Vittorino; international tours went to Lourdes, to Fatima, and then on to the place of the living saint.

And then the bubble burst. The date is June 1988. Three young seminarians submitted sworn affidavits claiming that they had been seduced into homosexual activity by Padre Gino. Vatican authorities immediately stepped in and removed Gino from San Vittorino, first to Austria and then to a parish in Tuscany, where he was placed under a kind of house arrest. He was forbidden to return to San Vittorino. Soon afterward four more seminarians claimed homosexual involvement with Gino. A long-time follower, Oblate Father Kevin Walsh, resigned from his position as Secretary General of the Oblates and was appointed to head up an investigation of Gino's alleged misdeeds.

Fr. Walsh took his investigation to the United States, Canada, and Mexico, where he talked to former seminarians. That summer he found three more cases of homosexual involvement with Gino, dating back to 1972, 1974, and 1975. It had all been kept under wraps, but we may well imagine that this behavior wrought a crisis of faith in the seminarians and was no small part of their decisions to quit the Order.

In August 1988, Fr. Walsh returned to Italy and interviewed a professed Oblate monk concerning the cases of homosexual involvement Walsh had found in America. The monk told him "Oh yes, it happened to me as well, in 1984 and 1986." The monk had informed his superiors, but nothing came of it.

Fr. Walsh's investigation was for him an agonizing duty, for he had been a devotee of Gino for over ten years. As Secretary General of the Oblates, he was housed in Rome, but San Vittorino was just up the road, and Fr. Walsh kept in close contact. Slowly, very slowly, devotion turned to disillusionment. One thinks of Fr. Walsh as an innocent soul, sensitive but observant. And what he observed finally wrought a crisis of faith.

Two incidents illustrate the way Gino's purported "second sight" was stage-managed for the benefit of the faithful at San Vittorino. An Eastern Rite Catholic Bishop from Columbus, Ohio, arrived on the scene, dressed in civilian clothes. At a gathering Gino picked him out of the crowd and asked "the bishop" to come forward. The bishop was of course flabbergasted that his disguise had been uncovered by the seer. But Fr. Walsh had previously identified the bishop to Gino.

More typical were the many occasions when Gino seemed to have telepathic knowledge of the hidden sins of seminarians. One young man had come to Gino to confess a shameful problem, but, before he could begin, Gino told him the nature, and even the details, of the problem. The young man was astounded, perhaps mortified, but surely impressed to the depths of his soul. Fr. Walsh was privy to the situation. It turns out the seminarian had previously described his problem to another youth and sworn him to secrecy. But the youth, a false friend, or perhaps a designated secret informant, had gone right to Gino and told him the whole story. So of course the "seer" had the information in mind when the first seminarian came to him. This particular incident among the seminarians is described by Fr. Walsh as one of many deceptive events he encountered that lead him to a deepening skepticism.

The extent of this system of informants, creating a magical atmosphere filled with a multitude of fictitious miracles, is unknown. That the tattle-tale system was pervasive in the seminary is suggested by the hot-house atmosphere in the convent next door, where nothing at all could be kept secret. Everything told openly or in secrecy among the sisters found its way immediately to the superiors.

The odor of sanctity is another supernatural sign that does not bear close scrutiny. When Gino was forcibly removed from San Vittorino—he did not go peacefully—his room was found to contain a collection of perfumes. What did Fr. Walsh find out? Once, visiting the area, he dropped in on a friend of Gino's in the adjoining village. He spotted a vial of Essence of Roses, smelled it, and told this friend that it smelled just like Gino's odor of sanctity. The man said, "Yes—Padre Gino mixes it with his pipe tobacco."

On one December 8, Fr. Walsh and some other penitents brought a number of religious statues, medals, and rosaries which the Virgin Mary would bless when she visited Gino in the night. The next day the objects were returned, as Fr. Walsh puts it, "reeking with the odor of sanctity." The objects were greasy to the touch, and the paint on one brand new statue was peeling off. To Fr. Walsh it seemed less a miracle than a crass drenching in sweet-smelling oils that had occurred in the small hours of the night.

But why did people smell the mystic odor often after they departed from Gino?—even many miles distant? There are two speculations to make. One is the suggestive power of faith. The other is that oils can be transferred to clothes, give off an odor for a time, the odor finally wearing off, then returning if the wind catches the clothes just right, or even when the body's position changes. Odors can come and go in any localized space—such as a car or a train compartment—depending on air currents.

If Gino's mental telepathy is a fraud, if his odor of sanctity is in reality the odor of attar of roses, what of the famed stigmata, penultimate sign of the favor of God?

When I first heard of Br. Gino back in 1983, one thing I learned struck me as significant: Gino's stigmata was not in the palms, but in the wrists. There have been at least 300 verified stigmatics in the history of the Church, but all of them had the wounds in the palms. Why the discrepancy? In my imaginings of supernal events, visions, stigmata, voices, messages from the angels, I had always thought the message, the vision, the voice, even the way the stigmata appeared, was sifted through the subjective belief of the mystic, or rather through the mystical river generated by the common belief of the ages. Traditional portraits of Christ always had the wounds piercing his palms; pious mysticism thought that this was the case, and so, if it was literally untrue, it was true enough.

I thought it was literally untrue because in recent years scientists have determined that a crucified body cannot be supported on the cross by driving the nails through the palms. The flesh would tear under the weight of the body. But if the nails are driven just behind the bone in the wrist, the wrist bone will keep the nail from sliding, and the tortured body will remain attached to the cross. Therefore (the scientists said) Roman crucifixions must have involved the practice of driving the nails through the wrists. I had heard this line of reasoning, and it made sense to me, and Gino must have heard it too: his stigmata would conform to the new scientific knowledge and, therefore, be exempt from debunking scientists. One could suppose it was God answering the critics. That's how I took it, until I learned something else.

It turns out the scientists had spoken too soon. More recent research into Roman antiquities has discovered another method of crucifixion. The nails were indeed driven through the palms, but then a rope was wrapped around the wrists and tied to the crossbeams. In this way the arms were firmly attached to the cross. This procedure may not have been universal, but it was common enough in the Roman Empire in the first century. The Shroud of Turin displays a trickle of blood from the palms to the wrists, where it is clotted, with a line of blood then changing direction and running across the wrists. The pattern is consistent with the crucifixion procedure recently discovered. Several Catholic mystics have received detailed visions of the crucifixion. They are in agreement on the procedure: nailed through the palms, tied around the wrists. All of which suggests that the 300 or more genuine stigmatics were right and Gino was wrong.

Part of Fr. Walsh's decline in belief in the Stigmatist of San Vittorino had to do with what he saw of the blessed wounds. He notes that Gino always wore mittens to cover the wounds in his hands. He notes that Gino has birthmarks in various places on his body, the brown patches suggesting dried blood. On the rare occasions when he was shown the wounds, he noted that from one year to the next they changed location. Nowadays Gino is forbidden to wear mittens, and, low and behold, the stigmata have stopped appearing.

Much is made in the Gino legend about a visit by Mother Teresa of Calcutta in 1975. After she left, Gino let it be known that she had returned to visit him privately via bilocation. This knowledge naturally spread through the seminary and convent like wildfire, causing, of course, a deeper adoration of the God-favored Padre. Fr. Walsh's 1988 investigation took him to an interview with Mother Teresa, during which he asked her about the supposed bilocation. Her response: "Gino has a big imagination." She scoffed at the notion of her reported bilocation abilities. As for Gino's own bilocation abilities, we have only his own word for it.

Fr. Walsh's comment on the religious paintings: no one has ever seen Gino in the act of painting, or seen any painting supplies. (The rumor among the nuns was that the paintings were supernaturally produced.) The two I saw reproduced in Fr. Fox's *Call of Heaven* seem the work of an amateur. The proportions are not quite right (in one the hands of the Virgin are too big), and the portraiture is slick and artless.

As to the alleged death and resurrection on Good Friday, it was never attended by more than a (friendly) doctor and perhaps a specially favored seminarian.

On a more mundane level, Gino's money management was highly unorthodox. Fr. Walsh personally knew of $100,000 he received and turned over to Gino. The money was never accounted for and none of it was used for the expenses of the Order. Is it in a Swiss bank account?—along with a lot more money never accounted for? The Vatican court investigating Gino after his removal from San Vittorino looked into millions of dollars of misappropriated funds. An awful lot of money poured into San Vittorino and was never seen again.

Fr. Walsh's final report to the investigating commission included the testimony of a number of ex-nuns. The convent seems to have been the arena for a nightmare of mind-control. It was dominated by huge, life-sized pictures of Padre Gino. Sisters were fed on a diet of Gino sayings and Gino slogans. Gino talks were taped and constantly played and replayed. An hour in the morning and three hours in the afternoon were set aside for talks on the "spirit of the order"—meaning essentially the spirit of Padre Gino and his exalted role in the economy of salvation. Padre Gino was explicitly referred to as "The prophet sent by God in the Present Age." The story was filled out for the benefit of the nuns: during Old Testament times there was a string of prophets from Moses to John the Baptist. In New Testament times a lineage of saints took over the prophetic role. They spoke for God. In this age that role had been given to Padre Gino.

It is curious to see so many exalted spiritual personages in these feverish times each insisting he is the one and only prophet chosen by God for this age. Mr. Plinio of the Brazilian-based Tradition, Family, Property is one such. Another is the Hindu Meher Baba. A third is the Rev. Sun Myung Moon.

Independent actions or thoughts were forbidden to the nuns. "Don't think! The Devil can use it" was a constant litany. In the formation community, control over even the most minor activities was total. If a sister wanted to borrow a pencil from another nun, she first had to go to Mother Master for permission. That permission granted, she could then ask for the pencil. The second sister must then go to the Mother Master for permission to lend the pencil. Permission granted, she could lend the pencil to the first sister.

Everything done, even a trip to the bathroom, was known by superiors. Permission to go to the bathroom was sometimes denied for disciplinary reasons. To put a brake on possibly rebellious thoughts, the rosary was to be recited silently over and over. No thoughts or feelings could be kept private. A mind that held anything back was a disobedient mind.

When no time is spent alone, when no privacy is allowed, when everything in the mind and heart is a matter for public knowledge and public manipulation, then the individual has been robbed of something essential to her humanity—the ability to say no, even inwardly. The resulting personality is a puppet on a string.

In the scene at San Vittorino—especially in the convent, but the same kind of thing probably took place in the seminary—we are seeing a classic case of a self-advertised holy man in absolute tyranny over his devoted followers. It is all astoundingly similar from one malignant cult to another, whether the malignancy happens within a Catholic context or not. Everywhere one finds the same methods of psychological control, the same outrageous claims ("The Prophet for This Age," "The One True Light"), the same prohibitions against thought, the same destruction of personality, the same dreary punishments. The Spokane, Washington-based Fatima Crusaders displayed the same malice posing as spiritual discipline. There also, an obedience impossible to perform was demanded. There also, people were encouraged to say the rosary ad nauseam to stop the doubts intruding on the mind. There also, thinking was denounced as a trick of the Devil. People who had been deprogrammed or had somehow extricated themselves from the Moonies, from the Way Ministry, from the Fatima Crusaders, were so ego-shattered they could not make a decision on any matter, no matter how trivial. They would sit in a restaurant staring at the menu for an hour, unable to decide between a hamburger and a grilled cheese sandwich. Relatives and friends of Moonies home on rare visits would note a characteristic vacancy about the eyes, rote speech, flat emotions, and robotic deportment. People who have come out of San Vittorino betray the same symptoms. A nun home on a visit in my own parish—a true-blue Gino believer—was described as "zombie-like."

If a Moonie thinks about leaving the cult, he is told he has been infected by Satan. If he actually leaves, his possession is total. The same horrific consequences lie in wait for a daughter of the Oblates who wants to leave the order. It is a prescription for fear and guilt so profound that long term spiritual counseling is often required. If there is one incontrovertible mark of a totalitarian religious cult it is this perfect malice hurled at deserters.

How was zombie-like behavior inculcated in the Oblate Sisters of the Virgin Mary? When the situation warranted it (such as when a sister was thinking of leaving the community), liquid valium was poured in drinks to calm the excitable and the guilt-ridden. And guilt was epidemic in the convent: it was constantly reinforced and never alleviated. Touching was prohibited, to kill natural affection and make sure emotional dependence was directed only towards superiors. Self-esteem was replaced by self-abasement. Initiative was stopped cold. Adults were reduced to children: Mommy, can I go potty? Mental life of any kind was hollowed out and filled with Gino, Gino, Gino, "The One True Light."

Not God, but Gino, was "The One True Light." The divinizing phrase stands front and center in the hymn sung in choir while the Sisters bow their heads to those gigantic pictures of Gino dominating the convent.

No one, of course, could interrupt the Mother General in conversation. One incident in Fr. Walsh's dossier: a sister stood by quietly while Mother General talked on with another nun. Finally the conversation was ended, and the sister could tell Mother General about the fire raging outside the window. (Mother General called the fire department.) This is an extreme case, but it suggests the flavor of a community terrified into "perfect obedience" to the extent of forgetting reality.

There is something else to relate about Padre Gino's dealings with the women Oblates. Several ex-nuns allege sexual misbehavior, presumably seductions. Here we can only surmise that the nuns involved had been so brainwashed as to think they were operating in a higher heaven, exempted from the moral law. It's not hard to believe, once you learn how common such things have been in enthusiastic, perfectionist religious communities down the ages. An adoring, obsessed woman can be stupefied by a demagogic man posing as a supreme religious authority.

Marriage, says Gino, "is a piece of flesh." The notion comes straight from Albigensian dualism: the flesh—all matter—is of the devil. Marriage is a false attempt to sacralize bodily urges. The "Perfect," the saved, are only of the spirit, for only the spirit is of God. Yet bodily urges remain and can become tyrannical. What is the saint to do? When the tension grows too great, a distorted reasoning saves the day. Since the body is of the devil, and the devil is forever split off from heaven, what the body does has no relevance to salvation. Lust can be indulged, even encouraged. Gino and his little adoration society are convinced they do not sin, though they sin.

After the Padre's removal from San Vittorino, two strongly opposed factions sprang up to bedevil the Oblates of the Virgin Mary: those in obedience to the superiors who had ordered Gino's exile and those who (now more than ever) violently supported the Padre. The seminary at San Vittorino was closed down, with the seminarians opposing Gino housed at Mondo Migliore and the disobedient Gino followers at St. Helena's. But Mondo Migliore broke into warring factions as well. Finally the Americans were sent to a third Oblate house in Boston. Apparently to this day every Oblate community has its Ginoites and its anti-Ginoites at war with each other.

In Rome, so Fr. Walsh tells me, the scene was so bad a couple of years ago that death threats were made, tires were slashed, and people were assaulted in the streets.

In January 1989—about six months after the first accusations and the removal of Gino from the scene—the Oblate order was put into a kind of receivership under the control and direction of the Vatican Congregation for Religious. A three-Cardinal Commission was appointed by the Vatican to look into the charges and allegations against Padre Gino. Behind the scenes was the then Secretary of the Congregation for Religious, the Most Reverend Vincenzo Fagiolo. Archbishop Fagiolo was a long-term associate of Gino, and Gino was his confessor.

A recent article by Fr. Robert Fox in his journal, the *Fatima Family Messenger* (Oct.-Dec. 1991), quotes a newspaper report saying that the Vatican investigation court has found Padre Gino not guilty of charges brought by members of the Oblate order. At the same time, Padre Gino has been forbidden to return to San Vittorino.

The newspaper report was not accurate. After a long silence the Commission delivered itself of an interim decision couched in bureaucratic euphemisms. Certain "indiscretions" had occurred, and therefore it was "not prudent" for Padre Gino to be allowed to return to San Vittorino for a period of two years, at which time the Superiors of the Oblate Order would make a decision on his return. The term of exile is now over, but Fr. Walsh informs me that the Oblate superiors are not at all sanguine about allowing Gino to return from exile. On the other hand, the convent at San Vittorino, stocked with Ginoite nuns, continues to exist and continues to live according to its odious charism.

What are we to make of all this? Gino has not been cleared, but neither has he been really condemned. He remains in a kind of comfortable limbo, with a few fiercely loyal followers as servants, in a parish house in Tuscany. Meanwhile the myth of Gino is allowed to fester in the deluded souls of millions of Catholics around the world.

Do those in authority ever think of the pain endured by debased and shamed former followers of Gino who must hold their secrets to their bosoms while the world thinks this charlatan is a spiritual hero? Can the victims never be vindicated, never tell even part of the story? And what about those thousands of others who remain in rapt adoration of the great man? Leaving Gino in exile, but uncondemned, is like leaving Napoleon on the island of Elba. Too many ignorant souls will think him not only innocent of all wrongdoing, but also that he has been positively maligned by evil persons. How can the Oblates of the Virgin Mary ever return to normalcy while everything hangs in a ghostly sort of silence?

Someone in authority refused to go along with the white-wash, or shall we say, the gray-wash. Fr. Walsh's dossier, delivered to the investigating Commission and then largely ignored, was leaked to a number of Oblate seminarians by someone very high up in the hierarchy. From there, the report made its way to the journalistic pipeline.

The resulting suspicion is two-fold: first, that certain Church personages must be kept from embarrassment at all costs. Archbishop Fagiolo was a confidant of Gino's. The Bishop of Tivoli had said the first Mass at San Vittorino. Other princes of the Church had been taken in. Yet the story of Gino's malfeasances must get out somehow—so, suspicion number two: let the press do the dirty work and take the heat.

The failure of nerve at top levels of the Vatican hierarchy means that there probably will be no confirmation of this exposé from that direction. Yet the Vatican has the evidence in hand: the exhaustive report of Fr. Walsh, which includes a multitude of sworn affidavits and a number of unsolicited testimonies from ex-nuns regarding mental and sexual abuse. It has evidence of financial crimes and evidence that Gino on numerous occasions broke the seal of the confessional. It has evidence that the alleged supernatural events in Gino's life are the product of Holy Week histrionics and elaborate deceit.

The spiritual life has its dangers. Did Gino start out as a genuinely pious mystic and devolve into a charlatan and egoist when his fame grew to international proportions? It is possible. Did he then feel it necessary to compensate for his sexual sins by creating an aura of supernatural hysterics? Throughout Christian history individuals and sects have been caught up in lurid displays of supernaturalism. The Holy Spirit possesses them. (So they think.) They quake and tremble and fall on the floor; they scream prophecies and howl like dogs. Or, in a quieter intellectual mode, they scale the heights of heaven so swiftly that they forget they are human beings. They must be perfect; they are perfect; they identify with Christ; they are identical to Christ. So identified, they think themselves excused from common morality.

Some years ago Msgr. Ronald Knox wrote an exhaustive account of fanatical religion which he titled *Enthusiasm*. Before I read the book, I thought he meant to portray (and indict) emotional excess like that found among charismatics and Holy Rollers and Pentecostals. But these riotous expressions of faith are a small part of his book. He describes bizarre emotional states and bodily convulsions among the sixteenth century Anabaptists and the eighteenth century Jansenists; but he also explores in detail the ultra-scrupulous original Jansenists of Port Royal, the ultra-contemplative Quietists, and the medieval Albigensians. Bizarre ideas are more dangerous than bizarre emotions.

Yet the common ground among all these spirit-struck individuals and all these breakaway movements, from Montanism to the Fatima Crusaders, is a supernatural dream that pretends to raise the person above sin and raise his particular sect above every other as the only road to salvation. Everyone else is going to hell. In the last degree of fanatical perfectionism are the Perfect elite of the Albigensians or the antinomians of later times, who feel that their bodies have no part in their spirit; that they have been saved in the spirit; that what the body indulges is of no concern to themselves or to God. At the same time, or in another expression, they think they have become as God. Msgr. Knox puts the stamp on this extreme of perfectionism in a subtle discussion of the seventeenth century Quietists, among them the Frenchman Fénelon, the Spanish Quietist leader Molinos, and the deranged mystic Madam Guyon:

> "The good man," said Eckhart, "is the only-begotten Son of God." Put that text from the Galatians to a saint like St. Catherine of Genoa and she will take it in her stride. Put it to a philosopher like Fénelon, and he (when he is writing in cool hour) will comment on it with the precision it needs. Put it to a psychopath like Molinos, and he will tell you that he has become as God, knowing good and evil; he enjoys that participated light which can assure you that you are not sinning when you sin. Put it to a hysterical subject like Madame Guyon, and she will say anything, retract anything, sign anything; "neither am I capable of giving any reason for my conduct, for I no longer have a conduct, and yet I act infallibly."

The most charitable thing to say about Padre Gino Burresi is that he is a Perfectionist in this scurrilous and disordered sense. He "enjoys that participated light which can assure you that you are not sinning when you sin." He cannot give you any reason for his conduct because he no longer has a conduct, but acts infallibly.

It is a wonder how the whole myth of the miracle-working Gino was allowed to grow and flourish in the first place. Why didn't the Holy Office send someone to verify the alleged stigmata when it first appeared way back in 1969? Surely the Church has a vital interest in these things. If anyone in authority was paying attention, the fraud could have been discovered and Gino discredited long before he achieved international status. Prelates would have been saved from acute embarrassment, the Oblates of the Virgin Mary would have been saved from scandal and turmoil, hundreds of young men and women would have been saved from delusion and mental rape, and millions of Catholics would have been saved from a delusive faith in a false saint.

People can be hurt when truth is left unspoken. Fr. Kevin Walsh joined the Oblates of the Virgin Mary many years ago, filled with a devotion for the Church. That devotion naturally fed on the aura of holiness at San Vittorino. Refusing to close his eyes, he came to realize that all was not right in the temple of the prophet. He saw too much trickery passing for miracle. When he was appointed to carry out an investigation of the charges made against Gino, he took his job seriously. Today he is disillusioned twice over. He is emotionally sundered by the fall of his hero, and he is frustrated to the core by the Commission's refusal to take firm action. What does it do to a man's faith when he is conned for a decade by a spiritual poseur and then conned by those who entrusted him with a painful duty? No one except Fr. Walsh can answer for Fr. Walsh's faith, but he has now taken a year's leave of absence from the priesthood. He has a lot to sort out.

I asked Fr. Walsh if his dismay was the result of his treatment at the hands of the commission he worked for, since in a previous conversation he had betrayed an outrage that his strenuous investigation had come to naught. He'd been very angry at the Vatican for its failure to condemn Gino. He felt he had been used and then left to twist in the wind. But his present decision to take a leave of absence? "The Vatican's inaction is part of the reason," he said. "But the main reason is Gino."

And then he said, "Look. You should ask Fr. Kent Burtner [an expert on destructive cults] about mind control and what it can do to you." The reference was to the destruction of personality that can occur in a situation of mental slavery to a false prophet. Attachment to that which has gripped you so strongly can war for years against the skepticism forced on you by what you have seen. The battleground is your own soul. I assured Fr. Walsh that I knew what he meant, since I had once been a Moonie.

Chapter Eleven

The Legacy of Marcel Lefebvre

When I began to investigate the Society of St. Pius X in the Spring of 1992, I had no idea I would run into a movement that at least in some locales fits in well with the Fatima Crusaders and the other tribes who devour souls.

Since the Vatican's excommunication of Marcel Lefebvre on July 1, 1988, the Society of St. Pius X has moved further and further into a posture of shoring up its existence as a separate church. Now that its leader has gone to his reward, the Society is a body without a head and so obeys the law of separation: schism breeds further schism, charity is lost in rancor, and the end is chaos.

Especially in the United States, unanimity has never been a characteristic of the Society. But before we get into this discussion, we should say something about the history of the Society in general, since with Archbishop Marcel Lefebvre we have a serious and relatively respected protest movement. It is a movement that kept communion with the Church through twenty years of struggle and diplomacy before going into formal schism on June 30, 1988.

But the fact that it did go into formal schism just on the verge of an accommodation with Rome illustrates a kind of general law about schism itself. It is the problem of egoism. Once you have taken a stand in opposition to Church authority, once you build chapels, once you have properties and benefactors and mortgages, once you pour into your people a crusading, persecuted spirit and become a kind of god to your world-wide flock—once all of this has happened it is tremendously difficult to bow your head again to the institution you have fought for so long, with the added humiliation of losing all your property and your power. It is why the Old Catholics, for example, still exist as varied dots of egoism after a century and a half, or why various Protestant denominations still exist after four centuries of drifting from the theology of their founders. Protest movements of any kind, once they build a separate church, take on a life of their own, even though it is a half-life. Almost never do they climb back into the Church (unless they are coerced, and that kind of stuff went out after the horrors of the Thirty Years War). Instead, the first infidelity makes the next one that much easier, until in the end you have ex-Lefebvrite and sedevacantist Fr. Sanborn with his own tiny sect in Michigan, or ex-Lefebvrite Fr. Kelly forming his own Society of Pius V, or ex-Lefebvrite, ex-Kellyite Fr. Dolan hooking up with the Fatima Crusaders in Spokane, Washington.

Marcel Lefebvre was born in Tourcoing, France, in 1905. He was ordained in 1929 and joined the Holy Ghost Fathers in 1932. The order sent him to the French colony of Gabon in Africa as a missionary, and on September 18, 1947, he was made a bishop. The next year Pius XII made him Apostolic Delegate for all of French-speaking Africa. His driving interests, according to the official (SSPX) biography, were a crusading anti-Communist spirit and a resolve to end religious ignorance. During his African tour of duty he created 21 new dioceses, built seminaries and schools and printing presses, and ordained a good many native priests. It was a huge accomplishment. In 1955 he was made Archbishop of Dakar, and in 1959 he returned to France.

Two continuing events apparently accounted for Lefebvre's eventually establishing his own priestly society. Firstly, he was elected Superior General of the Holy Ghost Fathers in 1962. In that capacity he sent promising young men for seminary training to Rome. The French Seminary in Rome became progressively more modernist after the Council, and complaints from his protégés came back to him with increasing frequency. The other concern was in the Council itself. Lefebvre had been appointed to the commission that wrote the papally approved documents originally presented to the Council for deliberation. Every one of these documents was thrown out in the first Council session. Soon afterwards Lefebvre "publicly expressed astonishment" at the presence on subcommissions of modernist theologians like Küng, Rahner, Congar, and Schillebeeckx. The alleged modernist takeover, or near takeover, of the Council, and later on the "spirit of the Council" as revealed in the French Seminary in Rome, moved him at last to found "An International House of St. Pius X" at Fribourg, Switzerland on June 6, 1969.

A year later the new Society moved to Ecône, and in November of 1970 the "Society of St. Pius X" was established canonically under the jurisdiction of Msgr. Charrière in the Diocese of Fribourg. But the honeymoon between the Church and the Society was short-lived. Pressure from Cardinal Villot, Secretary of State and spokesman for the (mostly liberal) French bishops, as well as a general clash of ideology between tradition and *aggiornamento*, brought things to a head in 1975. Lefebvre was called to Rome and informally tried by a papal commission; he was forbidden to ordain any more priests and told he must close the seminary and disband the Society.

The Archbishop refused, claiming he had been made victim of an irregular canonical procedure. He ordained some priests in June 1976; he was suspended by Paul VI a month later. From this point on, he and his priests acted without faculties. Some may think this a technical point, but it is sure that since 1976 there has been a very controversial situation in the Society regarding the validity of confessions and marriages.

In his sermon "Twenty Years of Struggle" during a retreat in 1986 the Archbishop anxiously argues his rights:

> But we did not stop there [ordaining priests] with our apparently illegal actions with regards to the particulars of the law, such as the hearing of confessions, [or] the blessing of marriages performed in our presence in the dioceses. Many of the things which we have accomplished are of themselves and strictly speaking against the letter of the law, but why do we do these things? Quite simply because we believed that that which was undertaken against us was illegal and that they did not have the right to suppress our Order.

There matters stood until the election of John Paul II in 1978, after which relations between Rome and the Archbishop warmed considerably. Right away negotiations began with the view to regularizing the Society. But throughout the succeeding ten years, intransigent positions bedeviled the diplomacy and finally resulted in formal schism. There is no space here to go into all that passed between Rome and Lefebvre until the summer of 1988. A few points only will be covered.

A conciliatory letter from the Archbishop to John Paul II dated March 8, 1980, contains Lefebvre's assurance that he agrees with the pope's declaration that the Council "must be understood in the light of all Holy Tradition," and that, though he has reservations about the *Novus Ordo* mass, "I have never said that it is in itself invalid or heretical."

The same two points appear in Lefebvre's letter to Cardinal Ratzinger on April 17, 1985, where a declaration of reconciliation is agreed upon:

> We have always accepted and now declare that we accept the texts of the Council, according to the criterion of tradition, that is, according to the traditional Magisterium of the Church. We have never affirmed and do not now affirm that the New Order of Mass, celebrated according to the rite indicated in the Roman edition, is of itself invalid and heretical.

Lefebvre goes on to "explicate" the declaration before appending his signature: (1) the Vatican II Declaration on Religious Liberty is contrary to the Magisterium of the Church, and should undergo a "total revision." (2) The liturgical reform "has been influenced by Ecumenism with the Protestants and is by this fact a very grave danger for the Catholic faith, [so] we ask that this reform be entirely revised so that it restores Catholic dogmas to their former honored status, along the lines of the immemorial Mass." (3) Communism and socialism must be formally condemned, and "Catholic states" must be "encouraged to recognize the Catholic religion as the only official religion . . . ."

Cardinal Ratzinger replies (May 29, 1985) that Lefebvre's "explications" in effect contradict the original declaration—which, of course, they do. In fact it takes considerable effrontery for Lefebvre to first say that the *Novus Ordo* Mass is valid, and the Conciliar documents are acceptable in the light of tradition, and then demand a return to the old Mass and a massive revision of a Conciliar document. The next year another letter from Ratzinger insists on fidelity to the Council:

> Of course you can express your anxiety over certain interpretations that may have been given to various texts of the Council; you may also legitimately criticize such interpretations. But it is not possible for

you to call in question the authentic doctrine of the ecumenical Second Vatican Council, the texts of which are magisterial and enjoy the highest doctrinal authority. (Jan. 20, 1986).

The line is drawn at the point of accepting or rejecting the Conciliar documents (however they are interpreted). But while this high diplomacy is going on, the Archbishop's true state of mind is a little more unfriendly. Nine days later, perhaps stung by the Cardinal's reply, he writes a letter to the editor of the journals *Itineraires* and *Present*:

> The plan announced in the documents of the Masonic Alta Vendita and published on Pius IX's orders is becoming a reality day by day beneath our very eyes. Last week I was in Rome, at the summons of Cardinal Gagnon, who handed me the enclosed letter [from Ratzinger, quoted above]. A very well-organized network is in control of all the Curia's activity, inside and outside the Curia itself.
>
> The pope is an instrument of this Mafia which he put in place and with which he sympathizes. We may hope for no reaction to come from him, on the contrary. The announcement of the meeting of world religions, decided on by him for the month of October in Assisi, is the culminating imposture and the supreme insult to Our Lord. Rome is no longer Catholic Rome. The prophecies of Our Lady of Salette and of Leo XIII in his exorcism are coming about. "Where the seat of blessed Peter and the chair of truth was set up for a light to enlighten all nations, there they have established the throne of the abomination of their wickedness so that, having struck the Shepherd, they may scatter the flock in turn...."
>
> You will see, in the reply to our letter [again, that reply of Jan. 20, quoted above], that Cardinal Ratzinger is striving once more to make Vatican II into a dogma. We are dealing with people who have no notion of Truth. We shall from now on be more and more obliged to act on the assumption that this new conciliar Church is no longer Catholic (Letter to Mr. Madiran, Jan. 29, 1986).

The accusation that John Paul is an instrument of a Masonic Mafia "which he put in place" seems to leave no ground for accommodation. After the Assisi conference of October 1986 (which the pope proclaimed was solely a prayerful convocation for world peace and had absolutely no bearing of the supreme truth of the Catholic

Faith), the attacks from the Pius X Society and other traditional groups will be a constant barrage zeroing in on this "blasphemous event." Lefebvre's deep distrust of Rome can only get deeper, and the diplomacy of the last days before the excommunication should be seen in this light.

In fact the Archbishop had been preparing the ground for consecrating new bishops for some time. In 1974 he had told a confidante (now an ex-Lefebvrite priest) that he would never consecrate a bishop, for this would mean "I would do what Martin Luther did, and I would lose the Holy Ghost." But by 1983 he was in the United States sounding out his priests on the possibility of consecrating bishops. He asked each in turn for his view on the subject. Those Society superiors who objected to what he and they knew would be a formally schismatic act, in a year's time were removed from their positions. They were replaced by those priests who went a long with the idea.

The groundwork was carefully laid among believers. At St. Mary's Academy in Kansas, every child and adult underwent a mandatory new "catechism" under the auspices of Society priests—a year and a half before the consecrations. They learned that following a false authority was evil; that the Pope had lost any legal authority; that the schism and excommunication that were sure to follow the consecrations were not really schism and not really excommunication. How far-reaching was this new "catechism"? If variations of it were imposed on all believers in 1986 and 1987, it would account for the fact that so few people left the Society in the summer of 1988.

On May 5, 1988, Lefebvre signed an accord with Rome that in principle gave the Archbishop most of what he wanted. He could have a bishop and thus provide for the Society's continuance after his death. The Society priests could say the Tridentine Mass. The suspension was lifted, and the Society could once again legally ordain its own clergy. Once again Lefebvre accepted the Vatican Council, "as interpreted by tradition," and the New Mass as "valid," if not welcome.

According to an interview in *30 Days* (July/August 1988), during the May 5 meeting Lefebvre asked Cardinal Ratzinger when a bishop could be consecrated. June 30? No, that would be too soon, says Ratzinger. August 15? No, perhaps in November. (All of this is Lefebvre's version of events.) Later that day the Archbishop decides that Rome is playing games: he'll never get a bishop. So he shoots off a letter to Ratzinger on May 6 threatening to go ahead and appoint a bishop on June 30 with or without Rome's mandate. On May 24, Rome said in effect: OK, you can consecrate a bishop on August 15. But now (on June 2) Lefebvre rejected the concord entirely. On June 30, he consecrated four bishops, and on July 1, he and his bishops were formally excommunicated.

What had happened to ruin the proceedings on the verge of success? One thing about this matter of bishops is usually not explained. Sometime around the May 5-May 6 disaster, Lefebvre had presented the names of potential bishops, and Rome had demurred. The selection of bishops is a touchy subject. With papal approval, it is perfectly legitimate. Without papal approval, it is a schismatic act and an excommunicable offense. The real problem of the bishops was not when, but who? Who would be acceptable to the pope? Presumably the priests who eventually were chosen as bishops were on the list presented by Lefebvre. Rome knew who these men were and knew they held the same views Lefebvre did in his more incautious moments: the New Mass is blasphemous, the Council is heretical, the popes that approve the Council are heretical, and maybe they are not popes at all. Whatever the deliberations, it is certain that Rome had an extensive dossier on the men favored for consecration, and that is why the Pope reserves to himself the right of approval and why it is such a grave act to consecrate a bishop without it. It is no technical matter, but a measure to protect the Faith. How could Rome ever approve a bishop who really believed that the pope was a tool of the Freemasons?

In truth, Pope John Paul would probably never have approved a bishop Lefebvre had chosen, and contrarily, Lefebvre probably could never have been satisfied with a bishop John Paul had chosen. (But now we will never know.) It goes right back to the deep division over the Faith, and the two unresolved questions: is the New Mass invalid, and are the Vatican II documents heretical?

Another revelation of what went on in and around the secret negotiations of 1988: at one point, Lefebvre demanded as part of the accord that all the world's Catholic traditionalists (those who wanted the old Mass) would have to become members of the Society. It was an absurd demand, impossible to fulfill even if it had been granted, but it speaks to the condition of Lefebvre's (now feverish?) mind.

Apparently in the last few years of his life Marcel Lefebvre was not always clear-headed. He was unmercifully manipulated by his lieutenants—Fr. Schmidberger (Superior General of the Order), Williamson, and the others. When he returned from Rome after signing the May 5 accord, these bishops-to-be, perhaps seeing their bishoprics about to go down the drain, told the Archbishop that if he did not repudiate the accord with Rome, the Society would split apart at the seams. There were too many in the Society (meaning Williamson and Company) who simply had no trust of Rome at all. Under that pressure the Archbishop changed his mind and hardened his position against all possible future diplomacy with the Vatican. This was his state of mind in mid-June:

> I entered these negotiations because Rome's reactions in the second half of last year had raised in me a faint hope that these churchmen had changed. They have not changed, except for the worse. Look at Casaroli in Moscow! They have spiritual AIDS, they have no grace, their immunity defence system is gone. I do not think one can say that Rome has not lost the Faith. As for an eventual "excommunication", its disagreeableness diminishes with time. (Private talk, quoted by Williamson's "Letter from Winona," August 1, 1988)

And so the new Church was born, by a willful man who had created a monster he could not in the end control—either as that monster infected his followers or infected his own mind.

Among Pius X defenders it is now common to refuse to admit that Lefebvre had gone into schism or that he had really been excommunicated. Lefebvre historian Michael Davies, who at first denounced the June 30 consecrations, now defends them in a disappointing article (*Angelus*, December 1990). It is disappointing because Davies, for all his knowledge and intellect, descends to a swamp of special pleading to convince readers that (1) there was no schism, and (2) there was no excommunication.

He claims that the alleged excommunication was not for schism (Canon 1364), but for "Usurpation of Ecclesial Functions" (Canon 1382), which reads: "A bishop who consecrates someone bishop and the person who receives such a consecration from a bishop without a pontifical mandate incur an automatic excommunication reserved to the Holy See."

But the excommunication from the See of Peter (published in *L'Osservatore Romano,* July 11, 1988) specifically mentions Canons 1364 *and* 1382. The simple logic is that Canon 1364 contains the general condemnation—for schism—while Canon 1382 reveals the specific nature of the schismatic act: consecrating bishops without papal mandate. There is nothing closer to the heart of schism than the act of providing for the continuation of a separate church structure—bishops and priests providing that continuation by the laying-on of hands generation after generation. Back in 1974, even Lefebvre admitted that to consecrate a bishop would be "to act like Martin Luther" and create a counter-Church.

Davies goes on to argue that the excommunication was not valid since Lefebvre believed that "a state of necessity existed." Anyone can make a theological argument to that effect, but the reality is that excommunication is a act performed by a competent authority, in this case Pope John Paul II. You can argue about the justice of the act all you want, but the fact remains that, when the pope excommunicates you, you are excommunicated.

But sliding around the facts of schism and excommunication are typical for defenders of a group in schism. The same arguments were heard in the Schism of Utrecht (1724), in the establishment of the Old Catholics after the First Vatican Council, and during the creation of Protestant churches in the sixteenth century. Always a self-proclaimed higher law is appealed to so that a specific law can be circumvented.

> These [church laws] hold good only so long as they are not injurious to Christianity and the laws of God. Therefore, if the Pope deserves punishment, these laws cease to bind us, since Christendom would suffer.
>
> Martin Luther

> In the Church there is no law or jurisdiction which can impose on a Christian a diminution of his faith. All the faithful can and should resist whatever interferes with their faith . . . . If they are forced with an order putting their faith in danger of corruption, there is an overriding duty to disobey.
>
> Marcel Lefebvre

Davies forgets that beyond canon law and the thoughts of canonists interpreting that law, and beyond the thoughts of pundits interpreting the thoughts of the canonists, is the court of last resort, which is none other than the Vicar of Christ.

Is there any hope that the Society will return as a whole to the Church?—that is, besides the many individuals priests and seminarians who have gone over to Rome? It doesn't look like it. The new counter-Church propels its own existence by turning up the heat on the "Conciliar" Church. In a "Letter to Friends" of February 12, 1989, Superior General Franz Schmidberger reveals a threefold "foreign occupation" of the Church. First is the Pope himself, "a prisoner of modern philosophy and modernistic theology."

Second is Cardinal Ratzinger and others close to the pope who share his beliefs. Third is "the conscious and determined conspiracy of the forces of Gnosticism, Theosophy, and Esoterism, headed by the Illuminati and the Freemasons, and allied with Marxist infiltration."

Well, if the Masons and/or the Illuminati run the show, there is nothing to be gained by dealing with Rome. It's no good making a pact with the devil. It might be said in passing that diabolizing your opponent is at one and the same time to give him superhuman powers and to provide yourself with an excuse for severing any and all connections with him.

> The Church of Rome, formerly the most holy of all churches, has become . . . the very kingdom of sin, death, and hell; so that not even Antichrist, if he were to come, could desire any addition to its wickedness.
>
> Martin Luther
>
> The See of Peter and posts of authority in Rome being occupied by Antichrists, the destruction of the Kingdom of Our Lord is being rapidly carried out even within His Mystical Body here below.
>
> Marcel Lefebvre (August 29, 1987 letter to the four bishops-to-be)

The point of such anathemas is that attempts to reform the Church from inside are futile; it is too late; and so we (Luther, Lefebvre) must go our own way and build our own true Catholic Church.

Followers of Lefebvre say that he was a saint. They point out that if not for the Pius X Society, there would be no *Ecclesia Dei*, which commands a generous application of the 1984 Indult allowing the Tridentine Mass. That is, there would be no opportunity for Catholics to return to the old rite—as they now have the increasing opportunity to do. Perhaps. But if an accord had been reached, an internal reform might have been more readily accomplished. All that power and enthusiasm working inside the Church might have accomplished much more much quicker. But, once again, we will never know.

Was Lefebvre a sedevacantist? It seems that it depended on his mood, or on the audience he was addressing. In 1980 he wrote to the Holy Father and protested "I have no hesitation regarding the legitimacy or the validity of Your election . . . I have already had to condemn these ideas and I continue to do so in the face of some seminarians who allow themselves to be influenced by ecclesiastics outside the Fraternity." But in his various tours, the ex-Lefebvrite priest informs me, he would speak a "faithful to the Pope" line to conservative Catholics and a suggestively sedevacantist line when talking to radical traditionalists. Like any politician, he played to the audience. But he threw caution to the winds in the preface of his 1987 letter to the four bishops-to-be. Here he calls the pope an Antichrist, which is a vivid way of saying the papal seat is empty.

Moreover there exists an audiocassette tape of a Lefebvre sermon given shortly after John Paul II's 1986 Assisi peace convocation. Basing his charges on that ecumenical gathering, the archbishop says, "I think that when a pope or bishop honors God in this non-Catholic way, they have the intention of going to God as a non-Catholic, thereby renouncing the Catholic faith. Never has it happened in the Church before that he who sits on the throne of Peter has participated in the cult of false gods. Are we then obliged to believe that this pope is not Pope?—because it seems impossible that a pope could be a public and formal heretic."

The sedevacantist question brings us back to the United States. Three previously Lefebvrite priests—Fathers Cekada, Dolan, and Sanborn—have now split from the Pius V Society (which Fr. Kelly had formed when he broke with Lefebvre), to become involved in varying degrees with the Fatima Crusader cult at Mount St. Michael. The Fatima Crusaders' pretense to Catholicism rests on its connection to the excommunicated lineage of Vietnam's sedevacantist Archbishop Thuc.

As Lefebvrite seminarians proposed for the priesthood back in the 1970s, Cekada, Sanborn, and Dolan encountered opposition because of their openly expressed sedevacantism. A delegation of American priests warned Lefebvre. But the Archbishop, knowing their standpoint, ordained them anyway. Then, in 1983, Lefebvre used that excuse—sedevacantism—to kick Fr. Kelly and the others out of the Society. The accusation must have rung hollow, given Lefebvre's own leanings. Especially since Richard Williamson, openly a sedevacantist as a seminarian at Ecône, was later made bishop for North America.

The real reason for Kelly's ouster was his greed and power-mongering—and Williamson's enmity. Kelly and Cekada had put their own names on a lot of Pius X property deeds in the Cincinnati area. There are strong suggestions that Kelly wanted to take over the whole Society in the United States. Williamson, who eventually came out on top, had bad-mouthed Kelly as long ago as the early '70s when the two of them walked the seminary grounds at Ecône. Now Kelly has his own little sect in Oyster Bay, New York, along with a few Pius V Society chapels dotted around the country. Many of these are engaged in property litigation since they were originally owned by the Society of Pius X.

Another mini-schism has just occurred in the SSPX. Bishop Williamson, a friend of Tridentine Rite Conference (TRC) Fathers LeBlanc and Wickens, wanted to attend their Tridentine Rite Conference meeting last year (1991) in New Jersey. He was to accept an award from the new pan-traditionalist lobby on behalf of Marcel Lefebvre. Fr. Terence Finnegan, a Lefebvrite priest at Our Lady of Sorrows church in Phoenix, got wind of the project and protested first to Williamson and then to Fr. Schmidberger in Germany. Fr. Finnegan's major concern was to protect the orthodoxy of the Society; he knew all about the TRC and its involvement with the odder sorts of schismatics and heretics—with the scurrilous Order of St. John, with irregular Feeneyite (Jansenist) sects, and with sedevacantists like Dan Jones in Colorado. Fr. Finnegan was also increasingly distressed at the strange doctrines coming from the mouth of Richard Williamson.

After a feverish exchange of letters between Finnegan and Fr. Peter Scott (pro-forma superior of the SSPX in North America), between Schmidberger and Scott, and between Scott and Williamson, Williamson was told not to attend the TRC convention.

By this time Williamson was seething. Fr. Finnegan was called to Europe for an interview with Fr. Schmidberger. Finnegan again warned Fr. Schmidberger that Williamson was ruining the Society in the United States because of the latter's incautious associations and intemperate statements. For his troubles, Fr. Finnegan was told he would be transferred. The choices were Ireland and South Africa. Fr. Finnegan refused, and on April 8, 1992, he was dismissed from the Society.

Our Lady of Sorrows in Phoenix now has a new Lefebvrite priest and a flock of about eighty believers, leftovers from Fr. Finnegan's tenure. Fr. Finnegan says Mass in a private home, and on Sundays rents a hall. He brought with him the great majority of his former flock, amounting to some 200 fiercely devoted followers.

That is the significant fact. When this mini-schism occurred, the great majority of believers dissolved their union with the SSPX and followed their local leader into an independent Catholic status. This kind of thing can only happen over and over again when there is no central authority providing a sanctified unity. In other words, without a pope there is only self-will and devotion to one strong personality or another.

Other Pius X parishes (technically, missions) around the country have recently been squeezed out or been isolated. In Post Falls, Idaho, the parish pastored by Fr. Rizzo has been the site of a battle royal over the sin of "Americanism." As this contention between American patriots and European fascists is ripping the Society apart, we will explore its ramifications later on when we talk about the politics of the SSPX. Fr. Rizzo was transferred to England, but as of early 1993, he is back in the States and has departed from the Society. His associate pastor Fr. Hunter wrote a book defending the origin of the United States Government and denying the Society's charge that it was all one big Masonic plot. Fr. Schmidberger and Fr. Scott refuse to allow the book to be published. A new priest thoroughly loyal to Williamson and his lieutenants, Fr. Doran, recently took over as pastor in Post Falls—there to teach the One True Political Faith. Fr. Hunter says the congregation is demoralized and worried about what is soon to descend upon them.

In Campbell, California, the faithful are up in arms over the ill-considered funding of a retreat house out of mission funds that were intended for a new chapel and school. Violence on the church steps and criminal litigation is the upshot. The parish priest—Fr. Foley—was condemned, slandered from the pulpit by USA superior Fr. Scott and by Bishop Williamson, and finally told to report to a mission church in Minnesota. Instead, he left the Society and took a portion of the faithful with him. Now he says Mass in a private home in Walnut Creek. The underlying cause of the brouhaha is local displeasure over imperious control from the Society superiors.

In Omaha, a former Society parish of about 50 people now attends a (papally approved) Indult Mass. The people were tired of hearing their patriotism indicted as a sin and especially dismayed by the "Gestapo tactics" imposed on their kids at St. Mary's under the dictatorship of Fr. Anglés—about which more later. These concerns underlay the decision by Fr. Scott to tell the folks in Omaha that, "due to the shortage of priests," they would no longer have a Society priest say Mass for them. Letters passed back and forth, Fr. Scott said there had been a misunderstanding, "a priest would be provided on certain occasions," and all would be well. But by that time the parishioners had had enough.

In Phoenix, in Omaha, in Campbell, California, and in Post Falls, Idaho, a variety of causes has brought schism or division to the SSPX. These four cases are only the tip of the iceberg. American priests, and Americans, have been mistrusted from the start by their elite European masters. Intelligent, discerning American priests—those with minds of their own—have been expelled or transferred abroad, leaving Williamson's foreign-born lackeys in charge of an increasingly demoralized laity.

More recently the SSPX chapel in Oak Park, Illinois, has broken up, a hundred or so of its members registering as parishioners at St. John Cantius Church in Chicago, where the Indult Mass is celebrated. That's the good news. The bad news is that a further portion of the Oak Park Lefebvrites has gone over to another self-styled, illegitimate Catholic parish. The primary reason for the break-up was Fr. Scott's shrill condemnations of American patriotism.

Are Richard Williamson and his cohorts wrecking the SSPX by their hateful and dim-witted opinions and their denigration of American institutions? Firstly we should recall the two-fold theology of the Society. It is faithful to Rome (no matter what Rome thinks), or Rome is the seat of the Antichrist, and the SSPX is the last repository of the True Faith. Williamson's recent talks more and more support the latter view.

In the December 1, 1991 *Letter from Winona*, Williamson decries Cardinal Oddi's (reported) statement that Rome is ignoring the Society since the death of Lefebvre in March. Williamson doesn't believe Oddi. After all,

> Rome cannot help keeping watch on the Society, or on any coherent group with large numbers of Catholics keeping the faith. The reason is not hard to find—such groups are the main obstacle to the advance of the Antichrist . . . . the One Worlders owed it to themselves to infiltrate Rome and harness it to the purposes of the Antichrist. This, with Vatican II, they largely succeeded in doing . . . .To sweep all Catholics into the clutches of the One World Government, to switch them from followers of Christ into followers of the Anti-christ, Rome must deceive them . . . . In this process, it is vital that the people should be persuaded that Catholicism is only what Rome says it is . . . [but] another form of Catholicism than that of "Rome" is after all possible . . . .

Given this malice, there is little hope for a reconciliation with Rome on any grounds. So it comes as no surprise to hear (from an ex-Lefebvrite priest whom we shall call Father "Abel") that Williamson, from his early days in Ecône, has been a sedevacantist, that he has often said "there is no pope," and that today, in Winona, he teaches that the real Society position is that there is no pope, "but that because of the controversy this issue causes, we deny this position in public."

If there is no pope and Rome's program is the program of the Antichrist, and only the SSPX keeps the faith alive, then another Williamson teaching follows: "If you are not in the Society, you are not in the Church." This is also taught to the seminarians at Winona and the faithful at St. Mary's. Moreover, since Williamson holds the literal interpretation of the doctrine that there is no salvation outside the Church, it follows that there is no salvation outside the Society, which brings into focus the strange statement in the October 1, 1991 *Letter* concerning "the needs of hundreds of millions of souls in danger of eternal damnation throughout the English-speaking world." In the *Letter* Williamson complains that only 18 new seminarians came to Winona in 1991, a small number considering all those souls who need saving.

As for non-Christians, there is no hope at all. In the Winona publication *Verbum* (Winter, 1992) he declares (though for dramatic purposes he lets an imaginary priest speak for him) that "other religions will only lead souls to Hell."

This is the sectarian mind at work. A wall is erected around the spiritual elite who subscribe to Williamson's One True Faith. Inside are the few thousand who may be saved; outside are the billions damned eternally. It is a grimmer program than Mr. Moon's, who will send to hell only those who oppose his movement. If Williamson's salvation doctrine is a little cock-eyed, his doctrine concerning the Jews is also. Since Catholics hold a wide spectrum of beliefs concerning relations with Judaism, it will be best to juxtapose the Church's statements with those of the bishop. The reader may then deliberate on how far the one view deviates from the other:

> The Church believes that Christ who is our peace has through his cross reconciled Jews and Gentiles and made them one in himself (cf. Eph. 2:14-16) . . . . Even though the Jewish authorities and those who followed their lead pressed for the death of Christ (cf. John 19:6), neither all Jews indiscriminately at that time, nor Jews today, can be charged with the crimes committed during his passion.
>
> It is true that the Church is the new people of God, yet the Jews should not be spoken of as rejected or accursed as if this followed from holy Scripture. Consequently, all must take care, lest in catechizing or in preaching the Word of God, they teach anything which is not in accord with the truth of the Gospel message or the spirit of Christ.
>
> Vatican II, *Nostra Aetate*, 28 Oct., 1965

> . . . Until [the Jews] re-discover their true Messianic vocation [by conversion to Christ], they may be expected to continue fanatically agitating, in accordance with their false messianic vocation of Jewish world-dominion, to prepare the Antichrist's throne in Jerusalem. So we may fear their continuing to play their major part in the agitation of the East and in the corruption of the West. Here the wise Catholic will remember that, again, the ex-Christian nations have only their own Liberalism to blame for allowing free circulation within Christendom to the enemies of Christ . . . . Remembering also that Annas and Caiaphas induced but never obliged Judas to betray Jesus, and that the Apostle's betrayal was a crime far worse than the Jews'

deicide, he will look at the state of the Catholic Church today and see why the enemies of Christendom are being given so much power....

Richard Williamson, *Letter from Winona*, Feb. 1, 1991

In 1989 Williamson delivered some speeches in Canada that caused some consternation and got him investigated for possible "hate crimes" by the Royal Canadian Mounted Police. In Sherbrooke, Quebec, he said, "There was not one Jew killed in the gas chambers. It was all lies, lies, lies. The Jews created the Holocaust so we would prostrate ourselves on our knees before them and approve of their new state of Israel .... Jews made up the Holocaust, Protestants get their orders from the devil, and the Vatican has sold its soul to liberalism."

Later he defended these statements, stating that "I was attacking the enemies of our Lord Jesus Christ, and that includes Jews, as well as Communists and Freemasons." (*The Globe and Mail*, Montreal, April 13, 1989.)

Williamson returned to the States before the RCMP investigation got off the ground, but now the Pius X publications *Verbum*, *Angelus*, and Williamson's monthly *Letter* are banned in Canada. A *Letter from Winona* (Nov. 3, 1991) quotes from the *Protocols of the Elders of Zion*, a scurrilous document purportedly written by Jews, describing a Jewish master-plan to take over the world. The document keeps popping up in Jew-hating circles as if it were a newly discovered proof of Jewish malice. It is actually a piece of disinformation written by a Russian in the employ of the Czar's Secret Police and has been known to be a fraud by all serious historians for nearly a century.

Along with many crack-pot historical revisionists, Williamson subscribes to the big lie that Hitler had no intention, nor much success if did have the intention, of exterminating the Jewish race in Europe. To believe that, you would have to believe in an impossibly far-ranging conspiracy of U.S. Army soldiers and officers, French and English soldiers and officers, numerous investigating commissions, hundreds of thousands of faked reports, faked death camp records, faked photographs, faked testimonies, and faked dead bodies. It is an insane hatred that causes such fervid denial of historical fact and which bestows an utterly superhuman power on diabolical conspirators (Jews, Illuminati, Masons) thought to be responsible for everything that has gone wrong in the history of the world.

Williamson's fear and paranoia regarding the Jews is shared by the Protestant sectarian Dr. Wierwille, chief of the Way Ministry. This sect also believes the Holocaust was a Jewish hoax. Birds of a feather? Yes, in more ways than one. In both sects hatred of a mythic enemy has overcome any pretense to doctrinal religion (Catholic or Protestant). Both are a remnant, the last true Christians, and so the devil trains his guns on them, and so they react with arms purchases and weapons training, defending themselves against an enemy existing only in their own nightmares. A recent *Letter* from Williamson (December 1, 1992) captures the mood:

> The latest election in the U.S.A. surely shifts the programme of the wreckers from forward to fast forward. It is up to every one of us that has the true Catholic Faith to put back into circulation by our example that truth, purity, and transcendence of Jesus Christ which alone can persuade the wreckers that they are making a mistake, and if it has to be with our blood, so be it! They have the prison-camps ready for us in the Dakotas? So help us God, we will be ready for them.

Who are "them"? They are the One Worlders-Masons-Jews, the KGB of the soul, rattling around in the stricken brains of the good bishop and his shock troops of Armageddon—or the Great Bagarre, as Dr. Plinio of the TFP calls it. It's the same dream with a slightly different cast of characters and different heroes to save the day. Each sect thinks it is the last remnant of true Catholics.

Richard Williamson is probably less controversial among American Pius X Society members for his religious anti-semitism than for his nutty attacks on the American Constitution and Government. In one of his *Letters* (July 1, 1991), he decides that the Constitutional principles of Liberty, Equality, and Democracy are responsible for abortion. A taste: "Democracy—we, the people, are sovereign, so if our laws have approved of abortion, then what can be wrong with it?" This idiocy is hardly worth a response. If democracy is to blame for abortion, on what shall we blame abortion in China? A venomous Zeitgeist can overwhelm a dictatorship as easily as a democratic republic, and in a country where the people have some voice in their government, it is easier to finally overturn that Zeitgeist.

The critique of American institutions does not stop with the denigration of democracy. For several years, an attack on the U.S. Constitution, the Founding Fathers, and the "Americanist heresy" has demoralized Pius X members and brought many of them to the point of rebellion. Washington, Jefferson, Samuel Adams, the signers of the Declaration of Independence, and the writers of the Constitution are all branded as Freemasons and their governmental products as imbued with the doctrines of Freemasonry. The First Amendment is attacked for "religious indifferentism" since it did not provide for the establishment of the Catholic Church. Patriots are accused of giving their first loyalty to their country instead of to the Catholic Church.

These attacks come from the Frenchman Fr. Jean-Luc Lafitte in Ridgefield, Connecticut, from the Spaniard Fr. Anglés at St. Mary's, from the Australian Fr. Scott at SSPX headquarters in St. Louis, and from the Englishman Bishop Williamson at Winona. There is not one American in a position of power in the Society in the United States.

Fr. Lafitte raves against "Americanists" through his *Letters from the St. Ignatius Retreat House* in Ridgefield. Under the heading "To Idolize Our Country," he says:

> This serious sin, opposed to the First and Fourth Commandment, is more and more frequent in the mind of many of our parishioners; by it, we worship our Country, our Constitution, putting our Country above the Ten Commandments of God. [It is] an infamy and a mortal sin.

Later in this *Letter* (Number 18, May 15, 1991), Fr. Lafitte attacks the John Birch Society as "an Americanist organization whose doctrine is in many points in open contradiction with the traditional doctrine of the Catholic Church." The list of charges against the JBS is long, but most importantly it seems the organization isn't anti-Semitic enough: "[it] refuses to understand the Jewish conspiracy behind the revolution. It is proven that the Jewish leaders have always been heading the revolution through Freemasonry and Communism." Along the same lines, the JBS is indicted for its 1990 Resolution that its members should "join a church or synagogue: this country was founded on the Judaeo-Christian ethic." Fr. Lafitte claims that "This is pure Indifferentism; furthermore I am curious to know how the Jewish ethic, which killed Our Lord Jesus Christ, and the Catholic ethic, which worships Him, can be put on the same table."

If Jesus Christ had been born an American in 1700, and some Americans had engineered his crucifixion by the ruling British government in 1733, Fr. Lafitte would accuse every American today of holding an "ethic which killed Our Lord Jesus Christ." If Jesus Christ had been born a Chinese, the Chinese would be indicted as "Christ-killers."

The practical problem of this exaggerated attack (by foreign leaders) on the JBS and on American patriotism, in general, is that the majority of Pius X Society members in this country are extremely patriotic and many are, or have been, John Birch Society members. Nor do people of any nationality like to hear their country run down by foreigners. One disgusted SSPX member told me that the Society seems intent on shooting itself in the foot.

The truth is that the Founding Fathers were not engaged in a Masonic plot to spread religious indifferentism, but were faced with a situation where many of the former colonies already had intact state-established Protestant churches of different communions. The new Federal Government could not have favored one or another (Congregationalist, Quaker, Episcopal, etc.) denomination, nor the Catholic Church, without committing suicide at its very beginning. The Catholics in this country are indeed lucky that no national Church was established, for such a National Church might have been "indifferently" Protestant, but it would never have been Catholic and certainly would have persecuted Catholics. The First Amendment to the Constitution should be considered as providential for Catholics. Without it we would never have been allowed to build churches, schools, monasteries, and convents, promote the Catholic truth, or make our presence felt politically and socially.

The bishop's attacks on Rome and on the United States have become more and more unfettered. Last year (1992), he spoke to a group of the faithful in Colorado. He said that "this Pope" is making Rome the spearhead of the "All Religions Church." He said that this "New World Church will then use the power of the State against the Society. It will be in perfect synch with the New World Order—then the police will come for you and me." (And incarcerate "you and me" in a prison camp in the Dakotas?)

The police may indeed come for Richard Williamson and hand him over for deportation proceedings, for just afterwards he said: "President Bush is a terrible traitor to this country. He is doing everything he can to dismantle the U.S.A. and integrate it into Russia and the New World Order, to the benefit of the Antichrist and to the absolute destruction of all that's best in the U.S.A."

Is it an exaggeration to say that this is the speech of a cult leader indulging in political paranoia? First he says "they" are going to come down on us, and a moment later he gives a reason why "they" might indeed come down on him. It won't be because his speech might be considered an incitement to political violence and thus make him *persona non grata* to the Justice Department, but because "they" are the Antichrist, necessarily out to persecute the last remnant of true believers.

Extremist politics flourishes at the Pius X Academy (the K-12 boarding school) and at the college in St. Mary's, Kansas. Since 1989 Fr. Ramon Anglés has been rector of the combined institutions. The children in the Academy learn to hate the American form of government. American icons are mocked. The Statue of Liberty is ridiculed as "a French prostitute." The only good government, the only Catholic government, is monarchy. Democracy is evil. But privately Father Anglés carries the critique further. It seems that good government comes to fruition in the anti-Semitic dictatorship of Nazi Germany. In an absurd transformation of good and evil, the mass murderer, demon worshipping, anti-Catholic Adolf Hitler is metamorphosed into a type of Christian King. Father Anglés has an apartment full of Nazi paraphernalia which he shows to favored boys. He shows them the Nazi ceremonial daggers worn by officers of the Third Reich. He is proud of the vintage Mercedes owned by his family which once was owned by Adolf Hitler.

A one-time student at the Academy was favored by a special meeting with Fr. Anglés a couple of years ago. In his private room on campus, Fr. Anglés treated him and a friend to a pizza and a showing of the Nazi propaganda film *Triumph of the Will*. He played the film back, stopping it in places, commenting with fervor, and reading from the stack of Hitler speech transcripts he had at his side. The film's producer, a chief propagandist for the Third Reich, is still alive. Fr. Anglés telephones her often (he informs his students) and boasts of the association.

St. Mary's, Kansas is a town riven by fear and controversy. When one father of a student at the Academy talked of "Gestapo tactics," he meant that a moral tyranny rules the campus, that children are intimidated, brow-beaten, and informed upon by other children belonging to a perfectionist cadre called the Children of Mary. He means that people who disagree with Fr. Anglés or cross him in any way are condemned from the pulpit, shunned, and even physically threatened. Thirteen Academy students were expelled or suspended in the academic year 1990-91 for various imperfections in themselves or in their parents. Another thirty-seven were withdrawn by distraught or shunned parents.

A grandmother is refused communion because her daughter has been shunned. A child is forced to kneel in the snow in the dead of winter for an hour as punishment for some minor infraction. Informants tell Fr. Anglés if they spot a Society woman wearing pants in town. She and her family are condemned from the pulpit. Children are taught to follow the rule of the priests and not their parents. If they follow their parents' authority instead, they are told that they are going to hell. They are told that their parents have "Satanic minds."

Sandy Cossette's daughter planned to marry a young man from town who was not a Society member. She was denounced publicly from the pulpit. Her family was shunned. Now that family, still living in the town, is condemned to hell—according to the priests at St. Mary's. This type of supernatural sanction, perpetrated on strongly faithful Catholics, who know there is a heaven and a hell and who have been taught that "Father is always right," is what brings St. Mary's right into line with the Moonies, the Hare Krishnas, the cult at Mount St. Michael, and all the other destructive cults that wield the stick of damnation over their flocks. "Outside the Society, there is no salvation"—and anyone who crosses Fr. Anglés is outside the Society.

It is no wonder that one priest formerly associated with the Society describes St. Mary's as "a Jonestown waiting to happen." A few members in the growing army of the ostracized, sick and tired of being threatened by Fr. Anglés, have bought guns to protect their families. Meanwhile a stalwart in the pro-Anglés faction says that, if criticism continues, "there will be blood on the streets of St. Mary's."

How have things comes to this pass? Not too long ago a woman who had dared oppose Fr. Anglés had an accident and went to the hospital. When she returned, she found her apartment had been destroyed in a fire. There is no evidence that Fr. Anglés and his henchmen were responsible for the fire, but loyalists take a kind of spiritual credit for it. A woman caught wearing slacks and shunned, later received a threatening letter from a true believer:

> And for your own sake take a lesson from recent history . . . Mrs. Chavez refused to live on campus as Father wished—her home burned with all her possessions.

This is the kind of self-serving magical message that comes from the pulpit and spreads across the town to breed fear and, increasingly, a kind of desperate rage.

A couple months ago a crony of Fr. Anglés purchased a shipment of 15 or 20 SKS semi-automatic rifles from a local gun dealer. An observer tells me that these guns are reappearing, one by one, in the hands of devoted Society members in the town. Not long ago a friend went target shooting out by the Kansas river and ran into a bunch of these amateur marksmen trying to hone their skills.

The hatred has gone beyond preparing for violence. Lee Gauvin, a critic of the Anglés regime, has had the lug nuts on the wheels of his vehicle loosened. The same thing happened to Andrew Convery, another outspoken critic, whose wife was driving with her children in the van when the wobbly wheels could very easily have caused an accident. The local police are investigating these incidents as attempted murder.

There is a virulent sickness of hatred and Hitlerism running through sections of the traditional Catholic movement. Why these folks have taken on the clothes of the very devil they detest is a matter for God to sort out. The strain runs through the Pius X Society in France, whose priests see Marshall Pétain as a hero and his anti-Semitic Vichy government of World War II as a paragon of virtue. Catholic traditionalism as a whole in France is imbued with extreme right-wing politics. On the one side is the historical dream of a restored Catholic Monarchy, allied often with pro-Hitler, anti-Semitic fascism. On the other side is Communism, liberalism, democracy, the French Revolution, the Resistance and the Free French of World War II, and Charles de Gaulle. And this odd alliance of past Catholic glory and present right-wing extremism in politics finds a home in the special education programs offered secretly, or not so secretly, at St. Mary's, Kansas and in Ridgefield, Connecticut.

Both in France and in the United States, there is a question in traditional Catholic movements whether religion is informing politics or the other way around. Early in this century the anti-Semitic *Action Française* supported the Catholic Church as a bastion against liberalism and socialism, but many in the *Action Française* were simply right-wing atheists who used the Church for their own purposes. Many of the priests in the United States who were to form the kernel of the traditionalist sectarians were originally members of the Orthodox Roman Catholic Movement. The ORCM was founded and run by Fr. Francis E. Fenton, who was also on the governing board of the John Birch Society. Now defunct as an organization (it was ripped apart by internal dissension), the ORCM's paranoid notions of wholesale Communist infiltration of U.S. government and educational structures still motivates many in the traditional movement. Fr. Fenton is now a sedevacantist, while the John Birch Society has been branded an Americanist heresy by the leaders of the Pius X Society. In sectarian movements, political or religious, your closest allies soon become your most dangerous enemies. Exaggerated political fears are often a deeper credo for some people than is the belief in God.

Impugning a person's religion because of his politics is a bad business, except when the religion disappears beneath the politics. This point was reached on the Left when parish priests in Nicaragua took up arms for the Sandinistas and when liberation theologians stole Catholic forms and rites and attached them to Marxist sacraments of revolutionary violence. It is reached on the Right when children are taught that Adolph Hitler was a "good Catholic" and that his Final Solution was an appropriate Christian solution to the "Jewish Problem." (The alternative draught of poison for the paranoid Right is the fantasy that the Holocaust never happened.)

With virulent anti-Semitism taught at St. Mary's and Winona and Ridgefield, with other deranged doctrines concerning the American government and the Bill of Rights, with the malice hurled at Rome, it is no doubt true that Richard Williamson and his clique are ruining the Society.

But it might be truer to say that the Society as a whole is ruining Catholicism in its members. I've talked to several Pius X parishioners locally. After ten or twenty years of propaganda, most are so imbued with a hatred for Rome that they seem content to remain forever in schism. They don't realize it, but they have found their identity as new Protestants.

To say "Protestant" in this connection is to say that the Society is preparing to complete its schism by establishing a fully separate Church. How will this come about? Williamson suggests the way in a bulletin of October 1, 1989:

> In the 1970s He [God] inspired an archbishop [Lefebvre] to give the laity a fresh start of priests and, in the late 1980s, fresh bishops. There is no way all these can give themselves a new pope, but if they stay with the Truth, God will finally give them a Pope of Truth. Within the Truth is within the Church, and without the Truth is without the Church.

The letter is certainly suggestive. Williamson is now apparently lobbying for Fr. Schmidberger's position as Superior General of the Order and may succeed to that status in the next convocation. Will the convocation end up turning into a Papal Conclave? Will the Pope of Truth descend from heaven? Will it be Williamson?

It will have been a meteoric rise for the Englishman. A student of languages at Cambridge, he was baptized at Ecône in 1973. Three years later he was ordained a priest, and in 1988 he was consecrated a bishop. Will he soon join the club of anti-popes that decorate the lunatic fringe of Catholicism?

My sense is that most Catholics in this country who deserted the Church for the Society of Pius X or other disobedient movements were not deeply concerned about any alleged invalidity of the *Novus Ordo* Mass or with conjectures of heresy in Vatican II documents. They were just looking for a place to pray. It was, and always is, a matter of *lex orandi, lex credendi*. Probably they are right in thinking that in the Old Mass there was a sense of mystery lacking in even the most reverently said New Mass. And there were, and continue to be, deplorable abuses of the New Mass in many parish churches around the world.

But now there is an opportunity to be both in the Church and to participate in the Old Mass, if that is your wish. One hates to pop the bubble regarding Marcel Lefebvre's movement since many pious

Catholics revere him as a saint. To these I say: continue to revere him as a saint, if you must, but please come back to the Church. The more of you who come back, the sooner recalcitrant bishops will be forced to allow the Indult Mass in their dioceses. If you stay outside, you will most likely divide and re-divide, and drink the gall of hatred poured out from the pulpit, and die alone and loveless. Or your sect will turn into a virulent cult. It is showing signs of doing just that around St. Mary's, Kansas.

Catholics who have gone over to the SSPX or to other schismatic groups should hear what Ronald Knox says in *The Belief of Catholics*:

> To believe in Catholic doctrines without believing in the existence of that infallible authority which guarantees them all is to hold, not the Catholic faith, but a series of speculative opinions. It is the first infidelity that counts.

He might have added that infidelity to the chief shepherd of that last, large, supernatural tribe that holds the world in its hands, whose little plot of ground called the Vatican City State provides a gate for the Angels to descend and ascend to and from the earth—separation from that distant, but final, authority will drop you into the sea of sects, where your faith will rise and fall according to the way you feel about Bishop Williamson or your local shepherd or any other unsanctioned egomaniac you choose to follow.

Chapter Twelve

The Keys of the Kingdom

The Moonie Pledge Ceremony I unwillingly attended in 1975 required a vow from the assembled disciples to follow the Rev. Sun Myung Moon through "blood, sweat, and tears" to bring about an Ideal World. Mr. Moon's thoughts were to be our thoughts, Mr. Moon's will was to be our will.

The "statement of commitment" pledged by Word of God charismatic community disciples says: "We are ready for every sacrifice, even death, if the Lord honors us by calling us to die for Him or our brothers. We are ready to serve until the Lord indicates that the war has been won. We will be loyal to our commanders, knowing that they are committed to defend and provide for our homes and families. We will serve where they direct us and in the way they direct us. We will keep our plans and movements hidden from the enemy and his agents."

This pledge came into use in the early 1980s when it was recited at the end of an intensive Training Course. The course consisted of some forty lectures by "covenant community" elders focusing on three primary areas: Ideologies of the enemy, specifically Marxism, feminism, and secular humanism; "Approaches to Christian Fighting/Strategy"; and "Home Front" teachings which focused on internal community behavior.

Perhaps we have learned enough about cults to see in these bare titles and militant words and "training course" strategies something unhealthy for souls. See how all the bases are covered and how the community is walled in. First there is an unlimited submission to one's leaders, a submission that covers the whole of life and explicitly includes the disciple's death—if required for the cause of Jesus Christ. The sheep are thoroughly bound to the shepherd. Then, tactics to deal with "the enemy and his agents," including deception and secrecy towards that enemy. The herd is psychologically isolated from the world. Remove the words "training course," "shepherding," "disciple," "covenant community," and "enemy," and look at the underlying reality; then project substitute titles on the movie screen, say, after a Friday night entertainment at Boonville: training session, subject/object, Following Center, Unification Church, Satanic world.

Or forget the Moonie comparison, and take a closer look at the Word of God covenant community. Steven Clark and Ralph Martin founded it in 1970 at Ann Arbor, Michigan, after some earlier attempts were made to promote Catholic charismatic renewals at Notre Dame and Duquesne University. The charismatic renewal itself took a page from the Protestant Pentecostals. The Catholic version was similar in most respects, except for the theological tenet that a Catholic had already received the Holy Spirit at Baptism and sealed it at Confirmation. While Protestants insisted on a vivid experience of the Spirit as proof of its reception, Catholics presumably stirred up that Spirit which had already been given by the sacraments. The Gifts of the Spirit vouchsafed to Catholics were, however, the same in character as the Protestant brand. Mostly they amounted to speaking in tongues, prophesying, and discerning spirits. The Word of God community had both Catholic and Protestant memberships. Its character or "feel" was that of Pentecostal revivalism.

After my Way Ministry experience, I am entirely skeptical that these Gifts of the Spirit are genuine. But I am not willing to rule them out. They happened in the early Church; perhaps they can happen today. One, however, must keep a tight rein on credulity when one hears of a Protestant Pentecostal group, the Kansas City Fellowship, "repenting of the use of prophetic gifts for controlling purposes." According to Tom Nash's article in *Fidelity* magazine (June 1991), this public *mea culpa* took place around 1988. The question immediately intrudes: if a prophecy is admitted to have been "used" to control followers, the prophet has admitted his own skepticism regarding the prophecy. Maybe it was his own mind, and not the mind of God, who had spoken. Once that doubt arrives, the whole theory of charismatic prophecy falls down.

Right in this area, the charismatic idea leads directly to cult control. A leader who speaks with the Holy Spirit is speaking for God. When God speaks, you had better listen. If Steven Clark, an unordained Catholic minister, receives the Word from God telling you exactly what to do, to think, or to believe, then Steven Clark has immense power over you—if you fall for it.

The germ of this power (unacknowledged, of course) formed in Clark's mind back in the 1960s when he was a student at Notre Dame. He conceived of the idea of Christian communities headed by unordained pastors who would be "psychological and spiritual counselors" for their flocks. In a 1976 book, *Unordained Elders and Renewal Communities*, Clark presents a model for his idea through a comparison with the ancient Desert Fathers, whose communities were often headed by holy men who had no sacramental orders. The comparison is off the point, since these Fathers were indeed off in the desert, physically out of touch with diocesan structures, and, wherever they were close enough to towns and cities, they came under the authority of the dioceses.

In any case, it is always an uncertain business to resurrect ancient movements or events and apply them or imitate them in the modern world. Imitations of this sort always tend to be out of synch with customs, cultures, and even souls. They are necessarily artificial constructions and often prove to be counterfeits. Human spirituality along with human culture has evolved or devolved over the aeons; what was fresh and powerful in the time of the apostles is no more. I have yet to see tongues of fire descending on the heads of "apostles" in a modern charismatic group, and no one can tell me that the contemplative spirituality of St. Antony or the hermit Paul is anything like the spirituality of Ralph Martin or Steven Clark.

Unordained Elders is not about charisms of the Holy Spirit, however; it is a defense of lay leadership in Christian "covenant" communities, effectively removed from the guardianship of the Catholic Church. The new communities, taking a "deeper walk" with the Lord, were deliberately removed from parish structures. The ordinary parishes were considered to be too dry and stale to provide a proper home for the outpouring of the Holy Spirit. But that very divorce in authority opened the door for a parallel church to develop. This is what happened to the Word of God community. It went its own way, ruled by Ralph Martin and Steven Clark and a few other "elders."

The control it imposed was total, as revealed by the pledge cited above and by *Patterns of Christian Community: A Statement of Community Order*. Published in 1984, the book is a compendium of "coordinator's decisions" in the group from 1971 to 1975. On page 51, Clark presents his notion of pastoral authority: "Those who belong to a Christian community are subject to its governmental authority for their whole lives.... They have committed their whole lives to the Lord and to one another. The government of the community, therefore, extends to everything in their lives." An earlier dictum from the "Decisions of the Coordinators" (May 1976), informs disciples that "the basic authority of the coordinators comes from the Covenant relationship . . . in matters which involve participation in the things we do together as a Community, the final decision about what a member does is the Coordinator's; in matters which concern what a member does outside of those things we do together as a Community, the individual is subordinate to the Coordinator . . . the Coordinator's authority is unlimited in scope. There is nothing in the life of the Community or in the lives of the individual members that it does not reach to."

Even the Moonies were never so brazen, at least until the recruit had been so thoroughly imbued with the life that he had no defense left against totalist control of his every activity.

But these Christians were filled with the Scriptures; they heard gobbles and gabbles translated into prophesies; they felt the rush of spiritual emotion; they felt themselves transported into the times of the apostles; they felt the world coming to an imminent end, with all things about to be transformed into a new heaven and a new earth. Caught up in all that feeling and expectation, they could accept without protest a "covenant" that ordered their lives absolutely.

I have no doubts about the existence of the Holy Spirit, but I have my doubts about the worship of the Holy Spirit these days, especially when He is divided off from the other Two Persons of the Trinity. It seems a form of instant emotional gratification masquerading as instant deification. It seems to be the self-worship of the God Who Gabbles in an Unknown Tongue. During these prayer meetings a person would "speak in tongues." Another person might then "interpret." The message from God has now moved from the unknown to the known. Glory to God in the Highest! It is reminiscent of the Way Ministry, and I have the same complaint here as I had then. If these events are real, they are tremendous. They are astounding. In thousands of charismatic groups across the country and across the world, God Himself is allegedly entering into people and speaking through them. Where is the overturning of the world that should come from such a flood of the Spirit? Where is the radical sundering of souls, the utterly transformed lives, the ten thousand new Mother Teresas, the five thousand new Isaiahs, the thousand new St. Pauls? Do people really believe that what they say is happening at these prayer meetings is really happening? Then why do they receive only an emotional lift and a tighter bond to the group, a warm feeling that they are close to God, and then go back to their daily lives as if nothing much has happened?

I think the answer is that nothing much has happened. Human beings have the capacity to relax and babble and think it's the babble of the Holy Spirit. Other people in the room can relax their minds and spew a string of pious words and think it's an interpretation of the babble. When I was a poet back in the 1960s, given the right musical accompaniment, I could mouth a half-hour's worth of rhymed couplets, made up on the spot. All it takes is a certain mental relaxation which allows the release of seemingly uncommon human mental capacities. Rap singers can do the same thing. There is nothing remarkable about it except that it demonstrates the rich, barely subliminal mentation going on in human souls. I think "Holy Spirit" babblings and interpretations and prophecies are in the same category, with rare exceptions. Would a man who really believed he had prophesied in the Spirit do nothing more than say good-bye to the folks, go home and mow the grass, and look forward to next Sunday's prayer meeting?

On the other hand, would not prophetic utterances coming from anywhere in the group produce constant crises of authority? If shepherd Steve held a doctrine which disciple Joe contradicted by prophecy, how would the community avoid anarchy? We'll turn for a moment from Michigan to Ohio to find the answer, in another covenant community that was, like the Word of God, part of the Holy Spirit cartel called the Sword of the Spirit. A "Manifesto" drawn up on October 30, 1990, by twenty-six distraught members of the Servants of Christ the King in Steubenville, Ohio, includes a testimony on the authenticity of prophecies. It says, "Pastoral leaders with the greatest authority screened the prophecies that were to be received. A clear slant towards the leader's interpretation was evident in which prophecies were given. It has become clear to us that the Word of the Lord has often been the word of the leaders."

Screened the prophecies? Again, the theory of charismatic gifts falls apart. How could these gifts be considered genuine when they were subject to human vetoes? Shall man censor God? Or are covenant communities so controlled that they cannot even reason on this most obvious level? The manifesto decrying the practice came twenty years after the charismatic bandwagon got rolling. It all says something about the strength of tribal submission, and nothing about the graces of God.

Tribal submission became pervasive over the years. On April 21, 1991, an unofficial report was issued by Muriel Mooney, Peter Clark, and Jo Noetzel of the Ann Arbor (Michigan) Word of God community. The report throws a spotlight on what can only be called a laboratory of cult control. Under various headings, each a generally accepted mark of destructive cults, the report details life in the Word of God's mental universe.

"Thought reform" is a loaded term introduced by the psychologist Robert Lifton in his research on Korean War prisoners who had been subjected to intensive reeducation in Communist P.O.W. camps. Under that title, the Mooney report quotes from a 1977 memo from Steven Clark to Ralph Martin and other coordinators: "We need an approach to the formation of the mind and thought of the leaders and influential people in our Communities . . . Discipleship should be the mode of training . . . We should provide a 'counter-environment' and 'counter-tradition.'"

The "thought reform" of members proceeded firstly along the lines of behavioral control: a highly-regulated life-style, with set services, rituals, daily prayers, Wednesday prayers for "God's people," disparagement of individualism, disdain of emotions, and control of information. People were to think only of the group and put a clamp on criticisms. Feelings were repressed, except, presumably, during Holy Spirit encounters. Guilt was inculcated by the failure to meet impossible standards of perfection; "excessive fear was present as it seemed difficult for some members to feel there was any security outside the group."

Reeducation consisted of a constant barrage of instruction at weekly gatherings, family forums, women's nights and retreats, men's nights and retreats, teaching weekends, district retreats, and, of course, the forty-lecture Training Course. The whole intent was to make people believe that the Word of God "represented all that was good and necessary to meet our needs." Analytical thinking was traded in for complete dependence on the thought of the leaders: "many members regressed to child-like dependency."

Outside the group was the "world," full of fallen souls, mistrusted, feared, despised. Inside the group, as WOG leader Jim McFadden confessed at a General Community Gathering on December 16, 1990, members were subjected to fear and guilt to keep them loyal to the program. The Mooney report comments: "We were led to believe that the world is rough without Community, that something bad might happen if we left the Word of God." When the WOG was struggling for independence from the overarching Sword of the Spirit in the summer of 1990, Steven Clark blistered the faithful with these remarks: "Each one of you, individually, is leaving the Community that you belong to [Sword of the Spirit]. Each one of you, individually, is dropping the covenant relationship you have with the Community you belong to and with other brothers and sisters who are in that Community ... You will be leaving a covenant relationship." This condemnation, ringing with Old Testament associations, was delivered at a meeting at Domino Farms on August 11, 1990.

The Mooney report reveals that WOG recruitment had much in common with Unification Church recruitment: "we used an initiation process which overwhelmed newcomers with love and acceptance at the onset. Our selective recruitment process did not include full disclosure of the Community's methods and purposes. We often used layers of truth, revealing our existing policies a step at a time as we felt they were ready. At some point, newcomers would be informed of financial commitments, dating policies, preferred manner of dress, uncompromising rules, men's and women's roles, and the authority structure of the Community." There follows a quote from the Training Course: "As new brothers and sisters and guests come into our life, we want them to confront issues in proper order. For instance, we want them to learn about our love for one another before learning that we believe in giving away a great deal of our money to the Lord's work, or we want them to experience the care of a head [a leader] before they learn about commitment to heads."

This is the time-honored strategy of Gnostic sects. Come into the life where all is peace and harmony. Then learn about the terrible burdens you will bear. Come in and learn all about God, and tomorrow we will teach you all about Satan. And you can defeat Satan only by becoming rigid, robotic, obedient, and ultra-puritanical—until the judgment of the elders rules every aspect of your life. And when the perfectionism and obedience wears you out, you are told, "if you leave, something terrible might happen."

In 1982 Steven Clark left Ralph Martin in charge of the Word of God community and formed the Sword of the Spirit, an umbrella organization to which various local covenant communities were affiliated. Its Catholic branch is Christ the King International.

Within the Sword of the Spirit, Clark formed an elite core of about one hundred celibates known as the Servants of the Word. Later Martin associated the Word of God group to the Protestant Prophetic Movement, itself formed primarily from two other Pentecostal groups, the Vineyard ministry and the Kansas City Fellowship. "Prophecies" or "discernments" from the leaders of these groups in 1989 and 1990 were the occasion for a split between Clark and Martin. The first event was a prophecy from Paul Cain of the Kansas City Fellowship, the purport of which was to indict Martin and Clark as shepherds whose work had gone bad in the eyes of God. In February 1990, at another conference, John Wimber of the Vineyard "discerned" that control and manipulation had infected the Sword of the Spirit groups.

Ralph Martin tells me that he noticed something going wrong with things, especially in the area of social engineering and dictatorial control, as far back as the initial formation of the Sword of the Spirit in 1982. Implicit in this contention is Martin's doubt regarding Clark's very formation of a wider controlling organization, set up so as to govern all the member communities, including Martin's Word of God.

In December 1990, Ken Wilson, "pastor" of the WOG, stood up in front of a Word of God meeting and begged forgiveness for himself and his fellow leaders for their abuse of authority, for their fostering of elitism and secrecy, their demands for absolute loyalty, their social engineering, and other sins of control. Six months earlier the Word of God community had voted itself out from under control of the Sword of the Spirit and into an "allied" status which translated to local autonomy in government, pastoring, and teaching. (This was the occasion for Steven Clark's malediction hurled at the covenant-breakers.) Seventeen other Sword of the Spirit groups followed suit. In 1991 Bishop Albert Ottenweller called upon the Steubenville,

Ohio local affiliate, the Servants of Christ the King, to dissolve its ties with the Sword of the Spirit and with Christ the King International. The bishop detailed some of the abuses in the community: members were forced to accept patterns of living, relationships, and even marriage partners in accordance with the desires of their masters.

Ralph Martin and his cohorts in the Word of God have (presumably) seen the errors of their ways: they have seen past the Christian trappings into the realities of the situation. Martin said (in 1991), "I almost feel like I'm in recovery. You know, I feel like I'm getting deprogrammed or reprogrammed or recovered. Like veils are being taken off. I'm seeing things in a way I haven't seen them before." One hopes so. But the report on the WOG quoted above declares that it "is not an official statement of any leaders of the Word of God." The situation may still be volatile.

Steven Clark has not seen the errors of his ways. He thinks the Word of God community developed troubles because discipline was lax. He sees Martin's association with Protestant groups as infecting the Word of God community with antinomian, leaderless religion. He claims that Martin's turnaround was based on Protestant so-called "discernments," which he should not have taken seriously. Martin denies his reliance on these "discernments." They may have been the occasion for the split, but Martin's disaffection had been growing for years.

Clark is the chief theoretician and disciplinarian of the prophetic duo. He retains the notion of "whole life pastoring," which he developed two decades ago. All those groups still within the Sword of the Spirit association continue to live under Clark's totalitarian idea. And most remain removed from oversight by Catholic or Protestant ecclesiastical bodies.

The intimate social engineering Clark's Sword of the Spirit imposes can be gleaned from the manifesto signed by twenty-six members of SOS affiliate Servants of Christ the King in Ohio in late 1990. "Whole life pastoring" meant that individual lives were ordered right down to hourly schedules. Dictated were the quality and quantity of marital sexual relationships, the correct program for child raising, who and how single people could date (generally, only within the community), the proper form of courtship, dress codes, hairstyles, careers, and major purchases, and even where people should move so as to be closer to their covenant "clusters." The "clusters" were another management idea—the division of the faithful into even more tightly bound little pods of communal living.

Individuals were subject to a "pastoral reporting system" that put their lives under a microscope. John Flaherty complains of a "comprehensive plan to 'form' me based on my perceived character weaknesses, [a document] professionally-finished on computer printout." Within the community private conversations were "reported up the pastoral chain" to provide a prurient feast for the overlords, and ammunition for control of persons. A wife could never know when her pillow talk might be loyally repeated to her husband's pastoral leader and then to his leader and so on up to Central Control. It is a frightening totalist system, more thorough than anything the Moonies managed to put in place.

The Sword of the Spirit's war on our progressively unisex culture took the form of a heavy-handed dictation of traditional roles for men and women. Men were to repress in themselves anything commonly thought to be feminine, like gentleness, sensitivity, emotion, and intuition. Cigar smoking was in, pink shirts were out. Women were seen as weak, emotional, and incapable of the measured reasoning that could make them viable contributors to household or community decisions. Even in the home, authority was limited to the husband and his pastoral leader.

If women were put into an artificially submissive position through a reckless application of certain verses in the Epistles of St. Paul, men were caught in the middle of the authority ladder. They must be obedient to other men, on higher rungs, for all life decisions, for character formation, for correction of faults, while at the same time fulfilling the role of household monarch. On paper, individual families were male-dominated entities, but in reality, they were slavish cells with their own privacy and unity blasted by the intimate control of a larger system.

A larger system of control seems a necessary consequence of any social engineering project. It might look good as a blueprint, but somebody has to build it and then enforce it. People are, after all, subtly made and obstinate and rich in personality. The artificial nature of an "imitation of things past" requires not only enforcers, but produces cardboard cut-outs of personality. Men can never be nurturing or emotional? Women can never be strong in character or thoughtful? The SOS ideal was narrowed to a caricature. The ideal leader (again I quote the Steubenville Manifesto) was "verbally zealous, never showing weakness, sharing 'only what he had to'":

> This allowed a false image of leaders to be promoted, facilitating a compelling tendency to lead a double life, maintaining a false front regarding one's own shortcomings. There existed a virtual refusal to allow a gap to exist between the high ideals of the Christian life and one's genuine, often serious, weaknesses. In many people's lives, this led to a judgmental, pharisaical approach to our personal Christian lives. People were "pegged," "judged," and/or "evaluated" by their pastoral leaders. Yet what the leader saw was sadly often a projection of his own weaknesses. A deep shame and harmful, unnecessary guilt resulted in people's lives.

This insidious internal government created its own spirit out of all that buried imperfection, criticism, fear, and shame. It is a spirit that seems to overtake all perfectionist cults. It collects to itself the whole psychic underground of human souls trying to live an ideal far from human realities. It becomes a kind of demon. But this dark side of sectarian existence is not what is presented with great fanfare and affectionate hugs to the disciples of the Holy Spirit. For its members, the Sword of the Spirit was "our family . . . often to the exclusion of our family of origin."

Our Family. Once again, like the Moonies, like the Way Ministry, this enthusiastic Christian tribe, united in purpose, zeroed in on the Holy Spirit, is "Our Family." Nor in this case is it a family that substitutes for one that is missing. Most cults fill their ranks from people removed from their families of origin. The Sword of the Spirit is a Family that insinuates itself so far into the little family that it collapses the little family as even a partially self-sufficient, self-ruling unit.

The manifesto which I have quoted was part of a grass roots initiative that finally brought in the local bishop and brought about a reform and a removal of the Steubenville group from the Sword of the Spirit's dictatorship. Bishops in other dioceses have become involved, and other charismatic communities have dissolved their allegiance to the SOS. But what about all those groups still existing within that pyramidal hierarchy at whose apex is the unregenerate Steven Clark? Will Clark and his Sword of the Spirit sheepfold finally be excommunicated and then go into the usual song and dance about the Church of Rome being in schism from the true Faith and themselves as upholding a purer Catholicism?

What makes people throw away their freedom and place themselves willingly under the consuming dictatorship of a self-proclaimed shepherd of souls?

A Christian in this country is not surrounded by a Christian culture. He must carry his religion around in his head. There are no crucifixes on the barroom wall or the classroom wall, and precious few on the walls of homes. Church bells no longer peal throughout the city on Sunday morning to call the people to worship. The greeting on the sidewalk is not "Praise be Jesus and Mary"; there is rarely any sort of greeting on the sidewalk. There is no help, only hostility, from the febrile arbiters of culture. Every day the believing Catholic, the faithful Protestant, the Orthodox Jew—anyone with a full sense of religion and religious strictures—is assaulted in the most sensitive parts of his being by the TV news, elementary school teachers, librarians, sit-coms, the *New York Times*, city councils, the universities, sculptors, painters, musicians, politicians, the feminist and homosexual lobbies, and most pervasively, the workplace.

Non-Catholics, non-Christians—atheists, materialists, ordinary faithless people—are all in a state of subliminal longing. They are as lonesome as the lonesome Christian, if on the public level they seem to have their own way. After the second abortion and the third husband, even those women still stuck in feminist ideology get lonely and frightened. Men without a religious faith play out their lives in a narrow range of getting and spending. Valium, booze, and cocaine provide a temporary comfort when there is no God.

This is the seed ground for cults. In an earlier chapter, I spoke of human identity which sends out tendrils of itself to the club, the company, the country, or the Church—or all of these. The problem in Western society (here you can go back to the break-up of Christendom four centuries ago) is the loss of a cohesive culture that can provide a secure larger identity for each person.

Let us take another look at the Moonie maid who drank wine for a year before she ran into the Unification Church. She was abandoned by her husband. Presumably there were no children. She had lost the nuclear family, which was the only larger identity she had. The Moonies got her. Immediately she got another family, complete with True Parents—which infantilized her. She was no longer grown up and lonely, but child-like and secure. She got a larger tribe, all unified and zeroed in on a single purpose. She got ceremonies and devotions and an image of God. (All she had to do was give up her free will.)

What does the outside world offer? A vaunted "pluralism," which means contending world-views and no unity of culture. A cosmos thought to be evolved automatically (Darwinism) or a cosmos thought to be created in all its parts. Political hatred between pan-sexual liberals and religious conservatives who try to preserve the family by putting constraints on sexual adventurism. Rampant divorce, homosexuality, murder of the preborn, feminists hating male dominance, and frightened men hating female dominance. Successful men who trade in one wife for another, younger wife. Successful women who can't find a man. No God or contending gods or imitation gods. Mammon and Dionysus. It would take an encyclopedia to document the chaos, but two things can be abstracted. The sexual revolution is killing the nuclear family, that social fundament of man, woman, and child. The extended family that once made up a real tribe of blood relation is gone except in parts of the American South. I got divorced, and I was all alone. The Moonie maid got divorced, and she was all alone.

So the one chaotic condition is the sexual revolution that is killing the family, and the other chaotic condition is that, when that little family is gone, there is nothing else. The larger culture just does not exist as a unity of ideas. And when that unity of ideas is missing, the little family can be split asunder, even while staying intact as a physical unit. The wife can be fiercely devoted to a sect of traditional Catholics while the husband plays along for fear of losing his wife— or he plays the field. Teenagers play demonic music in the den while grandmom prays the Rosary in her bedroom upstairs.

Let's put it another way. If a coherent religious culture is missing, the extended family is held together only by blood ties. It begins to dissolve as a cultural unit. When the extended, blood-tied family dissolves, it ceases to support the little family of man, woman, and child. That family in turn weakens. Then women turn on men, and men turn on women. Then women turn into men, and men turn into women. (Even sexual identity depends to some extent on a larger social identity. The homosexualist propaganda invading our schools—"maybe you're gay, maybe you're straight"—can only produce sexual ambiguity.) Freud's childhood phase of "polymorphous perversity" extends into adulthood and pervades the whole enfeebled cultural cosmos until the name of the culture itself is Polymorphous Perversity. Its god is Dionysus. The perverted social cosmos then provides no support for the extended family, which begins to dissolve as a unit providing probity, custom, and security to its members. Aunt Sally is a drunk; cousin Fred has just been indicted for securities fraud. The nuclear family is left all alone in the universe. Then women turn on men. Men get frightened and abuse women. Parents abuse children. And so on.

In other words, given the present state in the decline of Western culture, everyone is material for cults, most of which provide, or pretend to provide, proper roles for men and women, a family, a tribal unity, and a coherent religious cosmos. The full package is almost always called the Family, whether it is the Family of Moonies or the Way Ministry or the Sword of the Spirit—because it is the family, small or large, that has broken into pieces, and the family is the most intimate human thing and the most missed when it is missing. The word "family" has all the meanings in itself, from the little family to the tribal family to the family of God. It means togetherness; it means security; it always means love.

Cults pick up footloose people, travelers or the recently divorced or college dropouts or the recently graduated. Or whole families, sick of a bowdlerized liturgy that answers to no deep spiritual needs, join a sect that involves their religious needs totally, a sect which itself devolves into a cult that captures the family and kills it as a reasoning and reasonable unit. This is what is happening today in the Society of Saint Pius X, for example. It happened ten years ago in the Fatima Crusaders, and continues to happen today. And it happens by fiat in the Sword of the Spirit.

The cult, or the sectarian movement, gives you not only a totally lived religion, but, since you already know that the larger society has gone to hell in a handbasket, it gives you that delicious outlaw feeling of opposition to the society, that feeling of being a part of an elite reform, a remnant, a favored race, aristocrats of the apocalypse.

Why do sects become cults? That is, why do they become evil? Why, in the name of religion, do they dominate and then destroy personalities? I suspect it goes right back to fallen human nature. Cult leaders try to manufacture a whole world, separate from the world, without the backing of a genuine Revelation and with only their unacknowledged lust for power to sustain the effort. So they rule their scene, then rule it more closely, then rule it so completely that the people in their charge lose their very wills as they bow lower and lower to the ground, trying to please their Father as he demands ever greater proofs of obedience.

It could be that the ill wind that in the modern age has made a seed-ground for cults has also blown into the souls of cult-masters. If this is the age of the Antichrists, there are plenty to go around. Maybe that is why there is so much evil in sects and so much parallel evil from one cult to another. The strongest card that singular evil holds is the cultural disarray that makes disconnected people and disconnected families throw away their souls for a tribal identity.

Why can't you walk away when the god of the cult shows his true face? Because the release of gratitude for that high unifying identity has sundered your whole psyche. Generations of Americans (and Europeans and most of the world) have grown up and lived their whole lives without that tribal identity. Then they run into a cult and get what people haven't got for decades, maybe centuries. A deep human thing wakes up. An addiction results, like the strongest addiction of a man for his wife. So when the bliss and power turn into fear and slavery, that condition is of little account as compared to the attachment that has become the deepest part of your humanity.

Or a conflict develops in the soul. I remember that time back in the summer of 1973 when I grew more and more skeptical of the Divine Principle and more and more irritated at the forced emotion and forced praise we were expected to display on every occasion. At the same time I wished, I needed, to get closer to the center of things. It is very difficult to describe, this counter-pull that increased in intensity as my mind tried to pull away. The two contrary things were happening not so much on the level of reason warring with emotion, but on the level of identity as an individual at war with identity as a—what? A tribal person? Lost in the sea of love? Asleep in the womb of the cult? Metaphors fail me. It is something that the mind itself cannot describe since it is somehow lower or deeper or above the mind.

Whatever it is, the conflict introduces a constant, half-buried, gnawing anxiety. I think a lot of long-term Moonies and other cultists endure this anxiety, which cannot be expressed since it would indicate a less than blessed condition. A Moonie must always be happy—after all, he is a disciple of the Lord of the Second Advent. Then what happened in Moonie headquarters in 1980 when a long-term, "good Moonie" like Nick told me he was lonely? It must have been a momentary lapse, a moment's self-recognition, blurted to an outsider, a person not there every day, in contrast to his usual companions, cocooning him, clothed and clotted in the good Moonie role.

What happens is that the very soul gets mashed down in order to relieve the conflict. The conflict is not resolved, for to resolve it would be to heed finally the voice of the individual self, with its conscientious judgment of things, and leave the cult. Instead, the conflict is buried by burying the judgments of the mind. And then, in some cults, odd things begin to happen. Like irrational violence.

The Synanon cult had a jump start on violence because the Synanon Game ruthlessly destroyed conscience as it battered self-respect and then turned every concept upside down. "Irreverence is the mode." All meanings became valueless vomit to be spewed from one person at another. The Synanon tribal identity did not even have the pretense of sanctity or rationality. Loathsome things became the order of the day—beatings, torture, the forced transfer of sexual partners, abortions and vasectomies, attempted murder of perceived enemies, the forced demolition of any vestige of the little family. Synanon was very nearly a milder microcosm of the Khmer Rouge, with its instant mass murders and its brave new world starting with the Year One.

Synanon violence is comparatively easy to comprehend. But God-seeking cults end up in the same banality of evil. Leaders in the Hare Krishna cult started murdering each other in the West Virginia hills some years ago. (Why? Did the inner conflict between self and universal Self get too hard to bear?) The Rajneesh folks who had settled in Oregon awhile ago created a stir when they attempted a mass poisoning of their neighbors. Elizabeth Clare Prophet's Summit Lighthouse theosophists got in trouble recently for trying to purchase automatic weapons in Spokane, Washington. The weapons were presumably to defend the buzzing chanters of the Great White Brotherhood from the outside populace after an (imminent) thermonuclear war. Elizabeth's bunch has built a huge, well-stocked underground bomb shelter in Montana which the starving and ragged remnant will surely try to take over after the destruction of the world. The Great White Brotherhood will be ready for them.

Bishop Williamson of the Society of St. Pius X says he will be ready when the forces of evil come for him and try to put him and his Catholic remnant in detention camps. Meanwhile, around St. Mary's, Kansas, true believers are buying guns and putting up notices on the doors of critics saying "Your time has come." (I just got that news as this book goes to press.)

If there is one thing that ties all this violence and preparation for violence together, it is the fact that each sect feels itself a tiny elite, surrounded by a world of incarnate evil. The situation almost demands the development of a tribal spirit of paranoia. (The world is pretty big and the cult is pretty small. So it has to think big.) Individual alienation is replaced by tribal alienation.

But there is something I am missing. Why the paranoia and rifles in the Society of St. Pius X, and not in the Charismatic groups? Maybe the "covenant communities" are not so divorced from the outside world. Perhaps these minds are not so isolated and afraid. They can turn on the TV and see their spiritual cousins emote and swoon before a Pentecostal preacher. Maybe the madness of the Holy Ghost idolaters is closer to the madness of the wider culture. It has a wider resonance, and even a kind of respectability in the American world of spiritual entertainment. And since the Church hierarchy in various places is interjecting itself into the covenant communities, these communities may be saved, finally, from that social and spiritual isolation which ends in violence.

Each sect has its own mental parameters and its own motivations to peace or war, isolation or outreach. Still, it is a shock to see the tribal god so often demanding blood, even when the tribe is ostensibly a form of Christianity (which has its Ten Commandments and its Sermon on the Mount), or Hinduism (with its endurance and passivity and meditative practice).

There is no reasonable answer to the violence. Something in the group spirit gets twisted, and blood is spilled not only where you'd expect it, but where you'd least expect it, like in peaceful Hindu communities, or in the . . . Waldenses. Let us take a glimpse at Europe eight centuries back and see cult-like events happening there too. The cult mentality and its perverted twistings are not just a contemporary phenomenon.

Of all the Medieval sects, the Waldenses were considered the most peace-loving. Central to their belief was a rejection of all violence. Their elect, called the Apostles, claimed to receive their authority directly from the angels. The Apostles claimed to visit heaven regularly and contemplate God face to face. Naturally, they came to reject any earthly authority, including, of course, the Church. Their whole tenor was other-worldly in the extreme. But from time to time a furious spirit overcame them, and then Waldensian groups burned the houses of Catholic priests, killed deserters from their ranks, and put prices on the heads of enemies.

The sect had started in the late twelfth century as a reform movement that depended on the Scriptures alone for guidance and followed the sayings of Jesus literally. They embraced poverty, lived as mendicants, and entered on a program of lay preaching. It was this latter program that got them in trouble with the Church hierarchy. Lay ministers, lacking theological training or accreditation, unordained; a separate ministry, a separate life-style, a separate worship—all this is reminiscent of the modern "covenant communities." Under the influence of the contemporary Cathars, some Waldenses moved towards heresy, picking up the Cathars' hatred of matter, their notion that Christ was pure spirit, and their creation of a spiritual elite in intimate contact with heaven. Similarly, the unordained Steven Clark and his elite fellows in the Sword of the Spirit teach with the authority of the Holy Spirit.

The Waldenses were excommunicated in 1184, but managed to stay in existence for several hundred years, most of the survivors joining with the (Protestant) Anabaptists in the sixteenth century. Many Catholic charismatics today have likewise gone over to the Protestant Pentecostals. Ever since Protestantism has existed, and especially as parts of it have gone in the direction of religious enthusiasm and congregational autonomy, it has been a logical home for Catholics disaffected with hierarchical constraints.

A similar thirteenth century unworldly sect called the Apostolic Brethren considered killing a man for any reason to be a mortal sin. They were pacifists in a world where city warred on city and where brigandage was the order of the day. But this non-violent doctrine swiftly transformed itself into the doctrine that persecution of the sect was a mortal offense, justifying any action against the foes of the faith.

In that sudden transformation, we can see exactly what is happening in the Society of St. Pius X. Charity is at the heart of the Christian faith. Killing a person, except under carefully prescribed conditions, is a mortal sin. But another, more heinous sin has overwhelmed that fundamental law. That is the persecution of the remnant elect. So (imagined) persecution is met with homicidal fury. After all, if the Society contains the last and only people in league with God, everyone else is in the grip of Satan, and murdering Satan is no sin. So true believers at St. Mary's, Kansas, tamper with cars belonging to the sect's enemies with the intent to bring about fatal accidents.

Is there nothing new under the sun? From this distance we cannot get inside the Waldenses or the Apostolic Brethren to see if they commanded the same mental tyranny over their members we can see operating in the Moonies or the Fatima Crusaders or the Sword of the Spirit. But what we can pick up—the separate existence, the spiritual elitism, the isolation from the world, the developing hatred of outsiders as minions of Satan—all these are suggestive. It is possible that my list of social evils in today's world is no rare thing either. Perhaps my analysis is overheated, and perhaps Europeans enduring the Black Death or the invasion of the Huns had greater reason to believe their world was overwhelmed by a demonic horror than we do today. Perhaps the tribal life I encountered in 1973 always has the same consequences in any time and any place: a taste of heaven followed by a life that sometimes seems like hell. The pure tribe I thought might have existed sometime in the pre-technological past, in some degree, in some country (especially in thirteenth century Europe, at the supposed high point of Christendom), is perhaps an illusion, and must always remain an illusion this side of paradise. Maybe it is a general truth that as long as human beings are human beings, the tighter the bonds of the tribe, the more shocking the evil that results from a tribal identity.

There may be an avenue to understanding the evil of cults that has a partial application also to totalist political ideologies. In a cult your ego (your social identity) is first magnified and magnified again by tribal approval and tribal affection, which elicits from you a deep gratitude, devotion, and loyalty, and then the tribe as a genie, a spirit, pounces on you and demands you to give up your soul to it. "Pray harder! Work harder! Sell more flowers! Build the Material Foundation! Higher Truth!" Like any pagan god, the god of the cult is manufactured from the human spirit, which has a dark side. If publicly the tribe allows only perfection and rectitude, the collective psyche built from repressed parts of human souls forms itself into an independent spirit. It is a spirit that contains the unadmitted sins, shame, and rage of people pretending to be perfect. That spirit becomes the unacknowledged god of the sect. You start out as a tribe of harmony and love, and two years down the road you are buying guns to defend yourself against the alien Satanic world.

"Independent spirit"? It may seem fanciful, but I present it as one key at least to the theory of cults. Such a spirit is created instantly in a mob scenario. Sociologists have often remarked on the amorality of mobs. They ask: how can people in collective situations lose their moral inhibitions so swiftly and indulge their unfettered instincts for rape and riot and hangings in the night? I think it goes back to the point that conscience is an individual thing, or rather, it is a public thing that must be held by individuals. It requires thinking minds. In a mob, as in a cult, that self-contained capacity for conscientious judgment suddenly or slowly bleeds away. Individual identity is jettisoned for communal identity, with the loss of that capacity which comes with being an individual: the ability to think freely, to judge freely, and to reason out freely the consequences of this or that credo or activity.

Then what is it that thinks for the mob? And what is it that thinks for the cult? It is too easy to say that it is the rabble-rousing revolutionary leader or the cult-master or the calculating shepherd of souls. Followers are implicated in the sins of their leaders. Mr. Moon wanted to be my mind, and I was outraged. He also, being the great champion of God, would reap the judgment upon himself, for good or ill. Of course, it would be for good, and we would all share in that great blessing when God blessed our True Parent. A part of me relished the thought that if all my actions were given over to Mr. Moon, with the consequences coming to him alone and not to me, then I could "get off" in the karmic sense. The jots and the tittles would have nothing to do with me.

Even as I write these words I cringe. That night in the kitchen of the New Yorker Hotel comes back to me. I cringed then, too, and held back. Why? Because I am a human being. I am responsible for my soul. To make Mr. Moon responsible for my soul would be to give him my soul. And how many people in Weimar Germany, economically shattered, culturally in a juggernaut of perversion, sick of their freedom, sick of their high and moody intellects, gave their souls to Adolph Hitler?

What thinks for the mob or the cult or the tyrannical state is a psychic entity, created by everything human that is left when individual consciences have been excised, and individual minds have become communal minds, unable to judge what is good and what is evil.

In a mob scene, a riot, or a bacchanalia, the ripping out of mental integrity is acute and temporary. The soul is suddenly caught up in the action; it is voluntarily displaced, and as easily returns. In a political dictatorship the soul is ground down over the decades. Today Russia is experiencing the results of seventy-five years of dread and a billion cynical mental adjustments that have left most of its people passive and unable to assume responsibility for their lives. It is almost like a gigantic deprogramming.

Submission in cults is more voluntary than in police states, and so cultic disciples are more implicated in the make-up of the cultic god, and more culpable—though this statement should be varied according to the various cults and dictatorial regimes that have existed. However, the cultic god, or *egregore* (as these psychically created entities are sometimes called), is always closely entwined in the mentality, and even in the subconscious mentality, of the cultist, as it is not in the typical Cuban or North Korean citizen. It may be a different story with a Palestinian terrorist or a soldier of the Shining Path. A political cult may be more demonized than any religious cult.

The spirit of a cult, political or religious, is as tightly bound to each person in the cult as the cult itself is tightly bound together. It is as distinctively evil as the public persona and creed of the cult is distinctively good. It could ruin souls if human beings were not so wonderfully resilient.

When I entered the Catholic Church I thought it was the farthest thing from being a cult that could be imagined. It is just that, in its wholeness and its hugeness, its historical depths and its spiritual heights. Looked at as a society, it is a gigantic voluntary organization, ruled by a monarch who cannot command obedience other than by spiritual sanctions. The Pope cannot shoot recalcitrant bishops, and he cannot pull the whole mass of Catholics into slavish obedience by sending them all to a 120-day training camp in the Catskills. Particular parts of the Church can, and have, gotten themselves into the equivalent of a Moonie fortress, but only when little tin gods carve out minor kingdoms for themselves and attract innocently submissive people to their counterfeits of Christian life.

Today cults come to birth among Catholics because the world has changed chaotically, and the world has infected the Church. A lot of traditional Catholics who blame Vatican II or the post-Vatican II popes or the American Hierarchy, should realize that it is the world itself that has lost more and more of its moral grounding, its philosophical common sense, and its cultural cohesion. Vatican II may have been the occasion for this ill wind blowing into the Church, but it was not the cause. The ill wind was building and gaining force before the Council, and it would have entered whether or not the Council gave it a sudden opening. The so-called "spirit of Vatican II" is not the spirit of the Council at all, but the spirit of the world.

You don't have to be a Catholic to feel confused and upset by it all, and it is not only Catholics enduring banal liturgies and corruptions of the creed who endure banality and corruption in their lives. What I mean is that you can't blame the Church too much for what is happening in the Church. It is happening everywhere.

But what is happening in the Church—liturgical changes for the worse, with cheap music and cavalier approaches to the altar of God; a spirit of rebellion among priests and prelates who refuse to take orders from Rome, or who in a more subtle manner agree to those orders and then turn around and do the opposite; a people confused, ill-led, their churches ripped apart and redone as theaters-in-the-round; the loss of a Catholic culture in which a unity of ideas and morality gave the layman his Catholic identity; even the loss in many places of the sense of the supernatural—all these things have made Catholics try to reinvent the Church by binding themselves to a charismatic leader who takes them back, so they think, to the time of the Little Flower or the Council of Trent or all the way back to Pentecost. If in that process they remove themselves from the jurisdiction of the Church hierarchy, either legally or in spirit, they invariably fall into the trap of do-it-yourself religion. The resulting cultic isolation can lead straight to Boonville or Jonestown, or to the holocaust of 85 Branch Davidians along with their Messiah, in Waco, Texas, on April 19, 1993.

One major reason I knew the Church is for real is that it is the only world institution that upholds natural human things in this time of moral disintegration. The Church upholds the family; it insists on the sanctity of marriage; it promotes fairness in economic structures; it upholds appropriate roles for men and women; it says that abortion is murder and birth control is murderous to human love. It stays in touch with biological reality by saying (along with biology) that human life begins at conception and that the continuity of the species depends on children as gifts to cherish and nurture. Even in the years when I looked for love in all the wrong places, I knew implicitly that the Catholic social mandate conforms to social sanity—only I never gave a thought to the fact that it was Catholic. A while later I realized that the Church and only the Church is a final bastion against the sexual and moral and philosophical anarchy of the modern world.

The Church's social and sexual disciplines are in line with the natural law; the natural law is in line with Christian Revelation. Think of the principled action of *Humanae Vitae* and the debacle it engendered, and realize how the Church stands against the world (that is, for the natural law and against unnatural human proclivities), no matter what the consequences. And what about all the Catholics who dissent from these biologically sane teachings? That is the ill wind that blows up from the pit of the world to infect all institutions in the world.

I spoke before of growing up and becoming a Catholic. What it means is that I don't have to change teams when so many on my team are disloyal, especially since it is the only team. It is the whole ball game. I don't have to carry the Church on my shoulders. God does that. If a feminist-run guitar Mass in this or that parish affronts me, I go to a Mass (I'm lucky) where we sing the *Agnus Dei* in Latin and skip the kiss of peace and kneel for communion. If there's no Mass like that around, there's a Byzantine Rite across town. The kind of growing up I mean is that I accept limits and adjust to situations. If the Church today is going through a time of troubles, there was rarely a time when this was not so. Today, as compared to the 1950s, it is more up to me to be a good Catholic (if possible) in spite of the troubles in the Church. But as compared to the fifteenth century, when the constant cry all over Europe was "reform of head and members," I have it easier. Today, in spite of what the traditionalist schismatics say, the head needs no reform: it is the members who refuse to listen. If I still have the kind of mind that says, "If it ain't perfect, I won't play," then I have a cult mentality, like so many who kiss off the Church and create their own Catholicism and follow the road to ruin. All roads lead to Rome or all roads lead to yourself.

This is not to say I have matured spiritually and, therefore, have become a Catholic. It is to say that I am a Catholic, and therefore I have a chance to mature. It is impossible to mature inside a childish philosophy like existentialism or humanism or hedonism; it is at least possible to mature inside a philosophy that is as true as the Alpha and Omega. There are precious few adults in the world, in the sense I mean, and I can only hope to become one sometimes in some places. The point is to endure, even when you have to sing "Here I Am, Lord" in your local church. If you can't abide that piece of self-divinizing tripe, get up an hour earlier and drive fifty miles to a parish that still worships God. Make do. Look at the beast in your own heart, and put a lid on presumption. Try to love God, and stop picking on our poor pope, who is a faithful Catholic and who is doing the best he can in a world on the edge of moral ruin.

It is possible that since I had rejected the Faith back in 1973, God sent me on a trip of false turnings, showed me the ocean without a compass, so I would finally come back humbled. It is also possible that I learned things about the Faith itself in these other places. The Moonies bred intensity of religious endeavor and an insight into the tribal need and tribal capacity of the human soul (but at what a cost). The Way Ministry showed me how Pauline descriptions of early Christians could be misappropriated and how the modern charismatic movement is fouled by delusion. The scriptural frauds perpetrated by Dr. Wierwille led me to study the textual origins of the Bible on my own. My tour of Buddhism demonstrated to me that despite what Buddhism says, good and evil are real, and it is a delusion to try to rise above these things and pretend the Fall of Man never happened.

I guess the main thing I got from my twenty-year marathon in pursuit of this or that false face of God is a horror of man-made sectarian religion. God made the Catholic Church, and the gates of hell shall not prevail against it.

Sometimes I despair about this Bride of Christ, this Church, and about myself living within her. Sometimes I think I am too free in her, too free to choose this or that confessor, this or that parish, this or that part of her to love. The disunity is burdensome. But if she is going to ruin, it is truly the end of the world. In that case it is better to go down with the ship, still protected by the promise of Christ, than to jump off and drown in a puddle of your own making.

Four years after my conversion, I came across a book by Anne Muggeridge called *The Desolate City*, a beautifully written lament for the Church that was, and is no more.

She writes, "People have turned to cults, it seems, precisely because the Church has abandoned its certainty." And I turned to the Church because nothing else is certain.

The author describes the Church of her childhood as a culture, "a country of the mind." She might as well have said: a tribe. On the cover of the book is the picture of an abbey in Sussex, England. The abbey is in ruins. It struck me as a nearly exact rendition of the desolate scene confronting me in my dream of Joan of Arc back in 1980.

Perhaps the crumbling chapel in my dream was a warning, and I should pay more attention to the true and eternal Church revealed by a blessed saint strolling on a path in heaven. The real message of that dream was that even if the chapel is crumbling and the saint is burnt at the stake, it is the chapel and the saint and the Cross that hold the keys of the kingdom.